The Burdens of Aspiration

The Burdens
of Aspiration

*Schools, Youth, and Success in
the Divided Social Worlds
of Silicon Valley*

Elsa Davidson

NEW YORK UNIVERSITY PRESS
New York and London

NEW YORK UNIVERSITY PRESS
New York and London
www.nyupress.org

References to Internet websites (URLs) were accurate at the time of writing.
Neither the author nor New York University Press is responsible for URLs
that may have expired or changed since the manuscript was prepared.

Library of Congress Cataloging-in-Publication Data
Davidson , Elsa.
The burdens of aspiration : schools, youth, and success in
the divided social worlds of Silicon Valley / Elsa Davidson.
p. cm.
Includes bibliographical references and index.
ISBN 978-0-8147-2087-5 (cl) — ISBN 978-0-8147-2088-2 (pb)
ISBN 978-0-8147-2089-9 (e-book)
1. Education—Social aspects—California—Santa Clara Valley (Santa Clara County)
2. Student aspirations—California—Santa Clara Valley (Santa Clara County)
3. Youth—California—Santa Clara Valley (Santa Clara County)—Social conditions.
4. Educational equalization—California—Santa Clara Valley (Santa Clara County)
5. Polarization (Social sciences)—California—Santa Clara Valley (Santa Clara County)
I. Title.
LC191.6.C2D38   2011
379.2'60979473—dc22   2011007754

New York University Press books are printed on acid-free paper,
and their binding materials are chosen for strength and durability.
We strive to use environmentally responsible suppliers and materials
to the greatest extent possible in publishing our books.

Manufactured in the United States of America
c   10 9 8 7 6 5 4 3 2 1
p   10 9 8 7 6 5 4 3 2 1

For my mother, Marilyn H. Davidson

Contents

Acknowledgments

I first thank all the young people and adults who participated in my research for this book. Young people at the two high schools examined here, which I call "Morton" and "Sanders," gave me their time, thoughtfully answered my questions, and welcomed me in their classes and on their field trips, and sometimes in their homes. The process of observing them consider their own futures, and their places in the world was always fascinating. I hope that what I have written accurately captures their perceptions of themselves and their worlds as well as their acts of self-definition and aspiration during the fleeting time they were coming of age and attending public high school in Silicon Valley.

I also thank the school communities of Morton and Sanders. The staff at each school was extremely hospitable and forthcoming during my fieldwork. At Morton the school principal and a particular group of teachers graciously facilitated my fieldwork with students and gave vivid accounts of the student population they served, as well as the challenges they faced as they strove to provide an excellent education in the context of federal provisions associated with the No Child Left Behind Act of 2001, state budgetary constraints, and a socially, culturally, and economically diverse population. Staff at Sanders, my own alma mater, taught me much about how the educational environment had changed since I had attended the school during the 1980s. Staff members were especially helpful in highlighting the effect of the tech boom and shifting styles of parenting and being an adolescent in a middle class and affluent Valley community. In sum, I am sincerely grateful to the educators and administrators at both these public schools for their time and considerable insights. Much of what I learned about these schools, and about the conditions under which educators labor and students learn, I owe to them.

I am extremely grateful, moreover, to the parents of students at both Morton and Sanders for providing valuable information about their families, their hopes and dreams for their children, and their worries about pressures their children faced at school and within their respective communities.

I especially appreciate the time that parents of students at both schools spent with me, given the demanding work schedules of many parents.

The chapters of this book that provide information about the private-sector-influenced educational politics of Silicon Valley and the eroding security of Silicon Valley's educated middle classes owe their existence to the nonprofit youth-services and social services providers, corporate-community liaisons, city workers, clergy, and employees and ex-employees of local large high-tech corporations and small start-up firms who consented to in-depth interviews as well as to my presence at events and meetings. I thank them all for their candor about themselves, the institutions in which they worked, and their perspectives on the public culture and civic life of the region.

Apart from those who participated in this research, I would like to thank a group of people who helped me to conceive and refine this book, and have all along engaged my work in ways that have been illuminating and encouraging: Vincent Crapanzano, Ida Susser, Cindi Katz, Jane Schneider, and Shirley Lindenbaum. My exposure to their scholarship and thinking has shaped the questions I have asked, the ways I have interpreted the data I collected, and my writing. I especially express my deep gratitude to Vincent, Ida, and Cindi, who, following graduate school, have been truly great and endlessly encouraging mentors in different and complementary ways. Vincent's insightful questions and interpretations of diverse ethnographic situations have often caused me to reevaluate my perspectives on my own work and to think of entirely new avenues of inquiry to pursue. Ida's critical approach to the anthropology of North America and her wise suggestions concerning this book have been invaluable. Finally, Cindi's globally comparative analysis of youth contending with political and economic transformation and disinvestments in social reproduction has inspired this work in many ways.

I similarly thank the scholars who have read and commented on my work at various stages. Emily Martin, whose incisive analysis of emergent models of selfhood in American society and their relationship to economic transformation has inspired my thinking on many issues related to youth and their daily contexts, kindly served as the outside reader for the dissertation that this book grew out of. Her feedback at that early stage was much appreciated. Subsequently, as editors, panel discussants, or simply as fellow scholars working on related topics, Elizabeth Chin, Richard Lloyd, Robert Fairbanks, Caitlin Cahill, Rachel Heiman, Nari Rhee, and Jennifer Tilton have offered insightful commentary about my research or have inspired me with their own. Reviewers for this manuscript also offered extremely useful critiques of the text, particularly anonymous Reviewer 2 whose painstaking and detailed review helped me to refine each chapter. Although, perhaps unwisely, I have not taken every suggestion offered by these reviewers, they truly helped me improve the book and the flaws that remain are my responsibility entirely. In addition, Jennifer Hammer has been an insightful and patient editor at New York University Press. I thank her and Despina Papazoglou Gimbel for guiding me through the process of publishing this book.

Most recently, at Montclair State University, I have had the opportunity to work with a group of interesting and congenial anthropologists. I thank my colleagues in the anthropology department at Montclair for providing such an enjoyable and supportive environment in which to finish this project.

Finally, I thank my friends and family who have supported me through the seemingly endless process of pursuing a Ph.D. and writing a book. Miriam Greenberg, Nathaniel Deutsch, Jessica Jerome, Maria Gutierrez, Patty Kelly, and Laura Kaehler stand out in my life as friends and brilliant scholars whom I admire deeply. I especially thank Miriam Greenberg and Jessica Jerome, both friends since adolescence who continue to inspire me in multiple ways. Thanks also to Brian Albert, a great friend who kindly welcomed me into his home in Silicon Valley for months when I was beginning my fieldwork. I would also like to express my gratitude to Lisa Tharpe, Heather Caldwell, Dana Stevens, Robert Weinstock, Evan Spring, Penny Lewis, and Annie Polland, for enjoyable downtime in the past many years.

I am also extremely grateful to the wonderful women who have helped care for my children while I wrote and revised this book: Dawn Bood, Maya Earle, Hila Hakmon, and Reneé Leslie. I definitely could not have completed this project without the help of each one of these people. Reneé Leslie in particular was an invaluable support to my family during the period in which I revised this book.

Finally, my deepest thanks goes to my family. My mother, to whom this book is dedicated, has always encouraged me to pursue my interests, and her love and generous support along the way have enabled me to pursue a career path of my choice. I will be fortunate if this book is a fraction as insightful as she is. I also thank my stepfather, Charles Fidlar, a brilliant, talented musician and a generous and entirely unorthodox person, for his support and enthusiasm about my work. The other parents who have loomed large in my life during the process of researching and writing this book are my parents-in-law, Karen and Esfandiar Bahrampour. I give my deepest thanks to Karen and Essie for years of encouragement, fine company, and generous support, including shelter during the fieldwork years when Silicon Valley proved too expensive, and for all the time they spent with their grandchildren as I met many deadlines over the years. I wish I could thank Essie now and hope he knew how much I appreciated his sense of humor and perspective on life over the years. In addition, I also thank both sets of parents for the many times they took care of their grandchildren as I met deadlines over the years. I also thank my father, Eric Davidson, a biologist with a great appreciation for world history and cultures whose own scholarly path in life has served as an inspiration to me. My gratitude also goes to Suzanne Sharp, Tara Bahrampour, and Sufi, John, Charlotte, Soren, and Ella Rose Fox for all the enjoyable family time spent away from this project while working toward its completion. Finally, and most importantly, my husband, Ali Bahrampour, and my children, Nava Delphine and Giev Solomon, are the greatest joys of my life. Ali, your brilliance, stellar sense of humor, and encouragement, not to mention your editorial skill, have seen me through this process. No words can ever express my gratitude and love. Nava and Giev, I thank you both for existing in this world, and I love nothing more than exploring it with you.

I

Introduction

Phantoms of Success

*The Politics of Aspiration in
Post-Boom Silicon Valley*

Geography of a Myth

In a photograph accompanying a 2005 *New York Times* article titled, "Wheels and Deals in Silicon Valley," a young, goateed white man clad in the green and blue bike-racing garb of the Webcor/Alto Velo Bicycle Racing Club leans over his bike. Behind him, similarly clad men and women straddle their bicycles, preparing for one of the club's endurance-testing, long-distance rides. The caption reads, "Let the networking begin."

That Silicon Valley's information economy is founded on the practice of networking hardly constitutes news. But the hook here concerned a novel trend among Silicon Valley technology workers and entrepreneurs: the integration of extreme sports into the daily regimen of working and networking. Apparently yesterday's "skinny-armed computer geeks . . ." are today taking up adventure sports,

> Finding that a mountain road or a cresting wave can be an exhilarating place to integrate one's business, social, and recreational lives . . . Cycling is the new golf. And so is snowboarding, for that matter, and open-sea distance swimming, and kite-surfing [a sport that involves surfing in the air over water while hooked up to a parachute], and even abalone diving. (Williams 2005)

This article summons the Silicon Valley of popular imagination. In its vivid description of the work-time/playtime antics of Silicon Valley techno-entrepreneurs, it reinforces dearly held, enduring myths about the region that elide the multiple dimensions of its history and present: that it is a place-less meritocracy of innovators and that it exists, first and foremost, in the

| 3

mind, a province of ideas spun into technological innovation through competition and collaboration.

The techno-entrepreneurs whose extreme sports activities are featured in this *New York Times* piece represent the post-Internet boom version of the Silicon Valley myth. No longer simply the province of quiet, geeky engineers burning with intensity for technological innovation, the corporate culture of Silicon Valley reinvented itself during the tech boom of the late 1990s, becoming younger, wealthier, and hypercompetitive—a "culture mash" of risk-inclined people playing a market on a "crack high," Po Bronson (1999) wrote at the time.

In the late 1990s this new-and-improved version of a Silicon Valley "culture" personified by competition-mad and extremely wealthy techno-entrepreneurs emerged as a commonplace of American popular, indeed global, imagination.[1] For me, this representation produced a disjuncture. Having grown up in the area during the 1980s in a middle-class family with no connections to the region's high-tech sector, and having worked during the early 1990s as a patient advocate at a community clinic serving low-income immigrants in Santa Clara County, the geographic heart of Silicon Valley, I barely recognized the place or the young tech workers and entrepreneurs featured in the news stories that emerged as the boom gained momentum. My own memories of the place, of a childhood spent among graduate student families on the Stanford University campus, and of an adolescence spent in an income-diverse Palo Alto neighborhood home to middle-class professionals as well as moderate-income families and retirees, seemed to belong to a parallel universe. Though it had long been a hub of high-tech industry, Silicon Valley had, within a few cyber-crazed years, become an iconic symbol of globalization at its finest: multicultural, meritocratic, and borderless, a polyglot Eden of ultra-competitive techno-entrepreneurs and engineers starting companies and "going public," blurring the lines between extreme work and extreme play.

This mythologized representation of Silicon Valley and its idealized citizenry constitutes a social imaginary with global reach, one that, during the late 1990s, began to inspire Silicon Glens and Gulches and Deserts around the country and the world.[2] Indeed, the powerful and pervasive influence of this social imaginary recalls sociologist Henri Lefebvre's (1991) notion of "representations of space". For Lefebvre, such spaces are *conceived,* defined by people such as urban planners, architects, and the like, and expressly articulated, as opposed to *lived.* In Silicon Valley, this conceived space has been defined in terms of a "Silicon Valley culture" by the region's techno-entrepreneurial elite and its boosters in ways that flatten the complex history of the place into a simple narrative about highly competitive people who invent technology in a postindustrial landscape of corporate campuses and cubicles.[3] The multiculturalism of this mythologized Valley is somehow homogenized; cultural differences, though celebrated, are subordinated to the task of innovation. Moreover, such diversity seemingly exists without class divisions. In short, this regional space—the space, one often hears, of "the future"—offers a version of globalization and its subjects that is somehow conflict-free and ahistorical, a seamless cosmopolitan zone of "knowledge workers" and entrepreneurs.[4]

This version of the region stands in stark contrast to what Lefebvre would call the *lived* space of Silicon Valley, in which residents negotiate increasing economic insecurity, hierarchies of citizenship (Ong 1999), and conflicting class interests. My interest in this lived space, and its clash with Silicon Valley's dominant public culture, inspired this book. As I read and heard about the boom during the late 1990s and took in the almost evangelical talk of the information society and the "New Economy" flooding the academic and popular presses, I became preoccupied by working- and middle-class experiences of the region and its rapid social transformation, as well as such inhabitants' perceptions of the *conceived* Valley and its idealized, emergent techno-entrepreneurial class.[5] Moreover, I became fascinated by what I came to see as the *instructive* power of Silicon Valley's dominant public culture for the region's working- and middle-class inhabitants. What effect, I wondered, did representations of techno-entrepreneurial success, and emergent "new entrepreneurial" practices and values, have on the self-perceptions, self-defining actions, and imagined futures of working and tenuously situated middle-class people contending with rapid social and economic transformation?[6]

This book explores the lived space of Silicon Valley from the vantage point of those whose experiences of social and economic transformation are particularly formative and whose dominant notions of success and regional "culture" are especially powerful: local youth. It investigates how, as the boom morphed into a bust, working- and middle-class young people coming of age in Silicon Valley defined their aspirations and themselves in relation to a rapidly transforming social, economic, and educational context as well as to an unevenly experienced regional public culture.

I approach this subject comparatively. With the recognition that racial, class, and ethnic hierarchies as well as local educational inequalities insure no unitary experience of being young in Silicon Valley, this book examines the process of aspiration formation among youth from divergent class, racial, and ethnic backgrounds. Focusing specifically on the children of the Valley's low-wage service workers and those of its highly skilled tech and service professional classes, it explores how daily experiences of schooling and community shaped this process.[7] In so doing the book considers changing expectations of conduct and norms of success that such youth confront within these social contexts, and the extent to which techno-entrepreneurial values, skills, and social practices—by now an idealized model of citizenship in the contemporary United States—have become morally and practically instructive for working and middle-class youth.

My approach to the problem of aspiration formation acknowledges the role of processes of racialization, and, for many, experiences of racism and dynamics of ethnic identification, in shaping ideas about self, family, school, one's future, and one's class identity, and in determining one's relation to a dominant public culture. To be Latino, white, or Asian in Silicon Valley, or to be Mexican American, Chinese American, or Vietnamese American,[8] means negotiating particular historical experiences of exclusion or relative privilege, and particular structural conditions and stereotypes.[9] Hence this ethnography aims to shed light on dynamics of race and class that influence the ways in which young people forge aspirations and social identities, and thus engage dynamics of social reproduction and differentiation in Silicon Valley.[10]

Understanding the subjective process through which young people forge aspirations and social identities, however, requires a wider focus than young people and their immediate school and community environments. Because aspiration formation is a social and political process as well as an individual one, this book considers in almost equal measure the broader social, political, and cultural forces and circumstances that have shaped, and sometimes failed to shape, processes of aspiration formation and class identification. As a result, particular dynamics within the public sphere that profoundly influence young people's beliefs about themselves, their place in the world, and the ways they imagine their futures—such as the evolution of ideas about critical workforce skills, regional and national dynamics of educational reform, and expressions of adult middle-class anxiety—figure prominently in this book.[11]

The dimensions of this inquiry have been defined by the volatility of the regional and national economy under conditions of intensifying globalization and recession and widening social inequality in the Valley. The tech boom and bust wrought fortune and misfortune unevenly and in divergent ways across lines of race, ethnicity, and class. For many working-class children of immigrants from Mexico, the tech boom—before exposure to Silicon

Valley's corporate culture through school programs—meant absolutely nothing. Alternately it meant getting priced out of Silicon Valley and finishing high school in a less expensive area of California. For some of the children of white Silicon Valley tech professionals I encountered, the tech boom meant a remodeled family home, vacations to Thailand or Europe, parents who took frequent business trips, or even postponing college to start a tech company after high school. For many other middle-class youth, it meant feeling conspicuously "low-rent" in a place that seemed to be growing richer all the time.

Naturally the bust also meant different things to different people: for those performing low-wage service work such as ironing and washing uniforms for a company serving local tech corporations or working in construction, it meant an intensification of insecurity at often already insecure jobs or job loss; for an employee of a tech corporation facing job loss, with a mortgage and kids, or the person suddenly bankrupted by margin calls, it meant the potential dismantling of one's social world.

By the time I arrived in Silicon Valley to begin my fieldwork in the fall of 2001, my awareness of such variation and flux had shaped my plans for fieldwork and given rise to more specific questions about the relationship between schooling, aspiration, and expectations of citizenship. The design of the research and its theoretical orientation are best explained in relation to structural political-economic and social transformations within the region since the 1990s, and the emergence of a regional civic agenda focused on educational reform and workforce preparedness that relates to these shifts.

The Split World of Silicon Valley

During the boom years of the 1990s the region's wealth polarization intensified as recently arrived, highly educated tech professionals from other parts of the country and abroad filled highly paid and often stock-optioned jobs in the high-tech sector, and rents and home prices skyrocketed. At the same time Latino and Asian immigrants filled new low-paid service jobs spawned by the boom, thereby reinforcing a local racial and ethnic labor hierarchy inherited from the region's agricultural past and maintained throughout Silicon Valley's postwar history (Pitti 2003). The net result of this regional economic transformation was a sharper divide that outstripped by far the nation's much-discussed wealth-polarization during the 1990s. Within the County of Santa Clara, inflation-adjusted incomes of households in the bottom twentieth percentile rose a modest 9 percent between 1993 and 2001 compared to 17 percent nationwide. Indeed, between 1990 and 1999 wage rates of the poorest 25 percent of residents decreased by 14 percent (Sachs 1999). Simultaneously the local cost of living increased by 22 percent, making Silicon Valley 1.5 times more expensive than the national average (Joint Venture Silicon Valley [JVSV] Network 2003:19).

By contrast, inflation adjusted incomes rose 24 percent for those in the eightieth percentile income bracket. Thus, individuals with incomes in the eightieth percentile kept pace with the 22 percent cost-of-living rise during this period (JVSV Network 2003:19).[12] Of course those Valleyites able to "cash in" during the tech boom existed in an altogether different economic galaxy: the ratio of annual income for the top one hundred executives compared to the average production worker rose from 42:1 in 1991 to 956:1 in 2000 (Benner 2002:213).[13]

How did such socioeconomic polarization shape the social context of everyday life in Silicon Valley? The poor experienced continued socio-spatial segregation within the region: those whose incomes did not exceed the federal poverty guidelines remained concentrated in more or less the same census tracks within the county between 1990 and 2000 (Sachs 1999).[14] In geographic terms the socio-spatial pattern observed for Silicon Valley by sociologists Manuel Castells and Peter Hall (1994) in their landmark study of "technopoles" has held true: affluent Valley residents still live in the North and West of the county, and poorer residents in the South and East.

At the same time Valley residents in the middle found themselves awash in economic insecurity; at the turn of the millennium only 18 percent of Santa Clara Valley residents could afford a median-priced home for sale in Santa Clara County. Although this number jumped to 26 percent in 2002 as a result of the tech bust, it stands in sharp contrast to a national average of 56 percent.[15]

In experiential terms, the region's polarization of wealth and local increased cost of living during the 1990s exacerbated the sense of a place increasingly bereft of its middle strata, and instead divided between those barely able to survive economically and those able to flaunt their new wealth. Moreover, I found that these conditions also sharpened divisions in the region between different groups all considering themselves "middle-class." In light of my findings in this regard, I refer throughout this book to three distinct middle-class groups in contemporary Silicon Valley: a "new entrepreneurial," affluent upper-middle class comprised of young "dot-commers" and elites working in managerial positions in the high-tech sector; an established professional—and typically older—middle class comprised of technical professionals and others who work outside the tech sector as well as retirees; and a public sector middle class of teachers, firemen, policemen, nonprofit workers, and the like. These groups have experienced the dominant public culture of Silicon Valley, and the socioeconomic transformations in the region within the last fifteen years or so, in divergent ways. Indeed, for many of those in the established professional and public-sector middle class, economic insecurity, which ratcheted up dramatically during the recession of 2008–2009, has become a central reality.

The class polarization wrought by experiences of economic insecurity and increasing wealth differences among the Valley's middle strata has divided Silicon Valley's social space and intersected with local racial and ethnic hierarchies. Educated whites and Chinese, Taiwanese, and Indians often occupy highly paid technical and managerial positions in the high-tech sector, and Latino and Vietnamese, Filipino, Korean, and other Southeast Asian immigrants perform low-paid services and high-tech production work, creating ethnic and racial hierarchies and patterns of ethnic and occupational segregation (Hossfeld 1988; Ong 1999; Pastor et al. 2000; Saxenian 1996; Zlolniski 2006; Wadhwa et al. 2007). When I conducted my fieldwork this segregation was striking; Latino faces were typically absent from the companies I visited, except at the security gates or the Starbucks tent in the lobby.[16] Residential patterns reflected labor force hierarchies: highly educated South Asian and East Asian immigrants and their families lived and mingled with affluent white residents of Silicon Valley, whereas working-class Latinos, African Americans, Vietnamese Americans, and other Southeast Asians tended to live apart from whites in the region. The dramatic lack of public transit only intensified sense of parallel worlds.

Indeed, the combination of wealth polarization and socio-spatial segregation along lines of race and class made for a discordant fieldwork experience, despite my familiarity with the area. After moving back to the Valley in 2001 the social distances I traveled were far longer than my traffic-filled commute. In the morning I might sit in a dilapidated office building in an area home to low-income Latino and Asian families discussing the checkered relationship between corporate Silicon Valley and the region's Latino population or the young, white "yuppies" pushing lower-income people out of San Jose or the fact that for many families in the immediate neighborhood the boom and subsequent bust felt and looked quite similar. Later the same day I might listen to an engineer with "start-up" experience dissect the boom and bust at one of Palo Alto's upscale cafés. Language use exposed the distance between discrete life-worlds; a Mexican American teenager I once interviewed looked at me blankly when I mentioned "dot-coms," whereas the acronym IPO (initial public offering) peppered the speech of my more affluent high-tech connected interviewees.

A Techno-Civilizing Process

As I learned on a visit to the region in 2000, Silicon Valley elites were aware of these sharpening social, economic, and cultural divides along lines of race, ethnicity, and class. They saw them as a liability for a number of reasons, including the need for a homegrown labor force at many levels of the economy, and they sought to address them. Moreover, for some tech leaders, involvement on regional social issues stemmed from the belief that technological know-how, skills, and access engender social transformation and democratic participation. Thus, during the 1990s boom, local tech corporations collaborated with community groups, schools, and other institutions to address a host of social problems plaguing the area, including the educational and professional disenfranchisement of Latinos within the regional information economy, traffic congestion, and the shortage and cost of housing.

Significantly, these collaborations often promoted the application of technological products (like laptops for students, educational software, and web portals) and celebrated the values and attitudes of techno-entrepreneurship—often glossed as regional "culture"—as "solutions" to social problems often the product of local industry.[17] The conviction that the regional "spirit of innovation," and the social practices and products that spawned the growth of the regional high-tech economy, would solve the region's social and environmental problems was prevalent on websites focused on the region's quality of life, at public forums, and in conversations I held with many people in the private, nonprofit, and public sector.

Indeed, we might understand pervasive references to Silicon Valley's "culture," its techno-entrepreneurial elite, and the traits of its highly skilled workforce in discourse about the region's social ills in terms of sociologist Norbert Elias's (1978 [1939]) concept of a "civilizing process." Although Elias is concerned with the political project of civilizing the West, a process he links to shifting thresholds of shame and embarrassment and the emergence of new sources of fear, the broader message of his description is that the civilizing process entails a kind of self-regulation that becomes inculcated over time, and is motivated in part by fear of particular stigmas or desire for the status accorded those deemed "civilized." Thus the civilizing process involves a transformation of self-conduct that may be manifest in subtleties of lifestyle, and the attachment of particular emotional significance to certain everyday habits and rituals. Conversely, the act of not conducting oneself in such sanctioned ways implies belonging to a class of person deemed "uncivilized."

In its focus on often minute, daily forms of self-discipline and presentation that define a style of self-conduct, Elias's conception of the "civilizing process" calls to mind popular understandings of social class in the contemporary United States which tend to be conceived in stylistic as opposed to structural terms (Rouse 1995). This commonsensical understanding of social class in terms of markers of personal style, desires, and attitudes is in accord with a neoliberal rationality of rule in the contemporary United States; in a recycling of the liberal, individualist strain in American national culture that became pronounced during the second half of the nineteenth century (Emerson 1883 [1844]; Foner 1999), this form of governance stresses personal responsibility and choice. Stylistic meanings of social class promote this ideology: representations of an "underclass" with no sense of personal responsibility and a "middle class" that is morally deserving in its assumption of personal responsibility encourage the *choice* to adjust one's behaviors, attitudes, and desires, and thereby attain a respectable "middle-class" status.

The egalitarian message that it is simply a matter of personal choice whether or not one becomes "middle-class" is, of course, as much of a pretense as the notion that a time will come when all are "civilized"; just as the "civilizing process" paradoxically promotes normative behavior but can only proceed by creating differentiation, hegemonic ideas about class mobility in the United States implicitly encourage everyone to speak the language—figuratively and literally—of the dominant society, to observe the same customs, and to acquire the benefits of education that make it possible to belong to a "middle class." And yet the capitalist process requires a working class and thus depends upon socially meaningful markers of class. The requirements of a "civilized" status, like markers of class status, thus remain moving targets defined largely by the needs of capital.

The emergence in Silicon Valley during the late 1990s of a civic agenda around the local "digital divide," a gloss for gaps in educational and professional achievement as well as in technological access along lines of race, ethnicity, and income, offered a vivid example of a kind of techno-entrepreneurial civilizing process, one that resonated with an idealized middle-class style. Focused on cultivating the skills and values of youth in particular, as well as their access to technology and technological social networks, initiatives and discourse focused on the local digital divide articulated a preferred way of doing business, organizing society, and conducting oneself. Located within schools and other sites of social reproduction, such as workforce oriented after-school programs, agendas to bridge the digital divide often evoked Silicon Valley mythology and an idealized techno-entrepreneurial subject for pedagogical purposes, the techno-entrepreneur or highly skilled tech worker serving as a model of self-conduct and personal success. Implicitly, such modeling and emphasis on techno-entrepreneurial skills, knowledge, and values marked as "other" those lacking the right "social capital."[18]

Not surprisingly, the rhetoric of educational and workforce-oriented initiatives focused on the digital divide, and the cultivation of a "homegrown" workforce played with the cultural category of youth by focusing on young people as mediums of potentiality and malleability, as subjects "at risk," and as a category of person deserving of public- and private-sector help. In particular, deservedness was often tacitly conveyed in representations of the region's low-income Latino youth that emphasized their willingness to be exposed to new (techno-entrepreneurial) worlds, and their enthusiasm about the programs they participated in.

This regional civic emphasis on the *potential* of local youth provoked a number of questions. First, efforts to reform the education and training of the Valley's young people offered a lens through which to explore the role and effectiveness of formal exposure to techno-entrepreneurship in shaping young people's aspirations and, ultimately, patterns of social reproduction in the Valley. Second, I was interested in the ways in which local educational initiatives selectively invoked local high-tech traditions (Williams 1994), from the glorification of flexible work practices to the celebration of local CEOs who "think outside the box." Moreover, I also wanted to understand the relationship of a local movement to bridge the digital divide to a national politics of self-improvement targeting at-risk youth, one that reflects a global context in which children are understood to be increasingly at risk and to pose different degrees and kinds of risk to the body politic, depending on racial, class, gender, and national status (Stephens 1992).[19] In turn, these questions piqued my curiosity about how the potential of middle-class youth, whose connections to the regional dominant culture were less formal, and who confronted different kinds of risk and generally avoided the stigma of being labeled "at risk," was implicitly and explicitly framed by local middle-class adults and youth themselves.

This research agenda took on new meaning as the time approached for me to leave New York for fieldwork in Silicon Valley during the fall of 2001. After a series of downward slides in the tech markets during 2000, the Internet-fueled tech boom came to an end, replaced by a bust with devastating regional economic consequences. By 2003 the number of "gazelle compa-nies—publicly traded companies whose revenues have grown at least 20 per-cent for four consecutive years, beginning with one million dollars in sales—had fallen to nine, the lowest level in the region since 1992 (JVSV Network 2003:17). Real per capita income within Santa Clara County had slid for two consecutive years (ibid.:18) and large layoffs at local tech corporations were making the front page of local and national papers daily.

This shift in regional economic fortunes had a number of political and social implications. It added a bitterly ironic twist to pledges by corporate, community, and public officials to bridge the digital divide. Moreover, it placed boom-time techno-entrepreneurial success and values in a new and often less flattering light, and deepened economic anxiety for the region's already inse-cure middle-income inhabitants. Perhaps most profound, the regional trans-formation from boom to bust heightened social and ideological contradictions that, in turn, influenced the particular aspirations of different groups of young people in different ways as well as the extent to which middle-class, public-sector service workers and an established professional middle class identified with techno-entrepreneurial values, practices, and success.

Social Reproduction and Neoliberal Governmentality

These shifts transformed the conditions and sites of social reproduction in Silicon Valley, changes "on the ground" that alerted me to the complexities of studying social reproduction within and across divergent local social and economic contexts. In practical terms, social reproduction occurs within formal institutions such as schools or after-school programs or job-training centers and workplaces, informally in public spaces such as playgrounds, and within families and communities. Thus it involves emotively charged mean-ings associated with community belonging and social exclusion as much as it might entail participation, in, say, a job-training course.

Young people, then, whether at work, school, or play, constitute agents of their own social reproduction, and their acts of self-definition—as imper-manent as they may be—shape their futures in ways that may adhere to or diverge from expectations shaped by the political-economic interests of global capital. This perspective inspired my exploration of social reproduc-tion from the vantage point of young people's *strategies of aspiration manage-ment*. I have chosen the phrase "aspiration management," because it high-lights the active roles people play in defining self-expectation, hope, and a sense of the possible as well as the paradox of self-limitation and desire inherent to all aspirations.[20] The phrase hints at the existence of internalized structures of power and meaning that shape processes of subjectification and agency, a recurring theme in this book and in earlier works addressing the relationship of schooling, regional or urban environment, and political-economic process to youth aspiration and class identification, a body of scholarship on which this ethnography builds (MacLeod 2009 [1987]; Sullivan 1989; Willis 1977; Foley 1990).

The importance of structures of power to the process of aspiration management and, ultimately, to patterns of social reproduction has focused my attention on contemporary political-economic and ideological currents shaping local educational and social institutions as well as the everyday lives of my research subjects. The economic rationality of these formal and informal contexts, and the particular forms of self-discipline and presentation that I observed in the field, recalled Michel Foucault's concept of "governmentality," which he defined as a historically specific "art of government" (Gordon 1991:3) operant at the level of the individual's conduct as well as the conduct of a society or population (ibid.:36).[21] Moreover, I found that young people's conduct and their educational environments evoked a "neoliberal," or "advanced liberal" (Rose 1996) form of governmentality.

Foucault and other scholars who have engaged his concept of governmentality have defined neoliberalism as not just a political-economic regime but also as a rationality of rule in which "economics . . . becomes an approach capable in principle of addressing the totality of human . . . behavior" (Gordon 1991:43). Thus neoliberalism parts company from liberalism in the following way:

> Whereas *Homo economicus* originally meant that subject the springs of whose activity must remain forever untouchable by government, the American neoliberal *Homo economicus* is manipulable man, man who is perpetually responsive to modifications in his environment. Economic government joins hands with behaviorism. (Ibid.: 43).

This unification of the sphere of economic governance with individual behavior has significant implications for the dynamics of education in an American context, where education and training serve to augment human capital which ultimately can be converted into other kinds of capital. Education thus amounts to a consumer durable inseparable from its owner, a way to add value to oneself. Through education, people essentially become entrepreneurs of themselves (ibid.:44).

Hence the argument about neoliberal ideology in the contemporary United States goes as follows: the logic of the economic pervades not just society and goods and services provided by the state but the individual as well. Moreover, this penetration into the realm of the personal through renewed and reinvigorated emphasis on old national themes of individual choice, self-improvement, and picking oneself up by one's bootstraps dovetails conveniently and purposefully with policies of economic retrenchment of the public sector and the related privatization of once public services and goods.

As some scholars of neoliberalism and American education have argued, the nation's public educational system comprises one public good that has arguably become a vehicle for an enterprising of the self. In this view, an economizing logic now orders the ideology and pedagogy of schools; students are consumers of education, becoming "value-added" in order to compete in the global marketplace. Hence political effects of neoliberalized education occur at the individual and institutional scales. In the contemporary United States, then, public schools are both sites of social reproduction and citizenship formation; they serve to reproduce and differentiate the labor force just as they encourage children and youth to cultivate themselves in ways that meet the skill requirements of the capitalist global economy, and reflect priorities of a neoliberal state seeking to shift the burden for social and economic risk and security onto its citizens (O'Malley 1996).

In Silicon Valley I found that public education and community programs to address regional social inequality through supplementary education and training targeting low-income youth reflected neoliberal imperatives in a few particular ways. In addition to an economizing, "results-oriented" focus on standardized test performance and school accountability in the region, the emergence of local public-private initiatives (often in public schools) promoting techno-entrepreneurial skills for youth in the past fifteen years or so has resulted in the proliferation of local educational environments that encourage students—often low-income youth of color deemed at risk of not graduating from high school and, implicitly, of becoming economic burdens and delinquent—to learn the skills and acquire the desires and values of the "knowledge worker" or techno-entrepreneur. In other words, these programs focus on the crafting of identities as well as the acquisition of particular skills. Moreover, they frame the acquisition of such values and skills as a way to neutralize an at-risk status and avoid creating a burden to society, thereby privatizing responsibility for being at risk.

Like reforms that concentrate on standardized test performance and school accountability, programs oriented toward self-transformation are asymmetrically implemented within the unevenly developed social landscape of Silicon Valley. Students attending public schools in more affluent local communities are not subject to a school environment that "teaches to the test," and they typically have more informal connections to the techno-entrepreneurial world of Silicon Valley—connections that render techno-entrepreneurial work practices, lifestyle, and values commonsensical to them. This is not to say that neoliberal ideology does not influence local middle-class school environments or the aspirations of local middle-class and affluent youth. On the contrary, local middle-class youth who participated in this research learned, through schooling and informally within a community defined by techno-entrepreneurial success, values, and practices, to cultivate themselves in ways that suited global economic imperatives stressed within public education and that addressed the realities of eroding middle-class status and security—a status that the state, along with private industry, has failed to protect. In essence, the working- and middle-class youth who participated in my research were subject to a flexible form of governance, one that accommodates conditions of uneven development, educational inequality, and racial, class, and ethnic difference. Indeed, a central theme of this book involves the particular ways in which this neoliberal rationality of rule plays out within the educational contexts of young people, how it resonates with locally experienced political-economic conditions (also shaped by neoliberal priorities), and the ways in which it influences processes of social reproduction.

The Scope of This Book

This theoretical focus on processes of neoliberal subject formation as they occur within Valley educational institutions and communities divided by race, class and ethnicity determined the design of my research. The result is a study that is multi-sited and broad in scope, including ethnographic exploration of the daily environment and intricacies of two public high schools, everyday urban and familial worlds of youth, and the broader regional context of public-private educational initiatives designed to promote social equity across class, ethnic, and racial lines.[22]

To learn how public schooling shapes young people's strategies of aspiration management, I attended classes, observed school rules, and interviewed teachers, administrators, students, parents, school psychologists, and college counselors. Occasionally I attended student club meetings and observed teacher meetings and a few school board and PTA meetings. I also read program reports, collected educational and program materials, and attended field trips to corporations and school-community celebrations. Most important, I observed students and spoke with them sometimes in groups but usually one-on-one, during often intimate, informal interviews. I conducted random interviews at both schools, talking with every third student on a roll sheet. During that same period I was also on campus observing. Periodically, I went to students' homes, interviewed parents, or attended a social function outside of the school. Generally, however, my information was gleaned on school grounds.

Throughout my fieldwork on school campuses, my focus on young people's strategies of aspiration management meant that I paid attention to young people's modes of self-expression, self-discipline, and judgments about themselves and others. Moreover, I sought to understand meanings associated with the specter of social exclusion and hopes for social inclusion that the young people expressed implicitly and explicitly. These meanings, as I discovered, had everything to do with constructions of race, class, and ethnicity, and sometimes gender (e.g., the stereotype of Latina girls becoming pregnant or Latino boys belonging to a gang).[23]

Contemplation of these meanings in turn led me to consider political-economic anxieties confronting the families of my young research subjects and the political, economic, and ideological circumstances of their educational environments. In this way I broadened the scope of the project to include not only interviews with the parents of youth but also members of Silicon Valley's established professional middle-class. These interviews focused on their experiences of the boom and bust, the social and economic pressures they felt as a result of both, and their notions of success. In my exploration of the kinds of social and economic anxieties confronting these people, I followed what seemed to be key local issues of concern, a practice that ultimately led me to understand processes of class identification in relation to a techno-entrepreneurial ideal citizen-subject. Attention to the morally and emotively charged nature of these public discussions alerted me to the intensity of the social and economic pressures confronting particular middle-class fractions, and how these pressures shaped the aspirations, and attendant models of self-presentation and discipline, of middle-class youth.

In sum, the range of this book is quite broad. To grasp the dimensions of the argument I make, one must understand something about the divergent circumstances confronting my research subjects.

Asymmetries and Aspirations

The young people whose strategies of aspiration management are explored in this book hailed from two divergent social and educational contexts. One group lived in a low- and lower-middle-income area in the large metropolitan city of San Jose, California, which boasts an ethnically and culturally diverse population of just under nine hundred thousand people, of whom approximately 30 percent are Latino, 27 percent are Asian, and 47 are white.[24] There I conducted fieldwork in a state- and private-sector-supported "School to Career" Biotechnology Academy focused on developing academic, social, and technical skills and knowledge necessary to attain work after high school as a technician within the biotechnology sector of the regional information economy or to pursue higher education in the field of biotechnology. This Academy, which is limited to high school sophomores, juniors, and seniors, is a program within the public high school that I call Morton. The City Council District in which the school is located has a population that is 47.2 percent Latino, 35.8 percent Asian, and 25.2 percent white. In addition, this district had the second highest percentage of female-headed households in San Jose at 15.8%. Although the median household income for the City of San Jose is $70,243—compared to $74,335 for Santa Clara County—the median household income in the neighborhood area (meaning City Council District) surrounding Morton High School appears to be considerably lower, given that at least 54 percent of Morton students qualify for reduced-price lunches.[25] Moreover, this number is probably under-reported, given that 70 percent of students in the local elementary and middle school district that feeds into the high school district of which Morton is a part qualify for such lunches.

Morton High School, then, serves primarily low- and lower-middle-income families. The school community is made up of families that inhabit modest tract homes and apartments in complexes located on suburban cul-de-sacs in San Jose, and sometimes trailer parks and garages. It is predominantly Mexican American and Vietnamese, and during the time of my fieldwork the school was beset by a high level of student transience owing to the rising cost of living and unemployment related to the tech bust. The school and neighborhood were also reputed to be gang-ridden, and beginning in the 1990s both the school and the surrounding area became the focus of suppression and prevention efforts.

Furthermore, the parents of many of the Latino students I came to know there did not speak English and were educated only to the grade school or high school level. These parents worked in a variety of service positions, often holding down multiple jobs. Landscaping and janitorial work were typical occupations, but there were also bilingual professionals.[26] Students also worked in low-wage service jobs. Not surprisingly, for Morton students, life outside school offered little connection to the techno-entrepreneurial world of Silicon Valley.

The other school site was a twenty-minute ride north of San Jose on the 101 Freeway, in Palo Alto, a generally affluent, mid-sized town that is home to Stanford University and many tech corporations, and that became globally recognized following the tech boom.[27] Palo Alto is considered a particularly high-status place to live, partly because of the excellent quality of its public schools. Needless to say, it is home to many highly skilled and educated people who work in the tech sector, as well as other highly educated professionals. The median household income in Palo Alto is $140,900, and the median home price is $880,000. Approximately three-quarters of the adult residents who live there have four or more years of college, and 43 percent of adults over the age of twenty-five hold at least one graduate degree.[28]

The public school in which I conducted research in Palo Alto—which I call "Sanders"— has a student population that is approximately two-thirds white, 16 percent Asian, 6 percent African American, and 5 percent Latino. The school district includes two high schools, and 95 percent of the high school graduates attend two- or four-year colleges. Sanders has a nationally outstanding reputation, and links to the techno-entrepreneurial world of Silicon Valley are largely informal; there is little need there to bridge the digital divide.[29]

Moreover, talk of crime is rare in Palo Alto or at Sanders; in fact, despite student recreational drug and alcohol use, which, according to school counselors and staff, was ratcheting up, I had to actively seek out information on strategies for addressing youth delinquency, whereas I was inundated with such information at Morton.

These two schools, whose reputations and demographics remain quite different, reflect Silicon Valley's socioeconomic and educational divide, which is locally parsed in ways that intensify the reputations of each school. Whereas Morton suffered the stigma of its social demographics and the perception that it was a "gang school"—at least in the eyes of many with whom I spoke outside the school and the district—Sanders enjoyed a reputation of excellence; when I mentioned conducting fieldwork in Palo Alto, staff at Morton often raised their eyebrows in a gesture of mock snobbery, whereas parents and teachers in Palo Alto, responding to my work in San Jose, sometimes furrowed their brows in a look of concern and sympathy.[30]

The inequalities between Morton and Sanders, and their respective communities, are exacerbated by the state and national politics of educational funding. Since the passage of Proposition 13 in 1978, an amendment that rolled back property taxes in California by 57 percent, cutting property tax revenue for the state's public school system by 50 percent,[31] Morton's school district has primarily depended upon revenue from the state based on Average Daily Attendance (ADA), a fact that makes Morton's high rate of transience a disadvantage. The district amount per student in the 2002–2003 school year, the period when I conducted my fieldwork, was $5,332.[32] Although Proposition 98 (1988) insured minimum funding through state and property taxes, and Proposition 39 (2000) facilitated the passage of school bonds, and even with supplemental funding slightly increasing the amount per student, such funds are often the first to be cut in times of state budget retrenchment.

Moreover, the federal No Child Left Behind Act of 2001 has meant that schools like Morton, which are federally decreed Title I schools where over 40 percent of students come from low-income families, must meet Adequate Yearly Progress goals for the school's total population as well as for demographic subgroups. If they fail to do so, they will lose both funds and students; if a school is classified as "failing,"[33] students are given the choice of attending another school, and hence the linkage of state funding to attendance.

In stark contrast, the district of which Sanders is a part spent $10,670 per student during the 2002–2003 school year.[34] The school is in what is called a Basic Aid District, one in which local property taxes equal or exceed the district's revenue limit. Until 2003, this meant a constitutional guarantee of $120 per student in these more affluent districts in addition to property taxes.[35]

I belabor these political-economic facts because, taken together, they constitute the structural process that compounds educational inequalities resulting from the region's wealth polarization and socio-spatial segregation along class, race, and ethnic lines. Programs such as Morton's Biotechnology Academy attempt to address such inequalities. With the goal of transforming not only skills but values and aspirations, such programs are designed to reverse the effects of socioeconomic and racial segregation and exclusion that determine the extent to which young people are exposed to the techno-entrepreneurial world of Silicon Valley. Indeed, Morton's Biotechnology Academy was effective in getting students into four-year colleges, a significant achievement that should not be minimized.

But although the Biotechnology Academy might have leveled the playing field in this significant respect, I found that at Morton, and even at

Sanders as well, often contradictory school and community environments shaped students' aspirations in ways that ultimately reinforced class, racial, and ethnic hierarchies manifest in the regional labor force. In fact, I observed two distinct patterns of aspiration among the youth: whereas students at Morton expressed interest in public-service careers that emphasized "giving back" to their own communities and to society, students at Sanders learned to value self-exploration and intellectual and personal freedom, and expressed aspirations toward creative and intellectually fulfilling careers in highly specialized fields. Notably, however, the patterns of aspiration I observed did not seem to reproduce traditional gender hierarchies. Working-class young women expressed interest in traditionally male public-sector occupations such as that of probation officer, and working-class young men expressed interest in, for example, social work. Likewise, youth from affluent middle-class backgrounds seemed uninterested in modeling themselves and their futures according to traditionally feminine or masculine career paths.

Flexible, Responsible Citizenship and Social Reproduction

Putting aside these continuities and divergences in patterns of social reproduction, the process of observing contrasting patterns of aspiration at each school and exploring these two schools' disparate political-economic and ideological environments led me, ironically, to consider how each school and group of young people was participating in a common political project of citizenship formation in the United States, one requiring particular forms of self-cultivation among youth and their assumption of personal responsibility for social and economic conditions beyond their control. This politics of citizenship influences processes of social reproduction, encouraging young people's responsibility for social and economic risks and insecurities that might have been managed by the state or the corporate sector in the context of an industrial Fordist economy. Moreover, this "juvenilization" of responsibility for economic social insecurity and risk differentiates youth by encouraging divergent forms of responsibility depending upon racial and class status.

How does this flexible politics of responsible citizenship actually play out in the lives of individual young people and within educational institutions? I came to appreciate, in particular, how, within each school context, modes of self-cultivation, self-presentation, and styles of discipline that reflected regional ideals of success and a morally charged model of citizenship intersected with fears and experiences of social exclusion and desires for social inclusion borne out of everyday social and economic contexts. Such fears, experiences, and desires, whether related to one's social, economic, and political marginality as, for example, the child of someone who crossed the border illegally, or to the threat of losing one's status as a successful person within an affluent milieu, ultimately affected how young people negotiated ideals of citizenship and how they understood their place in the world. In turn, the ways in which young people engaged ideals of citizenship in the process of managing their aspirations and forging social identities helped to define local patterns of social reproduction and constituted a contested dynamic of citizenship formation.

This theoretical frame, and the evidence I provide to support it, raises questions of historical comparison, especially with regard to processes of social reproduction through education. For example, how might one compare the postindustrial, intensely globalized, and socially polarized space of Silicon Valley to, say, the industrial-era factory town in Midlands, England, that sociologist Paul Willis (1977) described in *Learning to Labour*? Or, to take a North American example, how to compare it to sociologist Jay MacLeod's (2009 [1987) searing ethnographic chronicle of the "hidden (and not so hidden) injuries of class" among the white, working-class youth coming of age in a de-industrialized, northeastern city during the 1980s? What continuities exist across these times and spaces in terms of young people's strategies of aspiration and the effect of school environment and political-economic and social context on processes of social reproduction? To what extent do the disciplines, options, and pressures confronting youth diverge from past eras? In addressing these questions I suggest that in the postindustrial "New Economy" era, public schooling promotes familiar patterns of social reproduction and racial and class hierarchy. Indeed, striking similarities are apparent between the findings of Paul Willis (1977) concerning "lads" he studied decades ago in an industrial English town and the Latino youth I met in Silicon Valley. There are also striking differences between them, for strategies of aspiration management among Latino working-class, white, and Asian middle-class young people reveal a different orientation toward the state than existed on either side of the Atlantic more than thirty years ago. Moreover, all the young people who participated in my research negotiated school, community, and familial contexts of intensified social and economic pressure and risk, and poor youth of color, in particular, faced a context of increasing economic marginalization and militarization targeting their communities and schools in a post-9/11 era of expanding U.S. military engagement (Lutz 2002; Saltman and Gabbard 2003; Perez 2009).

The intra-regional design of this work and its focus on subjective responses to social and educational conditions allows us to consider the circumstances under which social change might occur. Exploring aspiration within two disparate school and community contexts affords the opportunity to see how certain social and economic contexts shaped by the tech boom and bust, and dominant ideologies to which young people were exposed, offered contradictory versions of reality. The ways in which people negotiated these contradictory versions had profound implications for how they defined themselves and their futures, and the extent to which they identified with particular ideals of citizenship to which they were exposed, whether those models specifically celebrated techno-entrepreneurship, simply the management of risk, or a more generalized and well-rounded "excellence" informed by techno-entrepreneurship in a more ambient way.

Ultimately experiences of social contradiction similarly shaped responses to morally charged representations of techno-entrepreneurship among teachers, nonprofit managers, and established professional middle-class residents of the Valley. Such people's experiences of the tech boom and bust shaped the degree to which they identified with a "new entrepreneurial" model of how to educate young people, run a public or a nonprofit institution or simply behave as a worker.

Thus, in what follows, we explore the "success" of a flexible process of citizenship formation, one that selectively deploys morally charged representations of a regional "culture" and draws on a neoliberal ideology of personal responsibility, as it plays out within divergent socioeconomic and ideological contexts. Each chapter in the book, whether explicitly focused on youth or concerned with the educational, social, cultural, and political contexts that shape young people's daily lives and strategies of aspiration management, explores the relative success of this political project. Moreover, each chapter considers the role of experiences of social contradiction in determining patterns of subjectification and agency critical to processes of social reproduction within Silicon Valley's polarized and segregated social landscape.

A Preview of the Work

The structure of this book moves from a close-up view of two groups of young people coming of age on the downside of the tech boom and their particular strategies of aspiration management in a specific educational and social context (part 2, chapters 2 and 3) to a more panoramic view of the political, social, economic, and ideological contexts shaping processes of social reproduction in Silicon Valley (part 3, chapters 4 and 5). Part 4, which concludes the book, identifies patterns across the work as a whole and places my findings in a larger political and theoretical context.

In chapter 2 we examine a pattern of aspiration among first- and second-generation, low-income Latino youth participating in a public school biotechnology academy with corporate connections to Silicon Valley industry. We explore their desire, despite daily exposure to the themes, values, and technology associated with biotechnological entrepreneurship, to "give back" to the community through careers in public service, especially those that monitor and serve at-risk communities such as their own. Linking this pattern of aspiration to the school's emphasis on taking responsibility for an at-risk status and experiences of social contradiction and exclusion within their everyday school and community environments, students ultimately developed strategies of aspiration management that simultaneously supported a hegemonic social order reproducing race and class hierarchies, and reframed in ways meaningful to them a project of neoliberal governance which fused notions of personal responsibility and idealizations of the tech private sector.

Chapter 3 links aspirations and strategies of self-cultivation among the children of Silicon Valley's tech and service professional class to school and community environments shaped by daily exposure to techno-entrepreneurial social practices, values, and success, as well as familial experiences of social and economic insecurity. Focusing on expectations of self-cultivation and norms of success in school as well as students' fantasies of failure, we shall identify a strategy of aspiration management that involves defining particular passions and excelling in multiple areas at once. Linking this strategy to familial pressures shaped by a broader political-economic context of the erosion of middle-class security and, at a local scale, realities of the tech bust, we shall explore the effects of students' efforts at self-cultivation and school environment on students, and the particular conflicts and fears of exclusion that students experienced.

Chapter 4 places the educational environment of the young Latino protagonists of this book in local and national context. Here we consider an emergent civic agenda around the digital divide in Silicon Valley, and explore the political implications and historical context of this regional "civilizing process." Linking this regional civic agenda to bridge the digital divide to a neoliberal politics of educational reform on the national scale, we shall assess its political impact. We trace, in particular, the production of two kinds of disciplined "subjects" in need of saving: at-risk youth such as those we meet in chapter 2 and public educational and nonprofit social-service institutions.

In the process, we explore how the realities of the tech bust era have effectively rendered disenfranchised young people, and many who provide services to them, skeptics—not subjects—of neoliberal reform.

Chapter 5 examines the political, social, and economic milieu of Silicon Valley's established professional middle class. We examine the ways in which, during the boom and subsequent bust, middle-class professionals channeled frustration about their eroding security and status into a politics of nostalgia for a pre-"New Economy" past, a critique of a "new entrepreneurial" present. In exploring the political implications of this "cultural politics of class" (Rouse 1995), we identify expressions of adult middle-class anxiety and political entrapment that influenced young people's styles of self-definition and aspiration.

Chapter 6, the book's conclusion, returns to the young people and schools at the center of this book to elaborate a comparative argument about a contemporary, flexible process of citizenship formation shaping–but not entirely determining—strategies of aspiration management at both Sanders and Morton high schools. In exploring dynamics of subjectification and agency among these youth, and linking these dynamics to adult responses to social and economic circumstances, we shall consider the conditions under which a neoliberal politics of citizenship succeeds or fails. Such conditions have everything to do with potent meanings especially associated with class, meanings whose power may be encapsulated in daily interactions or status symbols.

Throughout these chapters, the idealized citizen-subject of the techno-entrepreneur figures unevenly, as does discussion of the tech boom and subsequent bust, given divergent working- and middle-class experiences of cultural transformation and economic change. Collectively, these forces give form to the stories of success and failure that young people and adults I encountered in Silicon Valley tell themselves, and determine styles of aspiration management. This ethnography, then, is my attempt to grapple with the disjuncture—and dialectic—between the way people live their lives and the way they conceive them in relation to the dominant public culture of Silicon Valley, and to the insecure and rapidly changing conditions of the global information economy and society. It offers a representation of the space and subjects of globalization that prizes historical experience—in all its contradictory and emotive complexity—over mythology.

Aspirations of Youth in Silicon Valley

2

Managing "At-Risk" Selves and "Giving Back"

Aspiration Management among Working-Class Youth

"Morton High School"

A few days after beginning my fieldwork in a "School-to-Career" Biotechnology Academy at Morton High School, a public school located in a predominantly low- and middle-income Mexican American and Vietnamese American neighborhood in San Jose, California, I visited "Suzanne,"[1] coordinator of the school's Medical Magnet program, which oversees its Biotech Academy.[2] Suzanne was familiar with my plan to conduct ethnographic fieldwork among the Academy's juniors and seniors—primarily low-income students from first- and second-generation immigrant families who were at the point of making at least some preliminary decisions about what path to pursue after high school—in order to gain a sense of Morton's school environment and how its students experienced and negotiated Academy curricula and goals.

Biotech's emphasis is on building skills through an integrated curriculum centered around biotechnological innovation and entrepreneurship. I wanted to know how the Academy's students—who had little contact with the world of highly skilled Silicon Valley professionals outside the Academy—were learning to define their aspirations in relation to both the high-tech skills and values to which they were exposed at school, and other social, economic, familial, and educational circumstances they confronted. Keeping in mind the paradoxical nature of aspirations, which can mask doubts and fears, and suggest limitations as much as goals, I specifically wanted to investigate what aspirations the students believed were possible to achieve and what their aspirations revealed about their doubts, fears, and feelings of limitation. I also wanted to know the forms of self-discipline and expectations that they internalized. I was curious as well about how Biotech students perceived the dominant public culture of Silicon Valley—meaning the work practices, values, and social style of high-tech companies and professionals—and the extent to which exposure to biotechnological innovation and entrepreneurship through school shaped students' aspirations for the future and their perceptions of their place within a Valley economy and society segregated by race and class (Benner 2002; Castells and Hall 1994; English-Lueck 2002; Hossfeld 1988; Pitti 2003; Saxenian 1996).

I had chosen the Biotechnology Academy at Morton for its corporate connections to the biotechnology sector of the regional information economy and for its student demographics. Many of Morton's students come from low-income and non–English-speaking families. At the time of my research 54 percent of Morton's students were Latino and 30 percent were Asian (primarily Vietnamese). There were smaller percentages of white (6%), Filipino (4%), African American (4%), and other students (California Department of Education, 2001–2002). The 150 students in the Biotech Academy reflected Morton's ethnic composition. The socioeconomic status of Morton's students was primarily low-income, though there were also students from middle-income families. In addition to the fact, mentioned earlier, that probably more than the reported 54 percent of students at Morton were eligible for reduced-price lunches, given that the local elementary and middle school district that fed into Morton's high school district reported 70 percent eligibility,[3] qualification for a state Cal grant offered another socioeconomic indicator: within Biotech, twenty-one seniors out of thirty-seven applicants for a state Cal Grant to attend a community or four-year college met the low-income eligibility requirements.[4]

In our private meeting Suzanne and I discussed the social, economic, and educational circumstances that Morton High students confronted at home and at school. Although some families held white-collar positions within the region's tech firms and a few owned small businesses, many students' parents performed low-wage, service-sector work as landscapers, customer-service representatives, medical and dental assistants, custodians, and secretaries. Others worked in construction, manufacturing, and electronics assembly. Many such jobs appeared to be unstable; some mothers of Latino Biotech students whom I interviewed reported that husbands working in maintenance and construction were having their hours cut because of the declining economy, causing mounting anxiety at home.[5] Further, many students I surveyed reported that their parents were unemployed,[6] and a number of students had part-time jobs in order to contribute to household expenses.

Many of the pastel and beige stucco tract homes and apartment complexes that line the suburban-looking streets and cul-de-sacs surrounding Morton's campus are inhabited by multiple families or large extended families.[7] Indeed, according to a Santa Clara County administrator in charge of school-linked services, Morton's student body is one of the most transient in the county[8] as families look for cheaper housing outside Silicon Valley or travel to and from Mexico.

The transient nature of the school and community places Morton at a budgetary disadvantage, since, as we have seen, school enrollment is directly tied to school funding. In addition to these challenges, as noted earlier, Morton was striving to outgrow a decades-old stigma of being a "gang-ridden" school in a "gang-infested" neighborhood. School officials, parents, a few students, and community advocates and religious leaders complained to me about gangs in the neighborhood, although most pointed out that the problem had abated considerably because of extensive suppression and prevention efforts coordinated by city, school, county, and community organizations.

The school's hard-to-shake reputation for gang activity contributed to the school principal's consciousness of the school's appearance, the quality of its facilities, and the way in which a school's physical and social space can define students' learning environment and expectations. Built in the late 1950s, when the surrounding area was filled with orchards, Morton looks like a typical, if dilapidated, California high school. Its beige, low-slung, and mostly old buildings house different academic departments and classrooms. There is a central asphalt quad with a student mural on one wall, where students at "brunch" and lunch, all clad according to the school's strict dress code, gather to eat and talk and then scatter to class. The school has a small pool and sports fields and a new science building (funded by a 1993 bond measure for school improvements and for building a new school in the district) but no theater or performing arts center, which the principal, Dr. H., regretted. The Biotech Academy, which program administrators described as a kind of "school-within-a-school" despite not actually being a separate school, shares this space. Biotech sophomores, juniors, and seniors use the same classrooms and outside space as the rest of Morton's students, so there is little, in fact, to distinguish Biotech students from the rest of the student body.

On these modest school grounds, Morton's administrators and teachers (including the teachers at Biotech, all Morton teachers who have been trained to teach in the Academy) serve as cultural ambassadors, helping immigrant families learn the educational and middle-class social expectations and norms within a public school system under pressure from the state to improve its standards and student performance. As I came to see, the need for ambassadorship was apparent; conversations with parents and teachers revealed an ambivalence toward the school on the part of Latinos, in particular; parents were both suspicious of the administration's motives and appreciative of the school and its teachers. They also depended on school staff for information about the social and educational expectations confronting their children. Although some parents praised Morton—and Biotech Academy, in particular—a few Latino parents thought that their children were being unfairly penalized for minor infractions or were not rewarded for success because they were Latinos. When an outstanding Latina student received an award from a Spanish-language TV station, her mother complained to the principal, and later to me, that she felt that her daughter's success was not as celebrated as were the successes of Vietnamese students.

At the same time parents sought advice on a range of issues from teachers, social workers, the director of the Reserve Officer Training Corp (ROTC), and county workers in charge of Spanish-language presentations to parents. According to teachers, some Morton parents asked teachers for advice about family matters. Parents' dependence upon teachers for such information and counsel revealed that many parents, who grew up in Mexico, Vietnam, or Cambodia, felt stymied trying to navigate a cultural gap with their own children, one that potentially compromised parental authority. Non–English-speaking parents complained that they had to rely on their children to fill out government forms and even explain mortgage statements.[9]

Morton parents' ambivalent feelings were reciprocated by teachers. Although the teachers habitually praised Morton's Southeast Asian and Latino immigrant families for the premium they placed on family, teachers also often expressed frustration with the priorities of some parents. Teachers complained about families that considered babysitting for younger siblings and family trips to Mexico a priority over school attendance; they also commented on the difficulty of getting Morton parents—especially Latino parents—involved in the school community.

As for Morton's students, and those in the Biotech Academy in particular, home and school expectations were often at odds. The Academy's dedicated teachers kept close tabs on their students, shepherding them through the sometimes rocky experience of high school, demanding explanations for absences, and trading information about students' academic performance and behavior in different courses. They also connected students to biotech professionals and corporate settings "up the peninsula," where many Silicon Valley firms and Biotech companies are located. Whereas Latino parents universally expressed a desire for their children to go to college,[10] many Mexican American and a few Vietnamese American students commented on the pressure they felt to live at home, work, and continue to contribute to household finances and provide child care for younger siblings after graduating from high school. A few Vietnamese American girls I spoke with reported that their parents wanted them only to attend a local school and continue to live at home.

As a middle-class, white outsider newly affiliated with the school, my quest to build rapport with students was shaped by these social conditions and conflicts. Generally I was able to establish better connections with Latino students than with Asian students. Many Vietnamese American students declined to be interviewed and generally avoided me, whereas Latino students tended to be more open to my presence. Moreover, I speak Spanish and not Vietnamese, which gave me better access to Latino households.[11]

As Suzanne and I sat discussing the circumstances of the "typical" Morton student and speculating on my ability to establish rapport, Suzanne worried aloud that Morton students' SCANS skills were not sufficient to compete for highly skilled jobs in predominantly white high-tech or health services industry sectors.[12] By SCANS skills, Suzanne meant the interpersonal and presentation skills that enable workers to communicate smoothly and be perceived as "team players" and "problem solvers" within the context of Silicon Valley's predominantly white, middle-class, and highly skilled information economy.[13] Suzanne's concern about the occupational barriers confronting Latino students was valid; a 1997 survey of local high-tech firms revealed that Hispanics hold only 7 percent of high-tech, white-collar positions (Benner 2002:220), despite comprising 31 percent of the populations of Santa Clara and San Mateo counties (JVSV Network 2000).

Armando

The talk about SCANS skills reminded Suzanne of one student in particular. Armando was an outgoing senior slated to graduate that semester. As a member of Biotech's first graduating class and the first to experience actual "high-tech work" in a major biotechnology corporation during a one-week Genentech internship the previous summer, Armando was the first "test case" of the Biotech Academy. Suzanne had known Armando throughout his four years at Morton, and she sensed that Armando, when recounting his internship experience, had told her "what [she] wanted to hear about industry." In musing about Armando's first experience with this other world, Suzanne "wondered about the culture, being Hispanic, fitting in there" and mentioned a mixed report Armando had received from his Genentech internship supervisors, who said that although he worked very hard, his social skills were not quite appropriate to the environment.

Despite a poor attendance record, and what many teachers described as his "extremely at-risk background," Armando, father to a three-year-old son, was one of the best science students that his biotechnology teacher ever had. In the opinion of this teacher, a former Stanford biology Ph.D. student, the kinds of questions Armando asked in class indicated a great aptitude for science: "He could be a Ph.D. researcher," the teacher commented. But this teacher also felt that other aspects of Armando's life, mainly his familial and economic obligations, distracted him from school. He was irked that from time to time his students, Armando included, simply "disappeared," failing to show up at school because of a mid-semester family trip to Mexico or perhaps because they were overwhelmed, he suspected, by events in their lives that he, a self-admitted product of a white, Midwestern suburb, found difficult to grasp.

The frustrations that Morton's middle-class high school teachers felt toward their students and their students' families was echoed by Armando's mentor at Genentech, a Latino research librarian active in the company's community outreach program, who confessed that he was "never able to penetrate the surface with Armando" or get a sense of who Armando "really was." The mentor was especially surprised when, after witnessing the enthusiasm Armando had expressed for biotechnological innovation and the possibility of working one day at Genentech, and after helping him apply for a Genentech Scholars grant for study after high school, he discovered that Armando had decided to join the Marine Corps immediately after graduation.

A few weeks after my chat with Suzanne, I had a chance to talk at length with Armando, a dark-eyed, gregarious teenager with a military haircut and a ready grin, whom everyone seemed to know and like. We met at a Biotech Academy event called "Lighthouse Day," a day-long celebration in honor of the program having been chosen as a Lighthouse Academy (a beacon of model practices) by the Career Academy Support Network at the University of California, Berkeley.[14]

A group of Lighthouse Day visitors—including representatives from biotechnology education groups in the Bay Area, a few teachers from other schools who had come to see a model program, and a few Academy Steering Committee members from Agilent Technologies and Genentech Corporation, two of the locally based corporations that provide financial, curricular, and mentor support to Biotech, gathered in the school's modest and usually empty library. Perched like cruise directors next to student-made poster exhibitions showcasing their work within the Academy, Armando and his well-coifed fellow students greeted visitors and described the program's social and pedagogical relationship to local Silicon Valley industry. Armando stood beside a poster that read "Agilent Community Service Components," and he and two girls, one of whom wore an attractive business suit, explained how, as Biotech students, they transported Agilent's scientific experimentation kits over to the local junior high school and taught local eighth graders how to conduct an experiment, with occasional guidance from Agilent employee volunteers.[15]

As we stood chatting, the conversation turned quickly to Armando's experience at his Genentech internship: "It was cool! A little lab work, and then back to the computer," Armando enthused, squinting dreamily as if reliving a luxury vacation. He recalled how the CEO of Genentech always wore shorts to work, worked half a day, and greeted him whenever he crossed his path. "I was like, the CEO!" Armando chuckled somewhat theatrically. In this group conversation, Armando portrayed his time at Genentech as a glowing success, commenting that the people at Genentech asked him to consider a job after graduation and a community college training course in biotechnological laboratory techniques. Armando had already learned how to perform "micro-pipetting" in his senior-year biotechnology course. He was also aware that Genentech would even pay for a four-year college education in a biotechnology-related field at a local university.[16] He seemed excited about this prospect, making it clear that he thought working with DNA to "cure diseases" was something important, and not without a little scientific glamour. And yet, after a glowing report of his experience in the Academy and at Genentech, Armando confirmed what I had already heard, that he planned to enter the Marine Corps upon graduation. In fact, he was already preparing for boot camp with five-mile runs every weekend.

Armando met his Marine Corps recruiter in an aisle of a Safeway supermarket. During senior year Armando worked at this Safeway thirty hours each week, and he happened to be on his shift when the recruiting officer was shopping. As he told the story, he asked the recruiting officer how old he had to be to join up, and he ended up spending three hours that day watching the boot camp video and talking to the officer about life in the Marines.

He recalled his impressions of the boot camp video, and commented on the practical reasons why entry into what he preferred to call the "United States Marine Corps" was an ideal choice for him:

A: I was like, this is *crazy*. There's a lot of worse things that I overcame in my life. I was like, this is gonna be nothing.
E: Like what?
A: Raising my son, providing for everything. I buy all our food and clothes, and medical insurance comes through Safeway . . . I wanna get all that training and become a Marine, and try to take college courses while I am there. I [will] have somewhat steady hours [in the Marines].

He went on to point out that once basic training was finished he would be eligible for a job in shipping and receiving on base, for which he would learn the Unix system and have his college tuition paid for. He referred to his need to earn steady money to support his three-year-old son, Armando Jr., and his girlfriend. Since Armando Jr. had been born, they had lived with his mother, father, thirty-nine-year-old brother, and "a white lady who is a family friend and took care of me when I was little," who had split the cost of a mortgage for Armando's parents' home. He added, as an afterthought, that he wanted to travel and to "experience the world."

I pressed Armando about the option of a career in biotechnology, perhaps at Genentech. He had, after all, gone through the motions of applying for a scholarship from Genentech and forging connections with people there, and he had teachers in the Academy as well as a Genentech mentor who would help him pursue this option. He answered philosophically:

It's like a lot of people say. You can't always have the best forever. I wanna have a little bit of struggle with a little bit of—I mean, I've been struggling here, but it's just like I've always seen the sun. I want to experience the cold or experience the super hot. I just want to have more experiences in life. Every man should do at least two to four years of service to their country.

I wanted to get more experience and get a little more educated before I go get a job. I saw what they did [at Genentech]. What they do is something I could do but a lot of the lab write-ups is kinda difficult for me, so I didn't want to stay. I was with a college student [at the internship] from San Francisco State University and I had a harder time with the lab stuff than he did . . . I wouldn't mind coming back to a job like that. I hope that same lady's still there if I do come back. She's cool.

He went on to say:

I want to join the United States Marine Corps. It's not just the military. Everything they [the Marines] do I like. A lot of people say, 'Why don't you go into the army?' And I'm like, those guys don't do nothing, man. Marines are 100% the best. They are the first to fight. They guard nuclear plants. It's like, *dang*. . .

Like many eighteen year olds, Armando entertained ambiguous imaginings of his future, saying at one point that he wanted to be a career military officer and, at another, that he would like to come back and do "more interesting" work for a biotechnology corporation at a higher level than "fourteen dollars an hour." These vacillations about long-term career plans notwithstanding, Armando presented service in the Marines as an act that was both practical, a source of the "steady hours" that would bring him financial stability and economic assistance with a college education, and a kind of higher calling. He spoke with genuine feeling about the chance to serve and sacrifice for the country, and he said that he thought that military service, particularly Marine Corps service, which he understood to be particularly demanding and dangerous, would build his character and his skills in ways that would equip him for whatever came next, whether that was an entry-level position at a high-tech corporation, a university education, or a military career.

How might we make sense of Armando's practical, moral, and psychological motivations? Certainly his decision to choose the Marines can be read as an effect of his economic and political circumstances. His status as a low-income Latino young man with a child and a girlfriend to support and a low-wage, unstable job, albeit one with medical benefits, made the prospect of stable employment and the ability to afford college via the military appealing. Moreover, this push factor intersected with a contemporary dynamic of militarization in the United States: the targeting of poor communities where inhabitants have little means to obtain dependable and secure employment or to pursue higher education (Lutz 2002; Mariscal 2004). As many have noted, poor at-risk youth, and Latino youth in particular, are increasingly a target of military recruitment in the post–9/11 era (Perez 2006: 54; Lovato 2007; Mariscal 2004), and the provisions of the No Child Left Behind Act of 2001, which give recruiters access to high school, junior college, and college campuses, have made their presence even more pervasive.[17] Indeed, the intensification of Latino recruitment reflects careful planning; the Pentagon aims to increase enlistment of Latinos from approximately 10 percent to 22 percent by the year 2025 (cited in Perez 2006.).[18]

At the same time Armando's particular situation as an Academy participant with teachers and mentors interested in seeing him fulfill his promise made his situation somewhat atypical. Moreover, his comments on the value of struggle and service to the nation make clear that, at least subjectively, the story of his recruitment is more complicated; for Armando, economic motivations intersected with profound feelings about struggle, exploration, and service as a means of self-empowerment, as well as an apparent insecurity about his ability to handle the rigors of an entry-level job in the tech sector.

Indeed, struggle was a familiar and affecting theme for Armando. He spent his first five years in East San Jose, a traditionally Latino and working-class area, before the family moved to a brown, stucco apartment complex right across from Morton High School, on the South Side of San Jose, a predominantly lower-middle- and working-class neighborhood populated largely by first- and second-generation Mexican immigrant families and Southeast Asian families who began streaming into San Jose in the late 1970s and early 1980s (Freeman 1989).[19] Armando's mother had been raised in Texas and the Mexican state of Chihuahua, and had come to California with a high school diploma "looking for a better life," he told me. Armando related the following well-worn story with pride: as the baby of a family of five, and the only child of his father—his mother's third husband—Armando grew up hearing from his mother how, before his father came along, she had to raise four kids on her own, working as a maid, while worrying about his two older brothers who got into trouble during high school and afterward.

His father, also a high school graduate, came from a small town in Michoacán, and Armando grew up watching his parents work together, his father as a landscaper for a large firm serving apartment complexes and corporations in Silicon Valley and his mother as a maid at the same complexes.[20] While they worked Armando would ride his bike around the apartment complexes, playing by himself, and sometimes with kids who lived there. When he was older he began helping his father with landscaping work. One day, when he was ten, his mother slipped on floor wax at a complex where she was working and was ultimately disabled from the accident. When I met Armando, his father owned his own landscaping company serving private residences and also worked for a large landscaping firm contracted, he told me, to Cisco Systems and Siemens Corporation. The family subsisted on the father's employment and his mother's disability payments.

At eighteen, Armando faced various struggles of his own: being a father to a son he had with his high school (and junior high school) girlfriend, working more than thirty hours a week at a Safeway supermarket while trying to graduate from high school, and confronting the prospect of supporting his family full-time. Paradoxically, Armando had represented his life as an easy one. "You can't always have the best forever," he had said. "I've been struggling here, but it's just like I've always seen the sun. I want to experience the cold or experience the super hot." He craved not simply new experiences but the test of strict discipline that the Marine Corps promised—military ordeal glossed in a metaphor of temperature endurance—and the experience of serving his country.

Although a person with Armando's life experience might grow accustomed to articulating that experience through idioms of sacrifice and struggle, thus making such sacrifice or struggle seem natural, the familiarity of struggle and sacrifice, like the promise of economic assistance, only partially explain Armando's feelings about the military, and his decision to join it. After all, he could have experienced sacrifice and struggle majoring in biology at a university, while simultaneously working and providing for his family. Why, then, did he feel he needed a disciplinary test, an obligation to serve his country for at least two to four years? [21]

The question of how a sense of obligation toward a common good translates into a desire to perform military service lies partly in what the Marines counterposed in Armando's mind. For Armando, the adventure and sacrifice of the Marines was in some sense an antidote to a default life of boring, hard work of the kind endured by his father, a struggling immigrant entrepreneur and worker:

Like my dad—he's—I grew up doing landscaping [with him] and I just hated it so much. And he kept telling me, he's all, "You hate it, huh? I can see you hate landscaping. Now you know why I do this to you, son? 'Cuz this is how you learn. You're gonna go to school and do something different than what I'm doing. 'Cuz like it's boring! You make a lot of money but do you like making a lot of money but cracking your back?" I'm all, "No." He's all, "You got nice shoes but how does your back feel?" He's like, "Use your mind! The only way I would'a had it better is if I'd had the money to go to school."

Military service in what Armando perceived to be the toughest wing of the military—the branch that guards nuclear plants—was also an antidote to the life that his neighborhood friends were leading. With perceptible disapproval, he viewed such friends and even certain family members as people who were, on some level, lazy and unwilling to improve themselves and take responsibility for their own circumstances:

The friends you make at home are like who lives next to you. They're like laid back, staying at home and working nine to five, doing jobs that are way boring. All they want to do is have fun and not sacrifice anything for life [he sounds disdainful]. I mean, they're making some money, but it's like, aaahhh! Anyone could do that.

Armando wanted to ward off the kind of existence he observed in his neighborhood, and, as the above quote indicates, he felt that personal advancement would require more than just "making some money"; it would involve sacrifice to something larger than oneself, and proving that you are not just "anyone." Armando's depiction of the Marine Corps, with its rigorous demands of physical and emotional hardship, suggests that he understood service in it as a means of providing such proof.

Career Goals as Expressions of Aspiration Management

In his articulation of a desire to perform public (military) service that might require personal sacrifice for a common good,[22] Armando resembled many of the Morton students, particularly Latino students, whom I interviewed and, to varying degrees, came to know.[23] I first noticed students' penchant for public and social service work during Lighthouse Day, when I conducted an on-the-spot straw poll of the future plans of graduating seniors. Although the exhibits the students created for Lighthouse Day showcased scientific, technological, and ethical aspects of biotechnological research and the social networking skills prized in Silicon Valley—one student recapped a classroom stem cell debate in which students played scientists and members of Congress, while another emphasized the connections researchers and other highly educated tech professionals at local corporations had made with Academy students through the mentorship program—no one I spoke with at Lighthouse Day seemed interested in a career in biotechnology at any level, with the exception of Armando.

By the end of my fieldwork those conversations were representative of a broader pattern of career aspirations that mostly—though not exclusively—was expressed by Latino students over the course of my fieldwork at Morton. The career goal most often mentioned by Vietnamese American and other Southeast Asian students was to become a pharmacist.[24] During my fieldwork at Morton, a few students of varied ethnicity confessed random passions: a Latina girl living in a garage with her mother and sister, all without legal status in the country, hoped to be a photographer,[25] and one day at lunch she showed me a book filled with her early attempts; another affable boy who performed a soul song at graduation confessed a secret desire to become a chef specializing in traditional Filipino cuisine. Latino Biotech students of both genders, however, repeatedly expressed interest in becoming probation officers,[26] police officers, social workers, nurses, teachers, or joining the military.[27] When the occasional student did express interest in biotechnology, it was often in the realm of forensic crime technology, a fusing of the aesthetics and morality of law and order with the scientific themes of the Academy.[28]

The point here is not to argue that the Academy directly tracked its mostly working-class minority and immigrant students into social or public-service jobs, although it is worth mentioning that, at the time of research, approximately half of the school's ROTC program, which includes some Biotech Academy students though not Armando, join the Army Reserves, the National Guard, or perform active duty in the military when they graduate.[29] Rather, we shall explore the cultural, moral, and political meanings that these jobs have for these particular students and how experiences outside and inside school shaped those meanings. Discussions I had with students about their career goals represent expressions of what I call "aspiration management," a term that highlights the active role students have in defining self-expectation, hope, and a sense of the possible, as well as the paradox of self-limitation and desire inherent in all aspirations. Aspiration management is a process that involves everyday practices of self-regulation, forms of narrative expression, and imaginings of one's present and future place in the world and one's community or neighborhood in relation to other people and places, all acts that inform students' self-perception, values, and aesthetics.

Of course, statements about future career goals is just one way among many in which students signal and shape their aspirations, but the pattern of career aspirations I observed among Latino students, in particular, serves as an aperture through which to explore the social and symbolic order that these students inhabited. What did these jobs symbolize, and stand in contrast to, in the minds of Biotech Academy students at Morton High School—low-income, Latino youth who were, as a result of their admittance to the Academy, being actively nudged toward an interest in biotechnological innovation and business?

Military work, police work, social work, and teaching have much in common. There is, of course, a practical dimension to the choice, as we have seen in the case of Armando: public-sector jobs tend to be steady, and therefore a valuable commodity in a mercurial tech-based regional economy known for its insecure, contingent employment (Benner 2002) which, in 2002, was in recession (JVSV Network 2003).[30] Indeed, in the contemporary United

States, the reality of diminishing opportunities for poor youth to achieve social mobility makes the promise of stable public-sector work or military service appealing (Perez 2006; Graeber 2007). Although a critical piece of the puzzle, this is only a partial explanation; economic considerations ultimately combine with multiple factors and power-laden "structures of feeling" (Williams 1994) that come into play as people negotiate life circumstances and attempt to define themselves and their aspirations.[31]

This point brings to mind another shared quality of public-service jobs, one that overrides the distinction that many would make between a job as a soldier in the military or a police officer, as opposed to a job as a social worker. Taken together, the jobs that these Biotech students preferred have a moral inflection; they suggest a collectively oriented vision of society and at the same time they involve overt and sometimes more implicit forms of policing. Morton's Biotech Academy students of both genders emphasized wanting to "give back." They expressed, in other words, a kind of obligation or debt to society. Moreover, they often envisioned "giving back" through the kind of monitoring to which they were subject.

Marteena, a Biotech Academy senior from a single-parent home whose housing situation during high school had been unstable, and whose mother received CALWORKS benefits in return for working at Target thirty-two hours a week, recalled an encounter with a community relations manager from Agilent Technologies who had suggested that Marteena consider possible employment at Agilent one day. "Would you be interested in that?" I asked. "No," she replied. "I want to be a probation officer or a social worker. I want to give back to the community." Marteena mentioned friends who had been helped by probation officers, and added, "You see about the past, what my ancestors put in, the civil war, civil rights, living in Arizona and Texas, so much has been given up for us." Marteena felt that she could best fulfill a debt for the sacrifice of her Mexican and African American ancestors by helping others in her position to avoid social marginalization.

Like many Biotech Academy students I interviewed and came to know, Marteena and Armando expressed their career aspirations in terms of obligation to a "community," whether to the nation, a "community" of historically oppressed people of color, or, as some students vaguely put it, "kids." What prompted such forms of aspiration and feelings of obligation? By exploring the meanings that students associate with failure and success, and the relationship of those meanings to forms of discipline and attitudes that students learned to cultivate at school and within the broader community, we can gain insight into the motivations for such aspirations.

The Specter of Failure

What does failure connote for the young people in the Academy? We return to Armando's perception of his friends, whom he found to be unwilling both to take a risk and to make a sacrifice. They reminded him, in fact, of his own brothers, whom he describes as recovering "delinquents" who "don't really do nothing." Armando's description of his brothers and his neighborhood friends conveyed an impression of people who won't help themselves. Who were these people? They were Latino youth or adults without much money who lived in Armando's neighborhood. According to Armando, their values contrasted with those that Armando had learned at school in the Biotech Academy and that he associated with his "school friends":

> The friends you make at school are interested in homework . . . They're bringing their mind more, doing other stuff than just staying at home and working. I see them saying, "I wanna go to San Jose State" and that's cool. It's like, my brothers, they don't really do nothing.

In the above quote, Armando immediately refers back to his brothers as a counterexample to the world of school. His description of the lifestyle of his neighborhood friends and his brothers evokes the specter of being an unimportant drone, in some way superfluous to society. It is a description reminiscent of many jokes, sarcastic comments, and fears I heard uttered by Academy students. In off-hand comments and private discussions, students expressed, in various ways, the racially coded stigma of being labeled "at risk" and of living in an "at-risk" neighborhood.

Like Armando, Juliana, a mischievous young woman with light-blue eyes, olive skin, and dyed blue-black hair, was a popular figure on campus. I knew her during the spring of her junior year and the fall of her senior year. She was one of the students who reached out to me, inviting me to come and "kick it" with her and her friends at lunch, and chatting with me when I saw her around campus or in class. During the first of two formal interviews (approximately six months apart) Juliana informed me, in her perennially congested voice, that she wanted to be a social worker "that goes to people's houses to check on kids," a career idea inspired by her own memories of a social worker who visited her home during a period of family difficulties when she was ten and eleven. Alternately she expressed interest in becoming a policeman or a private detective.

Over the months I observed that Juliana's apparent boldness and her perpetual expression of mild amusement masked feelings of vulnerability. When we discussed her future in our first interview, she had said with bravado, " I can do whatever I want in my life!" But at the end of the interview she commented: "I worry that I can't make it—I can't get into college. I think about it so much that I'm not going to make it. I'm the type of person, if I keep thinking I can't make it, then I won't." Juliana admitted this in a sad and seemingly urgent way, unburdening herself in the confines of a private interview. At the moment of this admission, she lost her amused expression and bantering style. Her backup plan, she told me, was to work in an office.

What did the prospect of not making it to a four-year college mean to Juliana? On a fieldtrip to San Jose State University to attend a Biotech career fair and listen to a panel of representatives from different biotechnology companies and NASA, the conversation turned to the University of California (UC) system. Juliana and her friends joked, "Yeah, we'll be going to UC Evergreen." Evergreen, a community college in East San Jose that many Morton students attend after high school, was an option that teachers did not openly disparage but portrayed during in-class discussions of preparing for life after high school as run-of-the-mill. Juliana made it clear that, for her, it was a lackluster option, a subtle failure, but one that couldn't be disparaged too much, since many of her friends planned to take the junior college route and she thought she might end up doing so herself. On more than one occasion I witnessed an administrator or teacher giving a pep talk during class and reminding Juliana and her classmates about the statistical unlikelihood of actually transferring to a four-year college from a community college. For those choosing community college, the odds, they were reminded, were against them; according to a nationwide study conducted by scholars of education at Stanford University, only 22 percent of those entering community college who wish to acquire a four-year degree actually attain one.[32]

Over the months I spent at Morton I heard Juliana joking and making sarcastic comments with her friends about status and about the future. With comic flair, she and her friends often reminded one another of the racial and class boundaries that circumscribed their lives, positioning themselves on the right side of the bridge separating those with secure legal, social, and economic status from those without such security. They designated their group of friends—all Latina—"the Mexicans" and greeted one another on campus with a shrill, "Hey, Mexican!" A collective nickname that signified solidarity and racial pride but also revealed constant awareness of their racialized status. During a social studies unit on World War II, Juliana and her friends joked to one another, "You're not a citizen! You're not!" "Yes, I am!" someone protested, and then the punch line: No, you're not! You used my social security card, remember?" Everyone laughed at this flip reminder of citizenship status which, for many students, was one generation removed and was, for a few students, an ongoing issue. Juliana, for example, had reported that her own mother "had to sleep on bus stops" when she came to California from Mexico. At the present time her mother, without a high school education, had a job making "little chips for the cell phone," and her stepfather had his own small landscaping business.

As was the case with Armando and many other young people at Morton, narratives about Mexico and the journey to a life in the United States were filled with parents' hardships and the poverty in Mexico relative to the United States. Students' parents also compared life in Mexico to life in the United States; a few recalled sending misbehaving teenagers to Mexico so they could understand the hardship and discipline they were escaping by living in the United States and become more grateful. Such references to Mexico and parents' experiences of immigration also signified the vulnerability of the present in San Jose.

"I'm a troublemaker," Juliana repeated a few times during our first interview. I asked her once where she thinks she'll be five years from now, and she joked, flippantly, "Probably pregnant!" "No, really," I persisted, and Juliana explained: "Everybody thinks I'm going to get pregnant."

Juliana applied herself intermittently in school. She worked part-time at Togo's, making sandwiches and operating the cash register, and her desire to be a social worker did not preclude a desire to own a Lexus and to travel. Though she was unsure of how to achieve these goals, or even make it to college, she was fully aware of the need to do so in order to maintain her position on the right side of the class and racial boundaries which she and her friends often joked about.

In the fall of senior year, one of Juliana's friends, Luisa, seemed to be slipping in the wrong direction. Another friend, Laura, gossiped to me about Luisa, complaining that she cut class too much and would probably end up being "a low-life." "What's a low-life?" I asked, and Laura explained that Luisa would probably just sit on the couch all day, without a job or maybe even a diploma, watching daytime TV.

Juliana and her friends also made "gang-banger" jokes about themselves and people they knew, while scorning the gang label that stigmatized their school. Along with making occasional jokes about scaring people from more affluent and whiter schools, they repeatedly described gangs as no longer cool and disdained "wanna-bes"; they also took world-weary pride in describing their neighborhood as "ghetto." These jokes, like the narratives about Mexico and parental hardship and flippant predictions of personal failure, signaled that, for these young people, the fact of belonging to a vulnerable and marginalized group was ever present, manifested in gendered and racialized fantasies of failure. They knew they were considered at-risk youth, and were aware of the moral and racial implications of this label. Being a "low-life" or getting pregnant while in high school connoted the possibility of being permanently relegated to a pathologized category of at-risk youth, associated, in a feminized way, with unemployability and unreliability.

Expressions of stigmatization or the threat of it reinforced a perceived need—on the part of both students and their parents—for forms of self-discipline to ward off threats of economic and social marginalization. The Biotech Academy in particular, and Morton more generally, provided antidotes to the threat of failure and models for student success in multiple ways: through learning environments and school community activities designed to promote students' sense of belonging to a school community, respect for fellow students, and positive goals, and through a pervasive discourse of risk management and an emphasis on regulations to promote what administrators and teachers felt to be school-appropriate behavior.

The Flexible Mission of the Biotechnology Academy

On Lighthouse Day Chris, the program coordinator for the Biotech Academy, distributed brochures about the Academy's mission. The statement read:

> In order to graduate students with biotechnology skills to enter the workforce, we will provide integrated academic classes, field trips, guest speakers, and the opportunity for work experience and professional mentoring. Upon graduation from the Biotechnology Academy, students will be professional, responsible citizens, and realize the benefits of becoming lifelong learners.

Although the phrase "lifelong learners" and the emphasis on responsibility seemed vocational in orientation, a welcoming statement to parents in the Academy's handbook made clear that the goals of the Academy were not necessarily vocational: "We are committed to giving your student a rigorous course of study that will enable him or her to either pursue an education in the biotechnology field or enter the field in an entry-level position." In fact, the handbook suggested that the Biotechnology Academy aimed to provide both academic and vocational education by emphasizing both "hands-on learning" and "critical thinking" within an integrated, biotechnology-themed curriculum. The handbook clarified this goal:

> The Biotechnology Academy is designed to meet the needs of at-risk youth as well as students from Morton's general population and those involved in its Medical Magnet program, and that it is a college preparatory program with a biotechnological focus . . . designed to motivate students to go on to college.

A range of industry and community "partners" actively supported this objective, including an array of local biotechnology corporations (Genentech, Guidant, Alza, Applied Biosystems, Incyte, Agilent Technologies, and Genencor), and health and educational institutions (Kaiser Hospital, the Central County Occupational Center, and a range of community colleges and local universities including Stanford University and San Jose State University). These private and public institutions guided decisions about the Biotech Academy's curriculum, provided guest speakers, and helped arrange field trips to biotechnology corporations, job fairs, and internships.

Teachers and biotechnology company liaisons to the Academy, representing very different interests, interpreted the Academy's mission differently, contributing to a certain ambiguity within the program. Teachers saw the Academy primarily as a way to keep close tabs on students, thus insuring graduation and the pursuit of college for almost all students.[33] Although no teacher I spoke to discouraged students from attending the Academy as a route to either entry-level manufacturing work or graduate-level specialization in the biotech field, a few commented, privately, that the program was unlikely to produce workers for the biotechnology industry.[34]

Chris, the head coordinator of Biotech, who had made contacts with people in the industry and has been successful at raising money for the program from local corporations, also emphasized the acquisition of SCANS skills as an important element of the Academy, along with the mission of providing entry-level vocational skills for the biotechnology sector. Moreover, she wanted students to expand the realm of the possible in their minds; to think: "Now that I've been exposed to South San Francisco [where many biotechnology firms, the largest being Genentech, are located] and down the peninsula [Silicon Valley proper], I'm not satisfied with an entry-level position."

Myra, a member of Biotech's steering committee, and director of community relations in Silicon Valley for Agilent (and also a former Hewlett-

Packard [HP] employee, prior to Agilent's inception),[35] understood that the Academy's goal was for students to pursue a four-year college education so that they could enter the fields of biotechnology or life sciences "and maybe someday work for Agilent." Myra saw industry as essentially rescuing Morton's at-risk kids, exposing them to the world of the future (biotech) as opposed to the past (electronics work making microchips) in which they could now, as a result of their Academy experience, play a vital role.

In addition to the corporate argument that supporting the Academy would ultimately produce a "homegrown workforce," corporations' support for local community and school programs helped to brand these companies as good corporate citizens. Myra expressed pleasure at the numbers of Academy seniors who plan to attend four-year colleges and universities. "We could have *lost* these kids," she said, "but we haven't, because of the Academy. You're looking at this huge mix of ethnic cultures in that community. Somewhat economically depressed, and a lot of ESL [English as a second language] in that area; it's a diverse group and we [Agilent] want to promote diversity." Indeed, Agilent Technologies emphasized its corporate citizenship. On a two-page spread in its 2001 *Annual Report,* titled *Agilent in Citizenship*, students from Morton's Biotech Academy were featured in color photographs working on science projects, smiling proof of Agilent's commitment to "diversity and inclusion" within their workforce.

The reasons Myra gave for Agilent's affiliation with the Academy echoed the goals of the School-to-Career program (goals which, in Silicon Valley, typically emphasize math and science).[36] In a climate of "sun-setting" federal funds, state programs like School-to-Career had become increasingly dependent on alliances with industry.[37] In Silicon Valley, the School-to-Career mission blended harmoniously with the educational agenda of the larger community of Silicon Valley firms and industry associations, which, during the 1990s, increasingly stressed "bridging the digital divide" and cultivating a "homegrown workforce" by transforming educational curricula and pedagogy to expose youth (particularly low-income, minority youth) to Silicon Valley industries, a regional entrepreneurial ethos, and skills. In fact, the tech industry considered existing School-to-Career programs a means to facilitate this goal; at the time of my research organizations such as NASDAQ, the National Association of Business, and the Silicon Valley Manufacturing Group (a powerful coalition of local corporations concerned with regional issues such as housing, education, and transportation) provided support to local School-to-Career programs to supplement their public funding.

Like other local programs that incorporated a digital divide discourse that invoked Valley customs and techno-entrepreneurial success as a way to achieve personal growth and advancement, the Biotech Academy emphasized the technological advances and entrepreneurial success of local biotech industry. The Academy's curriculum of corporate mentorship, field trips, and group activities, emphasizing team building, self-esteem, and familiarity with biotechnological techniques, was designed to provoke enthusiasm for local companies, generate social networking skills, excite students about the prospects of biotechnological innovation, and direct aspirations toward research and managerial positions within these companies.

On my first day observing a Biotech Academy class at Morton, I attended an early morning senior economics class to hear one of the Academy's guest speakers. In front of a room of bleary-eyed students, Sarada Anand, a biochemist from Alza Corporation, began a recitation of her life story, interwoven with a complex, topical lecture about the direction of current applied pharmaceutical research. Sarada described a middle-class childhood in India where she studied hard and developed a passion for cardiopulmonary research after an illness in the family. She then chronicled, step by step, how she had advanced in her career. At one point she showed slides of a cancer drug and spoke about Alza's advances in pain management. She concluded her presentation by telling students about the many different jobs that are performed within biotech or pharmaceutical companies such as manufacturing, sales, marketing, scientific science, and engineering. She did not discuss the option of post–high school, blue-collar work that one might perform at a biotechnology firm but focused instead on jobs that require university and often graduate education. Moreover, she did not connect the lab skills that seniors in the biotechnology class were learning with work in the industry. She ended on an upbeat note: "[Just as] the electronics industry was the excitement of the 1990s in Silicon Valley, the next decade will be the reign of the biological sciences." Although a few students asked questions about a heart device that the company had invented, the general feeling in the room was that of extreme boredom. The trajectory of a middle-class woman from India, transplanted to Silicon Valley, apparently did not move the class.

Nor did a presentation at a San Jose State University Biotech Career Fair, which I attended with a busload of juniors early on during my fieldwork at Morton. Students were asked to bring resumes to this event in order to take advantage of the presence of representatives from biotechnological industry by networking during a social hour in a university conference room.

Most of the audience was composed of undergraduates and graduate students at San Jose State, so, understandably, our high school group felt out of place.

Before the networking hour, the students listened to a number of panelists. A white-haired man with a doctorate in biosciences told the story of how he had become passionate as an undergraduate about "how cells got their instructions about what to do," and another woman described the importance of networking in propelling her toward her current position as a data manager at Genentech. A scientist from NASA began his speech with the words, "Welcome to the future! Biotech will be the defining engine of this century!" and went on to invoke the then president Bill Clinton's comparison of the genome map to Lewis and Clark's expedition across the continent. Students fidgeted during every presentation, and in the social networking hour that followed, many left, wandering the campus in search of snacks until it was time to leave.

Academy students seemed indifferent and at times alienated by the people and places associated with local techno-entrepreneurship, and the mentor program did not appear to significantly change their attitudes in this regard. During casual conversations and interviews, many students derided "spending the day in a cubicle" or a lab, and complained that they had nothing in common with their corporate mentors, who inhabited a Valley which they described—when prodded to talk about it—as "filled with technology" and "white." "She's so boring!" "I have nothing in common with her!" "She doesn't understand us!" Juliana, Linda, Elena, and their friends complained when describing interactions with their corporate mentors. Few students could tell me exactly what their mentors actually did at work.

In June, right before Armando's class graduated, the students presented their final projects for their biotechnology course, which was also their final exam. Their teacher had explained to me that he had calibrated the depth of the course towards the junior college level. Students learned about the concept of DNA, how it works, how it becomes RNA and protein, how DNA is used as a tool and how to work with it in the lab, and how to cut it and paste it into new organisms. The presentations were made in a new lecture hall on campus, on a stage equipped with a projector on which students mounted their own PowerPoint slides. A feeling of professionalism and nervous anticipation pervaded the room, perhaps partly because corporate mentors, Academy teachers, and members of the steering committee comprised the audience. Many students dressed up for the occasion, and a few girls wore stylish, corporate-looking blazers.

Each group presented a hypothesis, a procedure, results, and a conclusion in a bulleted list on PowerPoint slides. One group posed the question, "Do couples have the same DNA?" They described how they had taken cell samples from the tongues of couples who were dating. At one point a graph was projected on the screen, and the teacher asked: "What does the 3.5 on the Y axis represent?" "It don't mean nothin'!" one of the students called out, and everyone laughed. Another experiment hypothesized that "a domestic mouse will not do as well under the influence of alcohol as a feral mouse," but how the qualities of feral and domestic were determined and measured remained unclear. A final presentation concerned "Bacteria in the Mouth: The Battle of the Sexes." A slide read: "Do boys or girls have more bacteria in their mouths?" The results, students reported, were inconclusive; the bacteria they examined were varied and of different sizes. A member of the academy steering committee asked students if they had tried to identify any of the bacteria they saw, and they answered that they had not.

The biotech final was significant in that it highlighted a program that prioritized presentation skills, namely, dressing well, comporting oneself professionally, and using PowerPoint. On the surface the biotech final honed social SCANS skills important to industry and emphasized scientific inquiry by demanding that students conduct experiments and interpret results. The manner in which the preparation and performance were executed, however, focused on a display of professionalism through bodily discipline and technological practice; experimentation amounted to a prop with which to signal preparedness for work. In one sense, the comment, "It don't mean nothin!" might be interpreted as a flip, tension-breaking joke, but it also seemed to voice an implicit feeling among students that the presentation itself was more important than its content, a view with which mentors and Academy-affiliated corporate representatives observing the final exam agreed; both steering committee members and corporate mentors found that the biotechnological content covered during student presentations was watered down, a fact, they pointed out, that did not cultivate in students the creative problem-solving skills or rigor required for participation in the upper echelons of industry.

A few months later, after the summer break, I witnessed an event that ritualized the production of responsible, reliable student-citizens. The event was a team-building field trip that Chris had organized. We traveled to the affluent west side of Santa Clara County, to a nature preserve in the hills used for corporate and school retreats. Representatives of a company that provides training to corporations and schools, ranging from MBAs to high school students, met us in the parking area, and then we hiked to a cement clearing surrounded by forest. First we performed a series of competitive and team-building exercises, each followed by a "reflection session." These exercises emphasized learning to work together, to communicate politely and clearly, and to have patience with others.

In the afternoon I observed students participate in a ropes course. A high ladder was mounted on the side of a very tall tree trunk, perhaps thirty feet off the ground, which students had the option to climb. If they chose not to climb, they had to announce to the group, "My name is X, and I choose not to climb today." Those who decided to climb stated their names and told the group, "I choose to climb this tree." They were then asked to state a personal goal. After climbing to the top of the tree trunk, students stood on its narrow surface and leaped off (with a harness tied to ropes controlled by classmates), thereby symbolically realizing the stated goal. This exercise was intended to build trust and teamwork, but it also symbolized each student's potential. Most students muttered that their goal was to graduate from high school. A few said they wanted to raise their grades in individual classes or become more obedient to parents. Before jumping Suzanne, the head of the Medical Magnet program, told the group that she wanted to communicate better with other staff members. The company facilitators repeatedly uttered the phrase, "You are taking care of one another." After climbing and jumping, most students looked proud of their accomplishment.

At the ropes course event, being a "team player" became a euphemism for conforming to a particular norm, that of the reliable student-citizen. The individualistic act of stating a goal and taking a risk was at once designed to seal a group identity while forging an individual identity that was, ironically, defined by adherence to a norm. No student stated an idiosyncratic personal goal, whether creative, intellectual, or otherwise; participants clearly understood that they were executing a performance of obedience and that not to participate was, in a sense, to declare that one did not have the courage or discipline to be obedient or reliable. For the participants in this exercise, self-confidence and reliability were conflated.

Classroom discourse also reinforced an obligation to be reliable. Teachers often reminded students that they had an obligation to perform well on standardized state exams such as the STAR test not simply to learn the material but because state funding depended upon their performance. In this way the pressure teachers felt to meet state standards in order to avoid cutbacks was directly shared by students. Thus, despite teachers' emphasis on intellectual inquiry as a form of personal growth, intellectual knowledge was linked to a sense of collective social and economic debt.

In sum, the Academy curriculum intersected with political, economic, and social conditions at Morton to produce a paradoxical effect. Within the program's curriculum, Sarada Anand, the NASA scientist, the CEO of Genentech, and students' individual corporate mentors embodied success. These people personified the values associated with technological innovation and entrepreneurship. They were innovation-oriented cosmopolitans who felt comfortable moving between different social and geographical contexts, and valued experimentation and risk taking. And yet, simultaneously, the Academy taught students to equate success and self-confidence with displays of personal reliability. Students learned an art of self-marketing that cultivated their ability to define themselves as responsible citizens in opposition to an at-risk imaginary in the minds of potential employers. They learned a different language and a certain way to dress. They learned how to market themselves on a resume as they would at a job-training center, how to use PowerPoint, and how to present themselves to teachers, corporate mentors, and steering committee members.

These contradictions, however, existed within a broader educational context that shaped students' dispositions toward power and authority as well as meanings associated with success and failure.

The Biotechnology Academy in Context: The Social Space of School and Neighborhood

Morton's everyday environment appeared highly regulated and formal but nonetheless encouraging of particular kinds of multicultural expression and community feeling. Morton has one of the largest ROTC programs in Northern California, and the sight of groups of teenagers chatting with friends in immaculate military uniforms was common. Also common were homemade banners inviting students and their families to events such as "International Night" to celebrate the cultures and culinary traditions of Morton's students, and student government posters proclaiming "*Sí, Se Puede!*" echoing the refrain of César Chávez, a hometown hero.

In general, the campus appeared an industrious, disciplined, and respectful place. Teachers, predominantly white, and staff—mainly white, Asian, and Latino—closely supervised the students. Although students seemed to segregate themselves along ethnic lines, there were also integrated gatherings, especially among the school's smaller minority groups. Despite the tendency toward ethnic self-segregation, Morton seemed to lack cliquishness; as I would learn, popularity was not a constant topic, and the school's social world seemed less hierarchical than, for example, the field site of my other school in nearby, affluent Palo Alto.

This social environment, which reflected the desire of young people to socialize within their own ethnic groups and a sense of respect and pride for the school's diverse ethnic makeup, simultaneously emphasized the regulation of space and individual bodies. Despite administrators' and teachers' representations of Morton as a school home to a wide range of students, from the very at-risk to high-performing honors students, the ordering of the campus environment was designed to prevent at-risk students from succumbing to temptations that might impede their academic and personal performance.

The campus was the site of a pervasive discourse about at-risk youth. "At risk" was, in fact, a slippery term; teachers and administrators employed it to refer to students perceived to be in danger of not graduating from high school, but it seemed, judging from the contexts in which the term was used during my conversations with teachers and administrators, that it was also short-hand for low income, familial dysfunction, and deviant forms of behavior such as gang affiliation and teenage pregnancy. Indeed, teachers often described the students as being at risk right in front of them. They were described this way in teacher meetings, grant proposals, program materials, casual conversations, and Academy steering committee meetings, where a few student representatives were always present.

Staff often represented the school's history to me in reminiscences of a period of bad old days when the school was barely functional, suffering from a gang-ridden anarchical environment. Frequently I heard quotes about the number of gangs on campus—from eight to twenty-two, depending on who was speaking. Chris, the Biotech coordinator, offered statistics about gang presence on campus in a pitch for continued support to a Silicon Valley corporation.

Students' movements were tightly controlled on campus. Morton attendees were supposed to wear identification badges, and a district-wide policy called for having a surveillance video camera on every campus to catch students in the act of writing graffiti.[38] A district policy mandated that graffiti surveillance tapes be turned over to the local district attorney's office. Morton had a closed campus—it always had been—and within the campus were a number of prohibited areas. Students were not allowed to go to their cars during the school day (one administrator informed me that, when they do, they do "bad things"), nor were they permitted to lounge on the track and football fields. The quad was mostly empty while classes were in session, and faculty carried walkie-talkies, intervening when they saw a student not in class, late to class, or not dressed appropriately. Bathrooms were locked during classes, and students who were more than ten minutes late to the last class of the day were placed in a room the school secretary jokingly referred to as "the holding tank." It is notable, however, that the district had not adopted a "zero-tolerance" policy because of concerns about the overrepresentation of minority youth in the criminal justice system in California. At Morton, student violations of the no-weapons-on-campus policy, for example, were handled on a case-by-case basis.

In addition, although there was no school uniform, a strict dress code was enforced at Morton. Students wore black, gray, and white only. Any color, but especially red or blue—colors claimed by the Mexican American *Norteño* and *Sureño* gangs with a presence in the neighborhood—were strictly forbidden.[39] Students were also sent home for violating the dress code.[40]

On the edges of the school grounds, as I drove away from campus at the end of a school day, I might see police cars patrolling the school area, and occasionally I saw officers question a student leaving campus after school about where he or she was headed. Although some students complained to me about school rules, many did not. In fact, in a recent school survey conducted by an administrator, students reported satisfaction with the school as a "safe" area.

Although this regulatory environment ended at the classroom door—as at any high school, students at Morton passed notes to one another, whispered in class, sometimes cut class, and shouted out answers to teachers' questions—nuances of student-teacher relations seemed to indicate that students' dispositions toward power and authority, cultivated at home and at school, carried over into the realm of intellectual and academic performance.

The relationships between Biotech students and their teachers contrasted markedly with the relationships I observed at the Palo Alto school where I was simultaneously conducting research; seniors at the latter school—in the same state-required government class that I observed at Morton—enjoyed intellectual sparring matches with their teachers. At Morton students joked with their teachers and generally had closer relationships with them than did Sanders students with their teachers, perhaps partly because of the "small school" environment of the Academy. But the informal banter between students and teachers, while reinforcing a sense of shared humanity and temporarily putting students on an equal footing with teachers—"I'll beat you to the altar," an engaged Elena joked with her science teacher—tended to focus on personal facts or quirks. Students also felt comfortable engaging in joking flirtation or mimicry of teachers' habits; when an African American girl, known for her trenchant wit and general cynicism, donned a blond wig and held us all spellbound as she impersonated her blond teacher in a kind of carnivalesque depiction of authority, dancing and singing a made-up song, everyone laughed. In the realm of intellectual inquiry and course content, however, students unconsciously assumed a timid and at times infantilized style. When asked a question about *The Great Gatsby* in her Academy English class, Brenda, a friend of Juliana's, whined "I don't know" in a tiny voice. While students' disposition toward intellectual inquiry and discourse in the classroom was not solely determined by the school environment, patterns of discipline and dispositions toward authority ingrained in daily practice outside the classroom did little to diminish students' alienation toward course content. Students' classroom behavior echoed a disposition toward authority figures ingrained in daily practice outside the classroom.

Morton's principal, a thoughtful man whose service to Morton dates back to the early 1970s, and who wrote his Ph.D. dissertation on the effects of school uniforms on aspects of teachers' attitudes toward students, put Morton's "school culture" into perspective:

> There is a big shift on where we want kids to go, [a] shift of values . . . we went from a *"Lord of the Flies"* philosophy of no adult leadership—there was all that personal freedom, do what you want, liberate the mind, [and] now we have them back to basic values. For me, the shift was important. If you want to get philosophical about it, they have to know limits . . . and quite honestly, get your butt to school, get your hat out of the classroom; that's not polite. The red and blue [Norteño and Sureño gang colors], that crap's coming off now. Some of the young ladies, quite frankly, it wasn't appropriate. Boys with gross T-shirts—no more. And—this is before September 11—we say the flag salute, Pledge of Allegiance. We started the flag salute in 1997 . . .
>
> In this community what we find is that kids need more guidance. . . . In the classroom you'll find that it doesn't cut off your intellectual freedom in class. We are teaching them the values of polite society. You do need to get a college education, and you can't be talkin' Ebonics. We are trying to sell the values of polite—not white, European civilization, don't get me wrong—but polite society. Look at who controls society. Once you get there and you're an engineer or a professional, do whatever the hell you want . . . In the 1990s and 2000s, for this school to get its act together, these

steps were necessary. . . . When we implemented common dress there was a faction upset about civil rights. It was a statement to students about who was in charge. "Dress for Success" is the phrase we use—school is not about a fashion show; it's about coming to school to learn—you are here to do business, to work, it's like a job. We find students are more willing to comply when in uniform. You may think you have lots of rights, but at school, it's about learning. It [the dress code] was not disciplinary in nature.

In the middle of our interview Dr. H. abruptly stood up from his chair when the loudspeaker in his office suddenly broadcast the sounds of a student reading the Pledge of Allegiance, a daily ritual. As I sat observing but not participating, he stood with his hand over his heart as the pledge was recited. Afterward he commented that he considered it important to model this behavior for students.

Dr. H. advocated a rule-driven atmosphere as a path to freedom and class mobility. He specifically stated that students at Morton were subject to learning the rules of "polite society," rules they could jettison, he suggested, when they become engineers or professionals. Dr. H.'s motives were not punitive; he impressed me as a person who was passionate about providing a college-bound education for the low-income, minority students who attended his school; in his words, the rules he espoused and implemented were "about creating a level playing field."

As an ethnographer of youth in Morton's Biotech Academy, I don't want to impugn the intentions of administrators or teachers. On the contrary, judging from the school's success in meeting its API target, increasing school attendance, and graduating a number of college-bound students vastly larger than Morton's 30 percent, it appears that school policies were more than effective. And yet the combination of daily forms of discipline that structured the school and Academy environment and students' experiences of marginalization and social and economic constraint inherent to school and familial contexts produced certain effects. Against the grain of some of the values espoused within the Academy—those explicitly associated with techno-entrepreneurship—students learned to demonstrate reliability and an ability to manage their at-risk status. They also expressed a sense of debt or obligation toward a common good. In turn, this sensibility played a role in shaping students' identification with public-service and law-and-order careers.

Morton in a Political-Economic and Social Context: The "Right to Safety"

Like the school-within-the-school that is the Biotech Academy, Morton High School cannot be understood in a vacuum; the school environment and the position that Morton's principal advocates exist within a larger social, political, and economic context. The ordering of social and bodily space and the discourse of risk management at the school can be understood in direct relation to strategies of governance that played a part in transforming the City of San Jose and the County of Santa Clara during the 1990s. These strategies linked the social, political, and economic transformation of San Jose and Silicon Valley to racialized discourses of safety and delinquency that stigmatize particularly Latino youth. At a broader level such discourses reflect how class and race anxieties are experienced in contemporary California (Zavella 2001).

Redevelopment dollars had, since the mayoral administration of McEnery during the 1980s, been focused on revitalizing and "cleaning up" San Jose's downtown, a place long associated with vagrancy and crime. According to longtime San Jose residents and activists with whom I spoke, the transformation of downtown San Jose into a sanitized suburban landscape replete with expensive boutiques and a large sports arena galvanized many of the city's low- and middle-income residents, who organized to demand that redevelopment dollars be spent in their neighborhoods to promote beautification, safety, and economic development. The goal of "cleaning up" San Jose, advocated by the city's business and political elite, was well received by many residents across class and ethnic lines, including many in the neighborhoods surrounding Morton who felt that gang presence in their neighborhoods was imperiling their safety.[41]

During the late 1980s and into the 1990s the City of San Jose began an initiative called Project Crackdown, a multimillion dollar municipal initiative that encompassed efforts to promote community safety throughout San Jose through gang suppression and prevention efforts and to improve housing and neighborhood conditions in various low-income areas of the city (Zlolniski 2006).[42] According to Morton's principal, the prevailing attitude at the time among city bureaucrats, concerned residents, and school officials was, "We're taking back our city." For low- and middle-income neighborhood residents concerned about gangs and angry about city dollars being spent on an elite downtown whose shops they could not afford—"A shirt for $150 dollars!" exclaimed one Latina city worker and activist as she described an upscale group of boutiques added to San Jose's down-town—the discourse of the right to safety, like the right to clean schools and streets and basic city services, registered resentment about unequal access to city resources.[43]

A local, church-affiliated community organization, People Acting in the Community Together (PACT), was a major advocate for the focusing of redevelopment dollars in low-income neighborhoods. Members of a large, activist parish near Morton High School were instrumental in this effort. As Christian Zlolniski (2006) has noted, however, the concerns of community members were often sidelined as the Project Crackdown program was implemented.

During the 1990s the issue of gangs was of central concern to elites and poor residents alike, and during this time the City of San Jose focused intensively on it. Under Mayor Susan Hammer (1990–1998), San Jose formed a Gang Prevention Task Force, which the mayor's website proclaimed had helped reduce gang-related arrests by 47 percent since 1995, thus contributing to San Jose remaining the safest city with a population of more than five hundred thousand people in the country.[44] But San Jose's policies in this regard have been controversial, although they are in keeping with a county norm (during the 1990s, despite overall declines in violent and youth crime,[45] Santa Clara County dramatically increased curfew violation arrests of juveniles and also stepped up adult incarcerations) (Taqi-Eddin and Macallair 1999).[46] Despite overall declines in violent crime in San Jose between 1990 and 1998 (ibid.), in 1995 the city implemented an injunction, based on a public nuisance law that barred a specific group of thirty young Latinos from engaging in legal activities including "being seen in public with a known gang member, talking to someone inside a car, climbing a tree, making loud noises, wearing certain clothing, or carrying marbles, screwdrivers, pens, pagers, and sparkplugs."[47] During the same period the city also passed an "Anti-Cruising Ordinance," barring the pastime of cruising, a popular activity among local Latino and Asian youth (Best 2006:48). Similar injunctions to combat gang problems have been implemented in many California cities, including Los Angeles, and around the country.[48] The 1995 public nuisance injunction was ultimately unsuccessfully contested by the American Civil Liberties Union, which argued that "the City of San Jose is attempting to make an end-run around the criminal justice system . . . Simply because these men and women are suspected gang members, they are stripped of a variety of constitutional freedoms: the right to associate, to assemble, and the right to due process."[49]

During the same period prevention-oriented youth programs administered through the city and county of Santa Clara became more pervasive in San Jose. In 1994 the County Board of Supervisors designed a prevention-oriented collaborative system, called School-Linked Services, to address the needs of at-risk youth. According to the head of this system in Santa Clara County, the program was designed by "progressive" supervisors to coordinate services provided by multiple agencies as well as schools, thereby increasing cost-efficiency. At Morton, this has meant the creation of a multi-service student assistance program operated by the school, the county, and the city. The multi-service team consisted of a police officer, a guidance counselor, a student adviser, and social workers. In addition, one Morton administrator reported that in recent years the school had developed a closer relationship with the county probation department. In the eyes of the administrator of this program at Morton, the search for ways to cut costs at the county level, despite a notable increase in the county's budget during the tech boom,[50] had greatly improved the quality of prevention services to students. In this case, public discourse and policy emphasizing prevention were directly linked to local and national neoliberal politics of government efficiency and cost cutting.

Thus, in San Jose in the 1990s, a proliferation of discourse about youth delinquency, at-risk young people, and strategies to govern those at risk took different forms. At the city and county levels, the state promulgated tactics of suppression and prevention in response to gang activity. Between 1989 and 1998 Santa Clara County's overall juvenile felony arrest number increased (JVSV Network 2000). These shifts in governance tactics, initiated during the recession of the early 1990s, lasted throughout the region's tech boom, a period of great wealth polarization in Silicon Valley,[51] and into the post-boom economic downturn.

What is the broader political context of such local policies? In part, emphasis on prevention in the latter part of the 1990s can be understood to reflect local concern with the increasing criminalization of youth and minority youth within California, where since 1980 the incarceration rate has quadrupled,[52] and with a recent dramatic increase in incarceration in the state in general (Gilmore 2007). California currently incarcerates more young people than does any other state or, in fact, nation, and, within California, San Jose stands out as a city with particularly stringent enforcement policies (Taqi-Eddin and Macallair 1999). Latino and African American youth remain disproportionately represented in Santa Clara County's Juvenile Hall, although reforms, such as the Juvenile Detention Reform Initiative, have been implemented in the last decade to reduce these numbers at the county level.[53] Despite fluctuations and efforts to decrease numbers of Latino youth in custody,[54] Latino and African American youth remain grossly overrepresented in the Santa Clara County juvenile hall, comprising approximately 70 percent of the population.[55]

What is the larger picture for Latino, African American, and Asian residents of San Jose negotiating both a desire for a safe neighborhood and the known structural racism of the criminal justice system? One effect of an emphasis on the right to safety in the City of San Jose has been the erosion of freely usable public space and the heavy policing of communities of color. The contradiction posed between a right to safety and an intensively policed neighborhood environment registered among school officials and Morton families as well as county politicians and rights advocates. At a meeting for Spanish-speaking parents at Morton, I listened to a County Human Relations Officer address a group of mothers one evening. He reminded them that Latino youth comprise over 60 percent of the Juvenile Hall population, and stressed the importance of keeping close tabs on one's children to prevent gang involvement. At the meeting the mothers were concerned about gangs and safety in the neighborhood, but in subsequent interviews I conducted with a few of these mothers, they also expressed fear of the police and complained of increased harassment of Latino immigrants in the post–9/11 period.

Biotech Academy students expressed this contradiction as well; their identification with police work and other forms of community-oriented public-service work did not preclude irritation with profiling that they experienced in their neighborhood or when shopping in upscale areas of Silicon Valley. Daniel, an Academy student who, after considering a career in fashion design, decided that he wanted to work as a social worker with youth in San Jose, commented on a trip to a Banana Republic clothing store in the posh neighboring town of Saratoga with uncharacteristic anger: "They look at me like I'm going to steal something." Other Latino young men in the Academy commented that they were annoyed by police surveillance in the neighborhood. Although no Asian students complained to me about profiling by the police in the neighborhood, a member of the Gang Prevention Task Force and an on-campus worker for an Asian community youth outreach organization reported that Vietnamese American youth often complained about being harassed by police who told them that they fit a profile of an Asian gang member.[56]

Morton students grew up in this political and social context. The disciplinary environment of the neighborhood, like the environment of the Academy and the broader Morton school community, encouraged students to perceive themselves as at-risk youth, an identity that came with particular feelings of obligation, perceptions of the possible, and ideals of empowerment. These values encouraged a pattern of aspiration management that reflected a desire to demonstrate reliability and to "give back" to society, a form of self-government with ambiguous political implications.

The Political Effects of Aspiration Management

The Biotech Academy was purposefully designed to offer students a flexible range of options for the future. The curriculum aimed to cultivate skills and enthusiasm for work within a biotech-oriented techno-entrepreneurial organization at multiple tiers, ranging from entry-level technician work to employment as a research scientist or at the managerial level. Students themselves applauded the program, which was responsible for the admission of most of the Academy's first graduating class to four-year colleges, a notable feat in a school where 24 percent of students met UC/CSU entrance requirements. Indeed, almost all students with whom I spoke professed gratitude and appreciation for being permitted to be a part of the Academy, and some commented that other students, having a sense of the extra attention and perks they were missing out on, were jealous.

Yet the experience of participating in the Biotech Academy, inextricably bound up with a larger social, moral, and political economic order, also had the potential to generate outcomes that may have been unintended by the director of the Academy or the Academy's corporate supporters. Like James Ferguson's (1994:18) description of a development project in Lesotho (1994), the Biotech Academy is an "apparatus" that operates according to what Ferguson calls "authorless strategies"—he is borrowing from Michel Foucault—that turn out to have "political intelligibility." But the effects of this "political intelligibility" are not determined or total; complexities and contradictions of arrangements "on the ground" can produce unanticipated and even paradoxical effects.

Despite the apparent contradictions between the school environment and the Academy's mission and pedagogy, students were, in a sense, offered two pathways to the same form of neoliberal governmentality: whether they chose to identify with and accept technological innovation and entrepreneurship, and associate it with risk-management and self-empowerment, or whether they understood strict regulation of the self as the optimal strategy, as we have seen many did, students learned to cultivate themselves as responsible and reliable citizens at the individual level, to become "empowered" managers of their own risk (Cruikshank 1999; Kelly 2001). In the process they learned to view themselves and their community in terms of a racialized and often gendered idiom of being at-risk and to associate self-reinvention and individual responsibility for risk with self-confidence and self-esteem.

For some students in the Academy, forms of school discipline that encouraged students to comport themselves in ways that signaled their personal responsibility for an at-risk status meshed with positive experiences with role models to engender a sense of social obligation, or debt, to the community. Adults in the community served as such role models,[57] as did family members; in the case of Armando, for example, a brother-in-law in the military was someone he could emulate. Teachers within the Academy were also significant role models for many Academy students. I am reminded, for example, of the way students lingered around a particular Academy classroom and a particular social studies teacher after school, as she cleaned up the classroom, supervised homework, dispensed advice about life, and joked with her students. In interviews, students specifically invoked her as a role model. For others, such as Juliana or Marteena, role models came in the form of probation officers, police officers, or social workers with whom they had come into contact in childhood or adolescence. Such role models, who, as we have seen, became more prevalent in the community with the emergence of gang prevention efforts in San Jose during the 1990s, reinforced students' identities as at-risk young people and also elicited strong feelings of gratitude (frequently expressed when I was present) on the part of students.

Collectively, then, the daily experience of a strictly regulated school and neighborhood environment, the presence of significant role models at school and within the community, and the familial expectation that youth contribute to the household economy via money earned at after-school jobs or taking care of siblings provoked strong feelings about the need for self-discipline and the need to "give back" to the "community." Not surprisingly, Biotech students perceived public-service professions that governed at-risk communities such as their own as opportunities to contribute to society, and more implicitly, to demonstrate their own reliability, something that we have seen students, aware of their vulnerable status as at-risk youth considered to be economic and social risks, felt obligated to do.

Participation in the Biotech Academy may, in fact, have prompted identification with such careers for another reason: their privileged status as recipients of more teacher attention and perks as participants in the Academy emboldened them to see themselves as potential leaders or role models.[58] This possibility captures the contradictory nature of the cultural process: it may be that a desire to pursue careers in the "helping professions" and in the public sector reflects both a less than confident need to prove reliability and a measure of self-confidence sparked by participation in the Academy.

How do these observations about local subjects of school discipline and community environment relate to a regional and national political, economic, and social order? The kinds of self-discipline, self-perceptions, and aspirations that I observed among Morton's Biotech Academy students reflect a politics of citizenship emphasizing self-government and personal responsibility that has emerged in the United States with the shift from industrial-era, Keynesian form of governance to one guided by neoliberal ideas and objectives that emerged during the 1980s.[59] Academy students learned to interpret their social and economic circumstances via a pathologized idiom of risk (one that was racially coded and gendered) and, through their aspirations, expressed an obligation to take responsibility for that status. This subjective disposition has been forged within the broader context of a privatizing state focused on redefining the priorities of schools and individuals to suit the needs of capital and to reduce the state's role in providing social goods in a time of shrinking state provisions for social services and welfare and increased global competitiveness (Goode and Maskovsky 2001). Moreover, this form of responsible subjecthood has been encouraged as options for social mobility for poor youth continue to diminish (Graeber 2007; Perez 2008).

We can also understand Biotech students' aspirations and value orientation in relation to exclusionary dynamics of citizenship in a climate of social-service cutbacks that reflect the priorities of a neoliberal rationality of rule. In this political environment, those perceived to be stretching the state's social-service capacities experience intensified demonization (Zavella 2001; Chavez 2008). Given these historical circumstances, we can read the desire to "give back" through public-sector jobs in the "helping professions or military service as a means through which Academy youth, who we recall are the children of immigrants from Mexico who occupy a vulnerable and marginal status in this country, can offset the effects of an exclusionary politics of citizenship targeting Latinos now taking place in California and the rest of the country (Perez 2009; Chavez 2008).

In addition to reading these young people's desire to "give back" as a negotiation of a neoliberal politics of responsibility and risk in a context of limited opportunity—and as a response to a racist national politics of exclusion—one can observe an ironic and creative effect of such aspirations, one with local significance. Despite their embrace of what we may read, from the outside, as a neoliberal politics of personal responsibility for risk, Biotech students' identification with public-sector work and, specifically, their affinity for community-oriented careers—whether within policing institutions known to exhibit an increasing authoritarianism—represents a counter-position to a local neoliberal discourse equating youthful potential and personal success with the acquisition of values and skills prized in techno-entrepreneurship. Although students' identification with authoritarian forms of governance and their desire to serve the common good do not represent direct resistance to this locally dominant definition of success—such modes of aspiration management might not even seem contradictory to students such as Armando—the fact remains that few Academy students seemed moved by the prospect of a career as a biotech innovator or entrepreneur or by "Silicon Valley" as it is represented in the popular imagination. Thus, even if these students' strategies of personalized risk management were largely motivated by experiences of stigma as at-risk Latino young men and women and a practical desire to overcome economic and social marginalization, they ultimately embraced a vision of themselves and their futures that countered the objectives of regional elites concerned with a periodic and costly high-tech labor shortage or inspired to uplift a new generation of tech professionals with backgrounds very different from their own. The motivation to "give back" reflects a publicly oriented ethos of community building that was forged out of the collective experience of being part of a marginal group deemed to be at risk. This ethos counters a dominant public culture of Silicon Valley that celebrates individual advancement and the belief in the private sector as the locus of success and solutions. As such, the pattern of aspiration we have observed in the Academy is one that rejects the denigration of the public in an era of private-sector triumphalism, and may represent at the local level the transformation of a stigmatizing collective identity into a basis for community building.

For working-class Latino youth in contemporary Silicon Valley, experiences of schooling and neighborhood may be alienating in ways that result in a failure of schools and communities to ignite a sanctioned kind of striving, even when the youth in question are actively being lobbied to become strivers. Simultaneously such experiences may be generative, animating for young people different priorities borne out of social exclusion and awareness of social contradiction. These observations call to mind an ethnography focused on a different place and time: Paul Willis's analysis of working-class "lads" coming of age in a twentieth-century English Midlands factory town. I shall discuss the implications and limits of this comparison in the conclusion. For now, let us turn to a different world experienced by young people twenty miles up the freeway.

Marketing the Self

Aspiration Management among
Middle-Class Youth in Silicon Valley

Graduation

In June 2002, on a sunny afternoon at Sanders High School in Palo Alto, California, approximately three hundred capped and gowned seniors sat on folding chairs set up on the school quad, waiting to graduate. A casually but well-dressed audience of friends and family had gathered on the lawn with teachers and school staff to watch the proceedings. Before them was a stage with a piano on it.

A small group of graduating students—both male and female, and all white—gathered to sing the national anthem, *a cappella*. And then, after the student body president, a long-haired, fit, and smiling young woman (who later in the ceremony was awarded a plaque for outstanding academic performance and leadership), welcomed us to the festivities in rhyming couplets, four young women, clad in spaghetti-strap sundresses, sang a sad and wistful version of "Somewhere over the Rainbow." Their striking, minor-key harmonies were well received, an impressive setup for the subsequent commencement address by the valedictorian, which began:

High school is the pop whiz kaboom between the beep-beep sound of the alarm clock and the whine of the bell at the end of the day. The bell rings and students flee, into the open air, wild and free. Some gather with friends at brunch or lunch, pondering everything from the serious to the silly. Initial ramblings over how sweat pants are for people who just don't care anymore digress into lengthy political debates. [school name] brims with intellectuality, topped with a sprinkle of pure camaraderie.[1]

The audience chuckled when the valedictorian summed up high school in a series of "snapshots": sitting on the quad, sipping a Jamba juice while debating "metaphysical issues" during lunch; campus streakers parading across the lawn on a recent spring day; and a teacher's witty asides about Oedipus and Hamlet in an English class. At the end of this brief pastiche of memories, the valedictorian closed out his speech with a solemn reminder that the graduates were, after all was said and done, "*teenagers*," a statement of fact delivered in an incredulous tone that conveyed both the preciousness of youth and an implicit irony: that so many accomplished and sophisticated young people could possess such an ordinary status.

The student body president recalled for the audience her pride one day in class when, bored during a film, she looked around the room to take stock of her fellow students—an exceptionally talented pianist, a nationally recognized mathematics scholar, and a number of outstanding athletes. A young man then stood up, walked to the grand piano on the stage and played a ten-minute, original, concert-pianist-caliber composition that began with a tongue-in-cheek quotation of "Pomp and Circumstance." Next Dr. A., the principal of Sanders High School, approached the lectern to deliver his speech. Dr. A had come from a school district in a rural and less affluent region of rural northern California to assume the job of principal in Palo Alto during the height of the tech boom. His speech struck a decisively moral tone, focusing not on the future accomplishments of the graduating class but rather on the need to go through life with humility and grace. Linking Thomas Paine's phrase, "These are times that try men's souls" to the watershed event of the terrorist attacks on September 11, 2001, Dr. A. observed that the class of 2002 was entering a world defined by a "new perspective on war and peace, in which our graduates will become significant players in the years to come." He urged students to act according to their consciences instead of according to "convenience," and to have "a deep respect for themselves and others." Near the end of the speech he advised students, "Exercise patience with the pace of your success—don't expect to reach the top right away."

The Palo Alto ceremony hardly resembled the graduation I had witnessed the previous evening at Morton High School, where the ceremony had ritualized assimilation to an American ideology of meritocracy and personal advancement in a formal, even militaristic style. Homage had been paid to the sacrifice of Morton students' parents, and the ceremony had included the carrying of the national flag across the stage, a display of Morton's ROTC squadron, and a graduation speech structured along a meritocratic, dare-to-dream trope. "If you persevere and continue to work hard," a Morton vice principal had told the graduates, "one of you might go on to find a cure for cancer or AIDS, you might become a great innovator, or maybe find a solution to world hunger." The tone of the speech conveyed the impression that, with perseverance, some of Morton's graduates might potentially join the ranks of the great.

By contrast, the Palo Alto ceremony had no need to emphasize meritocracy or the goals of assimilation. Instead, the ceremony was designed to distinguish Palo Alto's students by showcasing their creativity, talent, and quirky individuality, as well as their personal and intellectual states of liberation. Eventual career or personal success was not conjured up as a future goal; it was assumed, mentioned only in reference to the need to cultivate certain moral attributes of grace, humility, and patience to accompany one's natural ascension to becoming "the best."

The Sanders High School graduation ceremony showcased the celebration of freedom of expression and self-cultivation through the honing of individual (often creative or intellectual) passions that define a public culture at Sanders. Indeed, attention to the language and habits of young people at Sanders revealed the extent to which their forms of self-discipline, modes of self-definition, and ways of categorizing others—in short, their styles of aspiration management—depended upon moral precepts of freedom of expression, diversity, and creative exploration of one's passions. Moreover, students' words and actions often suggested that they defined personal success in terms of the pursuit of individual interests and self-cultivation.

Simultaneously, however, despite the premium placed on freedom of expression and creative exploration at Sanders, there existed another, seemingly contradictory set of values and associations with success that subordinated creative and intellectual inspiration in favor of less personalized and more quantifiable markers of academic and social success. The tone and substance of Dr. A.'s speech—which, one might argue, contained a subtle admonishment to those in danger of succumbing to self-serving and shallow competitiveness—lightly hints at these seemingly contradictory values and definitions of success with which Sanders students grappled. As such, the principal's speech foreshadowed a central theme of this chapter: How did Sanders students understand and negotiate apparently contradictory values and aspirations that they were exposed to and encouraged to cultivate?

The children of Silicon Valley's established, professional middle class confronted intensifying social and economic pressures that shaped how they defined themselves and their aspirations. Schooling, as we shall see, played a role in compounding such pressures and encouraging particular strategies of aspiration management in response to them. Although this argument is based on fieldwork conducted at Sanders High School during the spring and fall of 2002, it also draws on personal experience: I spent my adolescence in Palo Alto and graduated from Sanders High School myself in 1988, during the last major recession to affect the region. The profound social and economic shifts in Silicon Valley and in Palo Alto in particular—a place that, between the 1980s and the late 1990s, transformed from a generally affluent middle-class city, home to high-tech and other professionals, to an elite epicenter of a globalized "New Economy" where even ranch-style tract homes sold for up to one million dollars—made Sanders High School in Palo Alto an apt point of comparison to my research at Morton High School in San Jose.[2] Moreover, the choice of Sanders as a research site allowed me to draw on my own memories of the school and town, providing me with some additional insight into the local cultural, social, and economic transformations shaping middle-class experience in particular.

In contrast to Morton, Sanders represents the best of California's public schools.[3] Its school district boasts a 97 percent graduation rate and over 74 percent continue on directly to four-year colleges.[4] According to a student survey reported in the campus newspaper during my fieldwork, approximately one-third of Sanders students wish to attend a top-tier school. Unlike Morton, there are officially no English Language Learners (ELL) at Sanders. Reflecting the class and race segregation of local industry, the Sanders student body is predominantly white with a sizable minority of Asian students,[5] and 8 percent of students in the district qualify for the reduced-price lunch. Further, because of Palo Alto's high property values, the district is classified as a Basic Aid District.[6] Simply put, this means that although the district in which Sanders is located receives less money from the state than most schools, it spends approximately ten thousand dollars per student per year in comparison with the state average of six thousand dollars (California Department of Education 2002–2003).

In further contrast to Morton, Sanders families tend to be highly educated; 76 percent of Palo Alto's adults are employed in management or in professional or related occupations (North Santa Clara County Census Report 2002). Responses to a questionnaire completed by seniors suggested that approximately 66 percent of Sanders students had at least one parent who held a graduate degree. Even in the midst of a recession, these families generally represented, in relative terms, an affluent middle class.[7] The student parking lot, like student wardrobes, reflected this fact; though some students drove Toyota sedans or Hondas or older model Volvo station wagons, many drove and owned new-model Mercedes Benzes, BMWs, Lexuses, or SUVs.

The community had changed, both socially and economically, since I attended Sanders. Skyrocketing housing values and cashed-in stock options had rendered many in Palo Alto's comfortable middle class wealthy. A concomitant cultural shift had also occurred; a techno-entrepreneurial influence had become more pronounced in the school and community. When I was doing my fieldwork, I heard much about techno-entrepreneurially connected parents at Sanders who helped garner extra perks for the school in the form of funds, fund-raising expertise, and technology. Their influence was pervasive; local high-tech leaders and companies were often invoked by students and teachers in the economics and government classes I observed. As one Chinese American young woman put it, "People at [school name] buy stocks. They pay attention to mergers, bankruptcies, new technologies. Some people know a lot about specific companies." The anonymous questionnaires revealed this fact, as many students commented on their families' declining stock value.

Thus Sanders was both familiar and unfamiliar territory, and my impressions of the place and the arguments I make about it reflect my own personal history in combination with observations and impressions made in the field during yet another local recession, one precipitated by a tech boom that had transformed Silicon Valley's social, economic, and cultural landscape.

Defining the Self in a Space of Freedom

In the intervening years since my graduation from high school, Sanders, like the corporate community of Silicon Valley, had become a place that celebrated "diversity" and freedom of expression (English-Lueck 2002). At Sanders "diversity" connoted racial and ethnic difference as well as individual tastes and interests. Students praised the school as a place where one could be whoever one wanted to be. The right to be different or look different or "think different"—as the Apple billboard demands— was prized regardless of gender, race, ethnicity, class, or sexual orientation, whether the activity was designing stage sets, producing a daily school TV show, or giving a graduation speech in rhyming couplets. As Alice Frost, an economics and government teacher whose classes I frequently observed put it, at Sanders, "being intellectual is really cool . . . being informed [is cool] . . . The school newspaper is a cool place to be." In my observation, it was, at least publicly, as "cool" to be, for example, a robot-building tech geek, a filmmaker, or a gay rights advocate as it was to be on the football team or an editor of the school newspaper. Students described Sanders as a place to explore and develop oneself intellectually, creatively, and socially, where it was "cool" to excel in school and devote oneself to exploring one's creative and intellectual passions. Evelyn, an Anglo American senior, was a self-proclaimed theater person. The child of a single-parent mother struggling to pay rent in Palo Alto on an office manager's salary from Agilent Technologies, Evelyn applauded the school's diverse atmosphere and identified herself by her passion and prowess in the realm of stage tech design:

> There isn't a lot of "you're popular and I'm not" here. It's like, "Whatever, you're popular and I can hang ten lights in an hour and get them focused and gelled, so there . . . I am pretty much lord goddess of the shop if you will . . . [a fellow student] and I are like the only people who know lights, so we are pretty high up in the stage tech echelon, if you will.

Students' career aspirations reflected this tendency to identify oneself by means of a personal creative or intellectual passion, or both, as well as a desire to cultivate oneself through creative exploration. Students' often precise descriptions of their career aspirations demonstrated familiarity with a vast array of professional options and a preference for exploring intellectual and creative horizons. For example, in discussing local high-tech jobs, one student delineated between "more creative" jobs such as being an animator for a locally based, prestigious company like Pixar or an innovator of a new technology and other jobs that required being a "drone . . . sitting in a cubicle," writing code for a small part of a larger project. Students' career choices generally tended toward the quirky, the artistic, the scientific, and the innovative; I was struck by the number of students, including athletes, self-described "preppy" young women, and more alternative-looking youth, told me they wanted to become film directors. Notably career preferences did not seem to be shaped or limited by traditional ideas about gender roles.

Moreover, unlike Morton, where students often framed career preferences in terms of a desire to give back to the community, Sanders students often justified a particular career path—whether conventional or unusual—in terms of individual tastes. Renée, a half-French daughter of a Stanford professor and a homemaker, planned to pursue a career as a researcher in the field of astrophysics. In talking about this aspiration, Renée indicated that she wanted to become an astrophysicist because she found the field to be "a very beautiful and interesting subject." Her classmate, James, a first-generation immigrant from a town near Shanghai whose father and mother held Ph.D.s in physics and electrical engineering, respectively, described his own motivation to become a physics professor: "In physics, I can look at really good pictures and think about them, but in biology I have to read the book, memorize." Both James and Renée were, by objective measures, outstanding students, taking between them eight Advanced Placement (AP) courses, which meant that the course could be credited toward a college degree. However, the tendency to explain career goals in terms of a desire to edify an intellectual passion was not limited to the most academically advanced students. Isabel, whom one teacher described as a "typical, smart but flaky A-student," told me of her longtime interest in working for an institution such as the State Department as a specialist in international relations: "I like law and its effect on people and culture. I'm interested in how laws affect international institutions [such as] NATO and the UN."

Like Silicon Valley's tech innovators who have, since the 1980s, decried rigid corporate bureaucracies as an impediment to innovation, new ideas, and productivity itself (Findlay 1993), young people at Sanders frequently depicted the classroom as a barrier to the personal project of intellectual or creative self-cultivation. James, the Chinese American would-be physicist told me solemnly, "When I'm not in class, I'm thinking." The classroom was, for him as well as others with whom I spoke, a meddlesome interruption of their intellectual train of thought. Some derided, as busywork, regular homework or certain required classes in favor of "project-based" work more common in AP courses. When students reported cutting class, the reason most often given was the need to pursue a project or to work more efficiently. As expressed by Zoe, a white, would-be diplomat whose single-parent father worked as a business manager for a start-up company: "I never cut [class] above my limit. I guess you could say I'm kind of a nerdy cutter. I cut to get things done."

Complaints about class time notwithstanding, the physical environment of Sanders High School inside and outside the classroom emphasized individual self-cultivation by encouraging freedom of expression and creative exploration through a broad range of activities. Every fourth-period class began with a student-produced, closed-circuit TV school news show, featuring a student's short video which was generally humorous. The school offered, among other options, the opportunity to participate in student-run theater productions, a robotics team, and an engineering class. During the 2002–2003 school year students launched a website that featured an interactive blog as well as searchable archives of student columns, animation, and Web broadcasts from the student television station.

In terms of academics, many students praised the freedom of choice allowed in designing one's academic schedule, and through chatting with students I learned that the school offered such collegiate-sounding courses as Sports Literature and Women Writers of Color, as well as a large number of AP and Honors classes, which were always in high demand.[8] In courses I observed, I watched students engage in the subject matter in an intricate and spirited manner. They analyzed stocks, often drawing upon personal or familial knowledge of a company's performance or the stock market, and they debated such topics as the merits of capitalism and socialism, speculating about the motivations of low-wage immigrant workers and the role of stock options on workers' attitudes. The atmosphere between students and teachers was collegial; students joked with teachers in the course of debates, and challenged each other's viewpoints.

Outside the classroom students lounged on the sprawling grass and open space of the campus. They headed to the shopping center across the street with their friends at lunchtime and during free periods. During lunch on campus, young men—and perhaps young women, though I never saw them—sometimes played music, setting up amplifiers, turntables, microphones, and instruments on a quad-like space called "the deck" to perform loud punk rock, rapidly screaming lyrics into the microphone or being the DJ for the crowd. It was extremely rare for a student wandering the campus during class time to be questioned. Also, the campus was "open," meaning that students were free to hop into their cars and go home or downtown or walk across the street to a shopping plaza for lunch or a trip to Starbucks; "It's a freedom thing that hasn't been squashed," said one of the vice principals. "Discipline is light at this school," he added.[9] During our interview I was told that Sanders had no network of parents, police, and school administrators working on the issue of school safety.[10]

Expressions of sexuality celebrated freedom and choice. Like at any high school, young people socialized and flirted and "made out" between classes, at lunch and after school. But unlike at many high schools—such as Morton—gay couples were comfortable enough to show affection on campus. Some students with whom I spoke were members of a gay-straight, transgender alliance, and the experience of transgender youth was a theme taken up in one issue of the campus literary magazine in the spring of 2002. During that semester I heard talk of nominating a transgender and bisexual couple for the yearbook distinction of "cutest couple."

Students often cited, as their reason for liking the school, the emphasis that it places on freedom of expression. As expressed by an extremely popular, blond senior, Rachel, whose father was a vice president at a globally prominent tech corporation and whose mother did not work: "I can't think of any ways this school is strict. People still come to school with fairy wings on sometimes.[11] They let you form your own clubs. I really like [Sanders]. People still wear whatever." According to administrators, students, and teachers whom I interviewed, the only clothing that was banned were T-shirts with alcohol brands or drug symbols, although I saw T-shirts with a beer logo more than once. Alice Frost described the style of young people on campus: "Really anything goes right now. It's Palo-Alto-casual, fashionable, a little earthy . . . The bohemian look is kind of in, and "Abercrombie and Fitch" is in and even the nerd whatever-you-want-to-wear look."

Although jeans and sweats with flip-flops were also common attire, many students dressed in a way that connoted sexual freedom and elite luxury. Walking around campus during the spring of 2002, I spotted that season's tight strapless sundresses and many $125 to $150 low-cut, distressed-denim jeans. Teachers occasionally pointed out young women's overly revealing clothing, raising their eyebrows at various outfits such as a pair of skin-revealing, lace-up leather pants that Isabel, the young woman interested in international relations and law, had worn to Alice Frost's economics class, or lamenting the common appearance of clothes skimpy enough to make thong underwear visible.

During an interview I asked the school's acting principle (Dr. A. unexpectedly left the position), Ms. S., a retired white educator with decades of experience in the district, what her philosophy was about discipline and freedom of movement and expression at school. She responded:

I feel very strongly that kids need to be empowered. I think we need to be teaching responsibility and we need to be . . . living by standards we set—examples which are positive—for kids. I do not believe that a lot of rules and regulations really make a difference in terms of how people ultimately behave. . . . like the dress code. I don't want to measure straps or how [much] skin is showing . . . We just try to teach individual responsibility.

The notion that freedom of expression and creative exploration promoted the empowerment of youth was a normative value at Sanders. The implicit message conveyed by the school environment was that a "free reign" would allow Sanders students to realize their potential. In turn, the need for a permissive atmosphere in which to cultivate limitless potential was fostered by a pervasive mantra about student brilliance and exceptionalism.

A Discourse of Brilliance

Teachers and other adults often commented that a particular student was "brilliant" or a "genius." For two semesters I listened to Alice Frost's comments about her students' idiosyncracies, scholastic habits, and intellectual and social qualities. As soon as I began my research, Alice, who knew I was also conducting ethnographic research at a public school in a less affluent area of Silicon Valley, described to me the exceptional academic, creative, and athletic ability of the students at Sanders. She told me that she taught "a big flock of really bright kids, maybe one-quarter or one-third are geniuses." This claim found its way into classroom discussions. "Why do people live in Palo Alto?" Alice asked her economics class one morning. "The educational system!" a Chinese American male student shot back. "Right, 'cause you guys are so brilliant!" Alice replied, only slightly tongue-in-cheek.

This offhand comment revealed a pervasive perception of Sanders students echoed by other administrators and teachers, who often marshaled evidence to this effect, listing prizes won by the school newspaper, literary magazine, or robotics team. Teachers spoke of students' accomplishments in two ways: at times they described them in terms of innate giftedness, implying a natural quality, and at other times they linked the exceptional creativity, motivation, and talent of the student body to social causes such as the fact that many of Sanders students hailed from families who were highly educated and competitive professionals in Silicon Valley. They used words like "successful" and "sophisticated" to describe these families.

Claims about the students' intelligence were often supported by references to the techno-entrepreneurial world of Silicon Valley/Palo Alto. Alice's classroom quip about the brilliance of Palo Alto students exemplifies what I observed to be a common association between Silicon Valley or Palo Alto and student and parent intelligence. I asked Sara, a thoughtful young white woman who loved the outdoors and had grown up with a mother and stepfather who occupied elite managerial positions in two high-tech firms, "Is the American Dream different in Silicon Valley or the same as in other places?" She thought a moment and replied: "Here the focus is on research. Intellect is just everywhere. It's being traded around." The sense of being exceptional in an exceptional school located at the heart of an area known for its highly intelligent people and share of famous innovators was a badge of pride. "People here are so smart," another white female student commented. "You can't get away with being stupid in Palo Alto, you just can't do it." This idea was widespread in the local media as well. In a news story about the Palo Alto City Council, the *San*

Jose Mercury, Silicon Valley's leading newspaper, described Palo Alto in passing as, "this center of innovation and intelligence" (Wong 2002).

Students often invoked the recent tech boom, in particular, as evidence of their own exceptionalism. The accomplishments and stock portfolios of Silicon Valley's local elite conferred upon Sanders students a sense of being a part of the epicenter of the global economy regardless of whether a student's family had experienced a sudden increase of wealth during the boom, had recently been laid off, or was tenuously hanging on to a house and upper-middle- or middle-class status in Palo Alto. Another student, Brenda, a white would-be engineer whose father had lost his job during the crash and had then been rehired at another biotech firm, and whose mother worked as an emergency room nurse at Stanford Hospital, described the boom and its aftermath and the sense of importance and possibility it fomented in her peers: "Sophomore and junior year—the economy—we were, like, really powerful . . . the United States . . . everything sort of revolved around Silicon Valley. It was like, everything was about us, you know? It was like we were the center of the world."

E: Why do you say Silicon Valley was the center of everything?
B: Everybody would be like, "Oh yeah, the market's up . . . it's all because of the tech people" and you'd be like, "Oh! That's us! (cheerily), and they'd be like, "Oh yeah, the tech market's doing really well." You'd see it in the paper everyday; it would be all about this area. My family in Florida and Ohio knew all about Silicon Valley. . . . A lot of people I know say, "I'll just start a company or be an investment person and get rich and then do what I want."

Other students referred to Palo Alto as "ground zero" of the tech boom and rattled off facts about Silicon Valley, such as its status as the world's eleventh largest economy.

Similarly teachers sometimes emphasized the quality of Sanders and its students by referring to the school's informal connections to the Valley's techno-entrepreneurial elite. A journalism teacher, responsible for the school's quarterly literary magazine, its video production, its newspaper, and its new TV station, recalled that during the boom eight former students had become CEOs. In the course of our interview, representations of Silicon Valley's boom blurred with a depiction of the excellence of the journalism program at Sanders. "It was unreal," she said, "*Fortune Magazine* came, French and German magazines . . . We [Sanders High School journalism program] were the number one place to interview."

A Posture of Privilege

In sum, emphasis upon freedom of expression and the exceptionalism of Sanders youth, their families, and the region itself defined young people's identities, sense of potential, and expectations. Moreover, school rules and values encouraged self-cultivation as a priority. For students, Sanders was more than a place to master academic subjects and desirable social and work skills; it was a zone of self-expression dedicated to the cultivation of inspiration and passion for particular pursuits. Discussions I had with students about workplace skills revealed a similar disposition. Questions about the skills students imagined they would eventually need in the workplace elicited responses which suggested that they conceived of the workplace as a place to pursue personal inspirations and to cultivate themselves. Mary, a white junior with aspirations to work as a filmmaker, opined that one needed, "passion! You have to love what you do." Jeremy, an Asian American junior who was unsure of what he wanted to do, simply said, "I could never do something I wasn't interested in." James, the young man who loved physics, said with conviction, "You have to be able to create."

The ways in which students framed personal life experiences also reflected students' celebration of self-cultivation. James described working once a week at a soup kitchen in East Palo Alto as an experience that allowed him to think clearly about history and philosophy. Sara, the student government leader, told me of a summer job learning environmental restoration in a wilderness area as an experience that had taught her a lot about herself. Similarly Katherine, a white senior, felt that a summer trip to Thailand to dig latrines for poor villagers had transformed her values and made her grow as a person.

Such emphasis upon self-cultivation produced a set of expectations about the role of the community, the school, and the workplace in students' lives. Some adults with whom I spoke at Sanders and in the community of Palo Alto interpreted such expectations, manifest, for example, in students' ways of inhabiting space or their demands, as obnoxious demonstrations of privilege. This critique of privileged youth suggests how class conflict within a community can be filtered through an idiom of conflicting generational mores.

For instance, a few teachers mentioned student "arrogance." Teachers sometimes interpreted a cut class as an expression of privilege; they thought the student in question considered his or her time too valuable or the class in question unimportant. Others objected to students' use of school space. One staff member commented:

There is an absolute premium on education and it's about me and mine. There's definitely in Palo Alto this sense of entitlement. Resources are supposed to be "at my disposal, 24-7." You have sixteen year olds driving Escalades (Cadillac SUVs) and then once they get here they park in staff parking!

Staff members also commented on parental relations with the school that indicated a similar awareness of school-community dynamics. Many hinted that parents were demanding, and a vice principal at Sanders, in reference to discipline issues, remarked, "Parents at [Sanders] have some input, but nobody should be dominating anybody."

Although the following letter to the editor of Palo Alto's daily paper by a local young man and recent Sanders graduate cannot be said to reflect the attitudes of all youth in Palo Alto, it nonetheless suggests a privileged orientation toward one's community. In what follows, the young man insists that local teen drug and alcohol abuse can be explained in terms of a lack of diversions for Palo Alto youth:

Dear Editor:

As a recent graduate of [Sanders] High School, I have firsthand knowledge of the alleged drug abuse that faces Palo Alto's and the nation's youth. For starters, I was horrified to see that Friday's article about the problem was devoid of comment from any of my peers—the people who were, essentially, the topic of the piece. . . .

I have been to parties in Palo Alto where alcohol was consumed en masse, marijuana was smoked by the ounce, and other "harder" drugs were readily available to those who wanted them. It is my opinion (and that is all it is) that 90 percent of us do these things not so much as acts of rebellion but as acts of desperation—there is absolutely nothing of any interest to do in this city or the surrounding communities.

My generation, especially among our specific demographic (white, upper class), is, in a word, bored. Until something of interest opens in Palo Alto or the values of Palo Alto's youth change dramatically, we will resort to illicit behavior to entertain ourselves. (*Palo Alto Daily News*, "Letter to the Editor," 2002)[12]

For this young man, it is the community's responsibility to come up with ways to amuse him, as opposed to his responsibility to care of the community, as was the case at Morton. The letter elicited a few sharp replies, one of which stated:

Dear Editor:

————, you live in one of the most beautiful, diverse, culturally rich, and intellectually stimulating areas in the world. This is not rural Oklahoma. The problem is not this area. The problem is what you have been raised to be.

You have been indulged. Parents have given you a home in a town that offers incomparable opportunities, driven you to school, AYSO [American Youth Soccer Organization] . . . and Little League, provided swim lessons, summer camp, gymnastic courses, riding classes, special programs at the junior museum, theatre, concerts, expensive vacations, ski trips, electronic gizmos of every description, JCC [Jewish Community Center], YMCA, and the list goes on.

Nothing has been demanded of you. You have never been required to work or improve the lives of others. Because everything has been done to keep you entertained, today at age 18, all you can think about is having someone to entertain you. What a shame that your upbringing and education have failed to inspire you, help you find a passionate calling, or think about something other than yourself (Letter to the Editor 2002).[13]

Although I am suggesting that, at one level, values and practices encouraged at Sanders and in the community of Palo Alto effectively created "structures of feeling" (Williams 1994) that served to promote expressions of class entitlement, observing and listening to students conveyed a more complex picture. Young people's conflicting values and aspirations, the pressures they faced, and the ways in which they felt vulnerable call into question the motivations behind the expressions of entitlement we have discussed thus far, and make clear that the process of reproducing class status and privilege was not seamless. Moreover, such considerations suggest that, at Sanders, processes of aspiration formation and self-definition could potentially reinforce class status and hierarchy and simultaneously undermine it.

Contradictory Values and Aspirations

Despite verbal and nonverbal displays emphasizing the commitment of young people at Sanders to creative and intellectual exploration as a route to self-cultivation and empowerment, and despite representations of the school itself as a bastion of freedom of expression and diversity, anxious comments students made about their future goals and about social norms at school and within their community told a more ambiguous story. Although students spoke enthusiastically about career goals in terms of an intellectual or artistic passion, a few sentences or paragraphs later, many of the same students—including those from extremely affluent and relatively economically secure families—would articulate the career goal of "a steady job" as a primary priority. Furthermore, many students quickly identified "having money" as the number one symbol of "success" at their school and in their community, despite the priority most placed upon creative exploration and the cultivation of excellence in intellectual, artistic, or scientific realms, and representations of Sanders as a place that promoted self-expression and acceptance of individual "diversity." Notably some experienced these contrasting ideals of success as a problematic and vexing contradiction, framing discussion of their goals in terms of an inner dilemma concerning whether to pursue a passion or a career with financial security.

Similarly students' focus on excelling academically complicated pat descriptions of Sanders as a place dedicated to creative exploration and the joy of learning for learning's sake. With great frequency, students qualified their academic performances to me, always clarifying whether the grade was "weighted" or "unweighted," whether the class was "accelerated" or not, or "Honors" or "AP." They often lamented an "unweighted" grade and begged for better grades or made hasty arrangements to bring up their grades through end-of-the-semester extra-credit work. With pride or anxiety, they confessed grade point averages and the number of AP classes they were currently taking. Four seemed to be a magical number: faculty referred to students taking "four AP courses" to illustrate the kind of academic ability of many at Sanders. Students referred reverently to friends taking four or five AP courses. As a young woman planning to attend New York University (NYU) in the fall and intent upon becoming a professional actor put it: "Everyone takes APs. If you don't take APs, you're just a big slacker. Here there's the sense, of 'Oh, you're only taking one AP' . . . My friends take APs. Right now I am taking two APs."

Students also frequently compared their performances unfavorably with other friends and acquaintances or even family members. "My sister just *looks* at it and gets an A," Susan, a Chinese American junior, despaired. Mary, the senior who wanted to be a filmmaker and served on the staff of the school literary magazine, commented, "All my friends are extremely successful. They want to go to Duke and Harvard, have 1400s on their SATS [Scholastic Aptitude Tests]. It's, like, unbelievable." Mary expressed relief that her parents had hired a private admissions counselor to assist her, a common trend according to many students. Indeed, such students reported spending between one and four hours per week with such private tutors and counselors.

The talk in class was often of college. As I sat in an economics class one fall day, around the time that college applications were due, I watched as three students, all white, chatted during "group work" on a project designing a mock company product and business plan. Fiona, an athletic-looking blond young woman whom I had begun to get to know during a particularly candid interview, was one of three participants in this group. Her collaborators were a well-organized and motivated young woman who had applied for early admission to Duke and a young man whom I had not met. Conversation focused on college and the merits of the SAT versus the ACT. With studied casualness, the three inquired of one another, "So where did you apply?" When Fiona replied NYU, the boy in the group replied, acidly, "I know a lot of people in New York, and I can tell you, no one thinks NYU is a big deal. It's not *that* good a school." Fiona stared distantly into space, while, in an effort to lessen her humiliation, I countered that NYU did have a good reputation. One's list of schools was an index of one's value.

This dual motivation to excel out of a dedication to one's passion or talent and also to conform to a set of social and material standards was also manifest in nonacademic realms. Attitudes toward certain markers of social status at Sanders reflected both the prioritization of a certain materialism and competitiveness, on the one hand, and an idealization of more "noble" aspirations and habits, such as the cultivation of maverick talent, creative exploration, and free expression, on the other. In marked contrast to student discourse at Morton High School, where young people seemed less fixated upon the issue of popularity, Sanders students inside and outside the "popular" clique of juniors and seniors were keenly aware of markers of popularity and social hierarchy, whether or not they decried them as "phony," as some, who were troubled by this dual motivation, did. Many students of both genders cited the importance of having a nice car—an elite brand or an SUV—and nice clothing as a ticket to popularity at school. At the same time students' communicative style when discussing such status symbols was often subtly derisive, as if to distance themselves from such values and norms. As one young woman, Sara, described life in Palo Alto:

> Everyone's like, 'Oh, we're so rich, we have money . . .'" The egos . . . In Palo Alto there's this whole status thing about where you buy your groceries. Do you shop at Safeway or Whole Foods? In school, money means a lot here. There are girls who will spend lunchtime [in the school library] shopping on the Abercrombie and Fitch[14] website.

As she made this comment, this young woman's facial expression conveyed mild disdain for the kind of person who felt compelled to spend lunch shopping online.

Despite the diversity of free expression manifest in the ordering of social space on campus—tech geeks favored the robotics lab; thespians and D&D-style role players often sat in a shady spot near the Social Sciences building; skateboarders and others were drawn to an overtly "alternative" lifestyle; and aesthetic types preferred "the deck" or across the street, on the edges of the shopping center parking lot—race- and class-based segregation on campus marked social status. The "deck people" were a predominantly white and Asian group of students both "alternative" and "preppy" in style. As various students informed me, the few African American students who liked spending time on "the deck" tended to come from middle-class or affluent Palo Alto families, as opposed to those in East Palo Alto, the adjacent working-class city, home to many of the school's voluntary transfer students. Those who sat at "the benches" were the most popular and, as some students observed, the wealthiest, young people in the school. This crowd was more "Abercrombie and Fitch," in style, and as I would learn from my time on the campus and in interviews, the car keys in their backpacks tended to belong to the nicer cars in the parking lot. The school's small population of African American and Latino youth, many of whom were voluntary transfer students from East Palo Alto, generally congregated in and around the Student Center, a cafeteria and common room. During my months on campus, various white students, with a mixture of humor and shame, informed me that this little area of the campus had a designation: "Little Africa."

In sum, although Sanders was defined by an ethos of freedom of expression, it was also bound by social rules. Markers of social and academic status at the school often coexisted uneasily with values and aspirations proclaiming creative exploration, diversity, and freedom of expression. Discussions I had with students about partying aptly express this ambiguous and, for some, blatantly contradictory social context. Although high school partying may be commonly associated with libertinism, with self-exploration and freedom, Sanders students who were interested and involved in the "popular" party scene often described partying in task-like terms. The status associated with "partying" (i.e., in its basic version, drinking with large groups of people) for many young people at Sanders belied the image of the person just "blowing off steam" after a hard workweek. While students stressed the importance of needing to decompress on the weekends—"Go to a party on Saturday night and you'll see stress manifest itself!" one girl commented—some spoke of the social competition and anxiety around being invited to the right parties and described a failed evening as not having a party to go to. "You are expected to have a party to go to at night on the weekends," a white young woman named Katherine commented, as if she were reciting house rules. Similar to their need to excel at schoolwork or wear the right clothes, students judged and compared parties and commented on the phenomenon of being excluded from entering certain elite parties.

Like the legendary Silicon Valley tech geeks of the late 1990s, who famously resisted a demarcation between work and play, it seemed unclear even to students, and certainly to many parents and teachers with whom I spoke, where the playing began and the working stopped. A school psychologist at Sanders described the ideal party in this way:

> A successful weekend is when you go to a party and someone gets into a fight, someone gets together, you're really drunk—just hanging out with a few friends isn't good enough . . . Kids want to pack drama, action, and activities into relaxation time. Playtime has become a job like homework.

Despite the pressures and demands of the multiple realms of potential accomplishment or failure that these young people engaged, they, school staff, and parents spoke about the school's freedom of expression, emphasis on diversity, and students' passionate interests as a sign of the healthy vibrancy of the school community. This collective appreciation for the context of Sanders notwithstanding, an exploration of student stress and meanings associated with failure reveals the pragmatic function of students' emphasis on freedom of expression and identities defined by personal passions, and, as such, the common purpose underlying often conflicting values and notions of success.

Student Stress and the Specter of Failure

Every teacher, administrator, and school district board member I spoke with described the stress, overwork, and anxiety students at Sanders and local affluent communities faced. Student stress, like creativity, was a major discourse on campus and in town. Alice Frost summed up the issue in this way: "Overall, kids feel hard-worked at this school. About a quarter of them—you really sense them crumbling under the pressure of having to achieve." Both a school academic counselor and a school psychologist reported that students often experienced such nervousness during tests that they took refuge in the school nurse's office.

A school psychologist commented on students' responses to stress: "Higher-performing kids have internalized the drive and motivation of their parents—they've internalized it so much that they somatize—illness, drinking." Most students commented on parental views of their school performance or future aspirations: "My mom was upset about my SATs"; "My mom wants me to be a pediatric surgeon"; "My parents want me to go to Stanford or Harvard." One young man confessed, "I worry about what I'll do [for a career] but my parents tell me just worry about SAT scores and grades."

What was the worst-case scenario of failure that induced such stress? During an interview Fiona, whose father worked as a computer programmer at Stanford and whose mother was, ironically, a child psychologist, tearfully recalled her sophomore year, when her parents had tried, "some weird experimental freedom thing: 'If you get good grades, you can have total freedom,' and they left everything up to me and I didn't know what to do with it." Fiona was filled with remorse for her poor performance in her sophomore year. With self-disgust, she said:

I thought, like, whatever happens, happens. I had my values really out of whack. I wasn't reading good books. I hadn't really learned critical thinking yet, or analyzing situations, and comparing and symbolism. I was going through a lot of changes—hormonal, puberty, I was kind of just at a standstill with my confusion . . .

[She starts to cry again.] I wish my mind was bigger. I was a ditz and didn't care about anybody but myself.

Fiona thought she had been lazy during this time of her life. She equated selfishness with a lack of intellectual sophistication, and felt pressure to cultivate herself intellectually. She commented that it was "good" how "intelligent" and "well-rounded" people were in Palo Alto and Los Altos (a neighboring town with a similarly affluent population), but she expressed an urgent desire to leave the area and her parents, whom she said made her, "read one college-bound book a week and write an essay on it" and who "forced me to do activities because I didn't have any interests." Fiona's mention of her lack of interests reveals the instrumentalization of enthusiasm at Sanders, and that, quite possibly, things Fiona enjoyed she had not learned, in the eyes of her parents, to convert into something she might check off on a list of accomplishments.

Fiona's parents' zeal and strictness seemed, in my observation, to surpass that of most students' parents, and the majority of students with whom I spoke were not so stressed as to cry uncontrollably during an interview. But

Fiona's self-contempt, revealed in a laundry list of intellectual deficits, was similar to the contempt other students I interviewed expressed for those who did not demonstrate their hard work in school or particular intellectual passion or talent. Fears of failure were personified in the image of the "slacker" who attends community college. Jeremy, a young Asian American transplant from New York City whose stepfather had moved the family to Palo Alto for a job at a start-up company that, at the time of our interview, had begun to falter, conveyed his feelings about the future and college: "It's not like I'm going to go to Foothill or whatever. I mean, it's a *junior college* [said with a great deal of disgust]. It's for stupid people. People at Foothill are slackers and stoners or druggies." He went on to speculate that these people, who "say they are going to a JC [junior college] for a few years and put off trying in high school and plan to fix things and then transfer to a UC [school] [with this his voice drips with cheery sarcasm] are deluding themselves."

Disdain for people who attended junior colleges was rife at Sanders. Another student, Linda, explained the moral meaning of attending Foothill: "Foothill's really good value for your money, but it's like, 'Oh, they're going to *Foothill*' [smiles]. They didn't work hard enough." The fear of going to Foothill was a fear of stasis, of literally and figuratively not going anywhere. For these young people, Foothill represented a stigma, a sign of an inner failing, of stupidity, shallowness (having no passions or talents), and laziness (an unwillingness to cultivate oneself intellectually), or even pathology ("stoners" and "druggies"). Like success, the specter of failure and its associated moral deficits threatened the wealthy children of what some students and teachers called "computer people" as much as more middle-class and sometimes economically struggling families confronting large mortgages, recession-related layoffs, or stock devaluations. Students monitored one another and themselves for evidence of these inner failings. "I'm a slacker," they often confessed to me, in self-deprecating and slightly anxious tones. Students whose focus was perceived to be too much on social life and partying were criticized by other students for being "shallow," for not *demonstrating* any creative or intellectual interests. Such criticism, often turned inward, was also racially and class-coded in ways that served to distinguish a white middle strata of strivers. The crime of slacking was leveled at those seen as a shallow elite (almost always white) or, alternately, working-class students of color. One school administrator explained, the general attitude of white students toward working class, minority students in the following way: "[They] might be called the losers, the not very academically curious, the "go-nowheres.""

The image of the lazy slacker points to one kind of freedom that was frowned upon by students: the freedom to choose not to compete. And what of those who chose not to compete? Evelyn, the self-proclaimed "lord goddess of the [stage-tech] shop," worked hard in school and was a good student who had already picked out a first-choice elite science and engineering college. But she expressed a kind of exclusion that she felt existed at Sanders for those who did not demonstrate academic prowess or a competitive spirit:

> Being able to get good grades in good classes is valued. Which is kind of too bad. Because it means that people who don't really particularly want to be here but who are smart and intelligent aren't valued as much. . . . A friend of mine takes lower-lane classes but is a really good artist. But she's, there's not as much for her to do here. There's sort of two groups of people here: there's the people that are going to get into four year colleges and are going to get Ph.D.s and going to make zillions of dollars—well, not quite but they wish—and then there are the people that aren't, that maybe are going to go to J.C., but maybe aren't even going to do that who don't feel the need to go to college and I think that group of people is less valued.

Evelyn's statement that "people . . . who don't feel the need to go to college" despite being intelligent and talented in some way, as in the case of her artist friend, are less valued at Sanders is significant, for it implies that talent is valued only insofar as it puts one on a college-bound path. Thus, as personal as talents might be, there was at Sanders a pragmatic aspect to having talent, exploring creatively, or expressing oneself freely. To not display signs of one's self-cultivation, as Fiona had failed to do, was tantamount to failure in light of the clear obligation to distinguish oneself in a highly competitive environment. The discourse around freedom of expression, which conveys an environment in which "anything goes," might instead represent the implicit command, "Express yourself!" Creative exploration and freedom of expression were inextricably linked to competitive performance.

Although in no way do I wish to suggest that all forms of self-expression and self-cultivation—from lunchtime punk rock performances to students' aspirations and dreams to become filmmakers, writers, mathematicians, or actors—simply represented a conscious competitive strategy or ruse to "get ahead," an in-depth exploration of how students negotiated often contradictory personal aspirations and values shaped by the competitive environment of Sanders suggests that students learned strategies of self-definition and aspiration that served at once to inspire them and distinguish them from others. Indeed, by examining the ways in which one particular student navigated contradictory values and ideals of success, we can illuminate common strategies of aspiration management and self-definition among Sanders youth.

Katherine: Registering Contradictions, Defining a Position

Katherine, the only child of a successful British house-painting contractor and a Swiss public high school teacher, was a fashionable, social, and articulate young woman who hung out at "the benches." Describing her social life, she emphasized a best friend who was "one of the richest people at the school," and made clear that partying, which she defined as congregating and drinking large amounts of alcohol, comprised a key aspect of her social world. It was common to party, she said, in places like the hills of Woodside, a wealthy and slightly more rural area with bigger lots, where neighbors could not hear any noise. At such parties Katherine and her friends often met up with other young people who comprised, as she put it, "this kind of network of cool party popular people who are friends with each other" from different schools in nearby affluent communities.

At school Katherine was an editor of the school literary magazine—which was an honor, as only journalism students from the school's award-winning newspaper were chosen to participate. At the time of our interview, the magazine's cover story concerned students at Sanders and other local schools who buy and sell prescription drugs such as Ritalin for recreational use. Academically Katherine was a strong student. She was taking two AP courses and worried about getting into the UC, Los Angeles, "because it's an amazing school and I tried hard and I want to go."

At the beginning of our interview Katherine described her family to me:

K: [We are] upper middle class. But in Palo Alto, I feel like I am at the bottom of the spectrum, but, um, I know compared to the rest of our family and every other place, if we can afford a moderate house in Palo Alto, that's pretty good.
E: Why do you feel like you're at the bottom of the spectrum in Palo Alto?
K: Um, just because my parents aren't Silicon Valley [laughs] computer people or affiliated with Stanford, and [pause] we don't drive, like, BMWs or live in a big house, like most of, well, you see a lot of that around here. You don't see that when you leave, like, the Bay Area.

We continued discussing her parents' tastes:

K: They don't like materialism . . . They like socializing with people . . . They just feel like here everyone is too into their own thing . . . Socially, like they don't feel, like, left out, but they're not, I don't know how to put it, they wish that they saw more people walking down the street and more people would say, "Oh, hi, how's your day," you know?

The conversation moved on to race and class dynamics at Sanders, and Katherine's own view of these dynamics and her family's place in the social order.

K: At first, [Sanders] seemed like a bunch of narrow-minded, spoiled kids . . . At my old school it was 40 percent Asian, and my best friend was Chinese and, like, I was dating an African American boy—it was very diverse. But here you don't see Asian people and white people hanging out as much, or whites and African Americans just being friends. Yeah, I do have friends of all races here, but it's not the same . . . Maybe it's just that in high school people branch away.
E: So you don't see whites and black people hanging out here?
K: I mean, you can. But it's not, I mean, if you saw a white [person] and a black person going out here you'd think, "Oh, her black boyfriend" . . . I don't think like that but I think that's how everyone else sees it. I mean, Palo Alto is very diverse but the diversity stays amongst itself . . . a lot of my friends are racist toward Asian people, and I've never seen that before.
E: In what way?
K: They just, just the comments they would make. Like, "Oh, they're all so smart in math," like totally the stereotypes but they [K's friends] all follow that. It's just, I don't understand where it's coming from. I mean you can't judge a whole race of people . . . They use derogatory comments, like, "Driving her *Honda*, Oh, she can't drive" . . . Like, my friend rear-ended an Asian family, and my friend said, "I think it was my fault," and my friend's mom was like, 'Oh don't worry, honey, it wasn't your fault." I mean, I don't see it like that at all . . . My friends would never want to date a black person. They just don't feel . . . like I had a black boyfriend, and it was like, "Oh, her black boyfriend." Like, everyone liked him; he was a cool guy, he was accepted, but it was [pauses] different. See, he lived in Palo Alto, and he was raised with other white kids, so that kind of set him apart. But he fit into, like, the "black

people crew." [She appears self-conscious about her use of the word "crew," a racially coded and potentially derogatory word.]

In our dialogue Katherine describes her discomfort with the racial dynamics of the school. She sets herself apart from her friends, whose ideas about race she does not agree with. After she described how her friends accepted her former boyfriend because he was an African American who grew up in Palo Alto and yet distrusted him for his associations with other, perhaps working-class African American students, I suggested that class was an issue. At the mention of class, Katherine began to describe her friends' wealth and compare her own situation to her friends. She wound up expressing hurt feelings at the way her parents had been excluded from this elite social circle of which she was a part. She was simultaneously proud of and hurt by what she perceived to be her own and her parents' marginal status.

Our interview had the tone of a confession. Katherine described her social world with some dispassion and embarrassment: being seen at parties, having the right accoutrements of success, and being smart and working hard in school and having interests made one "cool."

K: Traditionally all the cool, popular party people hang out at the benches [sarcastic voice] and that's where my group of friends hangs out.
E: And what makes people popular?
K: Just like, if you always have a party to go to . . . Basically, you are assumed to be out at a party when it's night out [on the weekends]. . . . The kinds of cars you drive, the clothes, the fact that you're part of a large group of people that [voice starts to change to satirize a bit] all hang out and all have nice cars and all have cute clothes and have boyfriends [laughs]. All people do this. Honestly it boggles me . . . because there are some people that don't have anything to them and they seem to be loved by everyone. I don't understand. My friends are part of this group of people but I don't like or respect a lot of the people that I'm associated with. I just feel like they're shallow and there's more important things in life than the way you dress and partying. This sounds corny, but I was dating this guy and all he did was party. And what he gets from a party I get from a really good conversation . . . Last year I said I'm not going to sit at the benches but like, the fact is, all my friends sit there . . .

The conversation turned to markers of academic status and success. Katherine expressed frustration at the prospect of having to attend a lower-ranked UC or state school with people who hadn't tried as hard as she had.

She offered a detailed analysis of what would be "cool" and what would be humiliating in terms of college, attending a private small school on the East Coast over going to a lower-ranked UC, and she summed up her worst-case, post–high school scenario through an example of a friend who had graduated:

K: He's going to *Foothill*. I mean, he's not going *anywhere* in life. When he turns twenty-five he's inheriting fifteen million dollars cuz his parents are computer people. And I would call him to party but I don't think he's a cool person. I mean, he's not going anywhere in life.

E: What's the perception of Foothill at this school?

K: That you aren't going to succeed.

E: What is success?

K: Money

E: Do you think your friends feel that way? Do you feel that way?

K: I think my friends feel that way. On many levels I feel that way, but I also feel it's important to be educated. . . . and you can't necessarily get that from high school. I mean, my father's a perfect example. On the outside he seems like a loser. I mean, didn't go to college and graduate. Like, *paints houses for a living* [said with theatrical disdain]. Like, that's not being successful—he should be a doctor or something. But my dad is one of the most intelligent, educated, proper people I've ever met . . . And, he's not concerned with materialism. He doesn't care about money. It's just something that doesn't worry him at all. I admire him so much because he doesn't care about that . . .

E: You are more materialistic than your parents?

K: Yes. Oh, by far. Yeah, I mean, I wanna have the new Tiffany's bracelet that all my friends have.

E: Is that what this is? [I pointed to the bracelet on her wrist.]

K: Yeah. Like every single person you'll see, everyone has it. And it's not even that I like it. I mean, when I first saw it, I thought it looked clunky and tacky but just because everyone had it and it was from Tiffany's I started liking it. But at least I'm not trying to tell myself that I like it for what it is and that I'm original. I like it because everyone else likes it and I wouldn't like it if everyone else didn't have it. I've grown to like it but not for what it is but what it stands for.

E: What does it stand for?

K: I don't know [uncomfortably]. I don't even like what it stands for. It stands for having money and style and class, kind of . . . I don't want to be surrounded by materialism cause it has empowered, no, it has taken me over.

Katherine went on to describe her life and career aspirations: to study, to be single and completely independent. She described her "genuine interest" in exploring and writing about the world in her discussion of furthering her education in cultural studies and theology in Bhutan and Nepal, becoming a journalist for *National Geographic*, and spending her life doing Peace Corps work. She wanted to be "just completely . . . rid of material items." What did the notion of becoming a journalist for *National Geographic*, studying religion and culture in South Asia, and volunteering for the Peace Corps symbolize for Katherine? Earlier in our conversation she had described a summer trip she took to do community service in Thailand. On the trip Katherine and other American teenagers wore the same clothes every day. Katherine recalled: "I wanted to get to know me and love myself for who I am and not what I was wearing and what I drove." She described the trip as a wonderful time when she wasn't "tainted by anything else." Community service in the Third World, away from the daily competitive materialism of Sanders, offered a route to an authentic self not compromised by wearing Tiffany bracelets, being seen at the right parties, keeping silent while friends made racist comments, or attending Ivy League colleges.

Katherine's communicative style—her "I don't knows," self-interruptions, and earnest confession mixed with sarcastic commentary about her own life—signals her ambivalence about her own aspirations and values and the social and economic order in which she found herself. She describes her participation in a clique that she finds racist. Caught up in a world of comparing schools and wealth that she finds shallow and stupid, she simultaneously distances herself from her friends' values and from Palo Alto. Bitter at people whom she perceives as having money and not working hard in school or lacking genuine interests, she nonetheless wants acceptance from those she describes as having wealth and high status, and she admits to a conflicted notion of what "success" really means to her. Her father serves in our conversation as a touchstone of authenticity, of *genuine* self-cultivation, a person for whom education meant more than a route to status and titles. And yet she readily disdains a friend for attending a junior college, and she ranks a hierarchy of college options that clearly shapes her own views of success, despite positioning herself, through sarcasm, hypothetical asides, and opinion, as an outsider observing arbitrary and rigid customs.

But in addition to signaling ambivalence about her circumstances, Katherine's narrative demonstrates her attempt to define a subject-position. In our dialogue divergent themes of race and class, self-segregation on campus, social and academic status symbols, her description of her family, and her aspirations for her future centered upon her struggle to steer a path for her-self between the seemingly magnetized poles of an original authenticity and what she perceived as a materialistic, phony conformism. She expresses the desire to develop a path in life that reflects her particular interests and dis-avows the entrapment of material status.

The Value of Authenticity, the Scourge of Conformity

Katherine's negotiation of opposing values and aspirations was typical at Sanders, as my introductory discussion of students' aspirations and defini-tions of "success" suggested. Students were aware of their own contradictory values and aspirations to varying degrees. Some students reconciled this contradiction by simply articulating their own hope that they would be able to avoid succumbing to materialism, as Katherine did. Sara, the senior whose parents worked in the biotech and software industries and who had subtly mocked the social competition surrounding markers of status such as gro-cery stores, said, as we talked about how Sara envisioned her future: "I go back and forth with . . . being into the Silicon Valley lifestyle. I could believe that I need a nice car and house to be happy. I am hoping that I won't get wrapped up in all this and be anxious."

For Rob, who in the past year had witnessed his father lose his job as an accountant at a software company, lose his apartment (his parents were divorced), and now was preparing to watch his father move back into his mother's house but only as a tenant in the unheated garage, a time when the dilemma of choosing to follow one's passion or succumb to the pressure for money and security was particularly acute. Sadly he recalled a time during freshman and sophomore years, before he let the pressure for good grades get to him, when he had envisioned becoming a film director and when, "I felt a little freer, my thoughts were freer and more abstract." As a singer in a local youth opera, he had considered becoming an opera singer, but then he worried about doing "something practical," even as he found himself "ques-tioning capitalism" and comparing his father's fate to that of Willy Loman in *Death of a Salesman*.

Typically students registered—and coped with—the pressure to compete for social and academic status in contradictory and ambivalent ways, as Katherine did. On the one hand, they compared and measured wealth and social and academic status. When I asked students to describe their family's economic circumstances, they never simply said "middle class." Instead, they gave detailed descriptions, comparing their own family's status with that of friends' families, much as Katherine did in her description of the wealthy best friend with the private movie theater. Students noted the kinds of cars driven by their own and their friends' families, compared vacation habits, the area of town where they lived as opposed to where their wealthier friends had homes. They sometimes also recounted the remodeling of a family home or stock options that their parents held or had lost.

Students particularly noted how their own families diverged from the perceived Silicon Valley norm of being wealthy and living in large houses with parents who worked for high-tech companies and were graduates of Stanford or Harvard. I am reminded of Lee, a young woman whose father owned and operated a school where the Mandarin language and Chinese culture were taught and who described her family as "so non-engineering," or Rob, the former football player and self-described loner who, when asked where his father, an accountant recently laid off from a San Jose software firm, had gone to college, replied, "nowhere significant."

On the other hand, in addition to comparing and measuring wealth and status, students from the school's many cliques simultaneously negotiated the pressure to compete for social and academic status by deploring or feeling self-conscious about personal materialism at Sanders. Such attitudes bring to mind a conversation with a young woman of the "benches" crowd, who, when discussing her fashionable SUV, self-consciously defended what she described as her love of "big cars," and she denied caring about a particular model. They also recall a discussion I had with Rob, who felt that a bald desire for status rendered even everyday social contact at Sanders a kind of commodity: "There's always like a status feel to everyone's interactions in general," he observed. Students representing diverse social groups within the school made fun of "grade grubbing," and I noticed that a number of "bench people" worried or were defensive about other people in the school finding them "shallow," too focused on clothes and popularity. A number of them said that they felt "judged" by other students in this respect.

Like the fear of becoming a slacker without interests, talent, or a work ethic, students feared being seen as a conformist or as shallow—as symbolized through material status symbols. Like Katherine, many students sought to create a case for their own authenticity and originality by describing particular passions and comparing themselves to those whom they felt were too materialistic, focused only on their social and academic status. The demonstration of authentic ability and passion was a way to separate oneself from the crowd. Students sometimes emphasized an outsider or maverick status. Similarly, they often made clear their lack of interest in the machinations of the school's social scene or in mocking imitations of people who were overly "freaked out" about grades, seeming to imply that those people lacked a passion or talent that made them authentic and original. Lee, the young woman cited above, disdained status-conscious behavior. She abhorred what she considered a boastful Asian Pride movement and spoke in sarcastic tones about the Sanders scene of "drugs, . . . parties, student government, playing volleyball, going to dances." In contrast, she applauded a fellow student's attitude and success in a way that made clear her own values: "Like N.—everyone respects his genius. He doesn't go around bragging about it."

Talk of career aspirations that revealed a desire for creative and intellectual discovery and exploration, and public presentations like the Valedictorian's speech that referred to a campus environment "brimming with intellectuality," where people "ponder everything from the serious to the silly," showcased not just authenticity and originality but also sophistication. Another common mode of expressing sophistication involved a knowing sarcasm that effectively conveyed depth and nuance, signs of authenticity, originality in a competitive educational and social environment.

One day in class, after having watched the student news show, Justin, a white senior and key player on the school robotics team, commented sarcastically: "Well, that was nothing short of scintillating." Everyone chuckled. His comment reflected cultural capital and depth; purposefully pretentious, it simultaneously demonstrated sophistication and mockery at the arrogance of the kind of person who would make such a comment. Classroom sarcasm often revealed students' cosmopolitan awareness of their own positions within a global capitalist order characterized by inequality. One white young man, Eric, the son of a divorced acupuncturist and a makeup artist, who aspired to become an actor or a musician and whose personal style fused the long-haired, messy, hippy look with the ascetic-looking black clothing favored by fans of anarchist punk rock, held up a cartoon he had drawn of Korean child workers for his presentation titled "The Life of a Tennis Shoe." "That's who makes the clothes," he said with cheery sarcasm, clearly disgusted with this example of capitalist labor exploitation. On another day, during a discussion of clothes, Josh, a white senior and captain of the school robotics team, joked, "Clothing? I don't know, I just think of the little Pakistani kids making my shirts." And then, addressing no one in particular, he went on in mock-callousness: "I'm serious, Mexican shirts don't fit me. I go into Eddie Bauer and they've got shirts made in Guatemala, Honduras, Mexico, and Canada. The Canadian fits the best." A group of young women giggled.

Unconscious and Conscious Strategies of Aspiration Management

We have observed the apparent value that students placed upon authenticity, originality, and sophistication, and the disdain or ambivalence that many felt about obvious signs of materialism and expressions of conformity. The pattern of identifying with particular kinds of self-cultivation associated with authenticity and originality reveals a compunction students felt to set themselves apart from others. This raises a question of intent: were students' expressions of authenticity, originality, and nuance purposeful, pragmatic, and conscious or were they spontaneous, deeply felt, and unconscious? In fact, they were both. Students expressed a sense of pride in their achievements and pleasure in discovery associated with the cultivation of the creative self—evident, for example, in the graduation ceremony described at the start of this chapter, in students' descriptions of the extent to which they were engrossed in solving problems (such that going to class was an interruption), or in Katherine's desire to learn about religion and culture in South Asia. But, simultaneously, students expressed awareness that, in the immediate preparation for college and, ultimately, for an adulthood that met upper-middle-class social and economic standards, good grades were not enough; they needed an edge. And so, consciously and unconsciously, they learned to market their authentic, individual qualities, shaping their aspirations and identities in advantageous ways.

A key term stood out during my time at Sanders, one that I came to realize held a paradoxical meaning that belied the pragmatism behind some students' passions, talents, and extracurricular activities: "well-roundedness." I first heard the term "well-rounded" in an interview with an interim principal at Sanders, Ms. S, in the fall of 2003:

> E: How would you define success here (for students)?
> MS. S.: Ideally success that we as a staff would have for students is that students leave here loving to learn, and wanting to learn more. Success as defined by students is probably, um, 'Do I have good enough grades to get into a good enough college?' . . . I feel that there are certain students that— the girl who is currently student body president has intentionally taken a lighter load because she wants to be a well-rounded person. I applaud her. I fear that too many kids don't feel that they have the time to do that. In principle, everybody wants to be well-rounded, everybody wants to do athletics and some extracurricular activity and do community service and be successful in school—they want to do it all, and so I guess maybe success is for students to be able to lead a balanced life.

The notion of cultivating oneself as a "well-rounded" person comple-mented the notion of cultivating a passion or talent. As the above quote indicates, the central tenet of "well-roundedness" is, ostensibly, leading a "balanced" life. In fact, Sanders was in the process of institutionalizing this principle while I was on campus. Ms. Smith, a guidance counselor at Sanders, described how Sanders was in the process of undergoing its periodic recer-tification as a member of the Western Association of Secondary Schools and Colleges (WASC), and that the creation of an environment in which students were able to achieve "balance" was one of the WASC goals that Sanders had set. Ms. Smith offered that one of the challenges of her job was to impress on parents the need for their children to be "well-rounded," especially parents extremely focused on their children's high achievement.

Parents with whom I spoke, however, needed little convincing about the merits of being "well-rounded." Christine G. was a white Sanders parent mar-ried to a software engineer who had worked for Netscape and, at the time of the interview, was working eighty hours per week at a start-up company as vice president of engineering. Christine worked as a part-time nurse practi-tioner at a women's clinic in a nearby town that served women she described as mostly "affluent." As a result of her husband's work in Silicon Valley, they had been able to buy a large house in Palo Alto during the late 1990s. I asked Christine, one of whose daughters was a high-achieving junior at Sanders with interests in computer science, math, art, writing, linguistics, and com-petitive water polo, if she felt that Sanders encouraged students to cultivate diverse interests—to be, in other words, "well-rounded." She replied that the school was too focused on grades, that Sanders was not doing a good enough job in encouraging diverse interests. For Christine, well-roundedness was a virtue to be encouraged and cultivated in youth.

To what end was "well-roundedness," "balance," and "slowing down" encouraged at Sanders? The principal, Ms. S, saw the effort of the Sanders administration to produce "well-rounded" youth as a panacea for the overly stressed or overly extended young person, whose singular focus on grades and acceptance to a "good enough" college was depleting a sense of joy in learning. Similarly Kimberly, a white school psychologist who moonlighted as a private college counselor, pointed out that many parents phoned her with concerns about the need for their children to "slow down." Although I do not doubt these intentions, my conversation with Kimberly revealed an alternate motivation behind the cultivation of a "well-rounded" self: the creation of a "package" for college. Many students I spoke with employed such private college counselors, who worked with them on test preparation as well as on their profiles and essays for college admissions. Kimberly pointed out that demonstrating well-roundedness provides an edge to high school students competing for a place at the country's elite private colleges or the competitive UC system. Activities pursued during "down time" to achieve "balance" and "well-roundedness" was also a competitive strategy for admission to college.

In retrospect, young women's fashion choices at Sanders can also be understood in relation to the concept of "well-roundedness." The presence of so many spaghetti straps, of visible thong underwear, and super-tight jeans can be read, like the compunction to go to parties on the weekends and take AP classes, as a competitive act of self-cultivation aimed not at securing the "right" man but at broadcasting a general "well-rounded" excellence, at being a "contender" in all senses. It also conveys the willingness to take risks, to lead and to perform on multiple fronts simultaneously. Thus, for young women, the "well-rounded" ideal is gendered; at the symbolic level, girls serve their own interests not just by excelling in multiple areas but also through conveying sexiness.

To sum up, "well-roundedness" is essential to the list of traits to be demonstrated by a high-achieving young person—the student who writes poetry but is also a National Merit semifinalist and volunteers at a soup kitchen on Saturdays—in putting together his or her "package." Moreover, "well-roundedness" is ideally paired with a specific passion or ability. A mother I interviewed in the nearby affluent community of Los Gatos, who had employed a private college adviser for her child, described an attitude toward children's performances: "The feeling is, take one activity and excel at it—you can be well-rounded, but you have to have some sort of edge."

Kimberly's frank description of the process of "spinning a profile" for college applicants confirmed the view that a strategic move for college admissions is to match well-roundedness with an "edge." Kimberly spoke of "refining and manufacturing an identity" for applicants, centered around their "thing," a passion or talent that "sets them apart." At a lunchtime meeting of the Entrepreneurs, Pioneers, and Innovators Club (EPIC)—at which five Asian American students were present to begin work on their plan to patent a club invention—a timesaving computerized printer that would print book chapters without anyone having to stand over the book and turn the pages to make copies—one club member, Susan, commented: "Colleges want to see me on [the school literary magazine]." She also felt they wanted to see her starting clubs, which was why she had founded EPIC with a few friends. Similarly, in interviews, many students described their volunteer work as an effort to look good for colleges.

Whether one had a private college counselor or not, at Sanders the idea of passions, talents, and the process of creative exploration as part of a "package" coexisted with a sense of the inherent virtues of such qualities and practices. Although many students simply described a sense of pressure to demonstrate well-roundedness and an "edge" in addition to getting good grades, others, usually those who identified with and cultivated an "alternative" or "bohemian" lifestyle (who, I noticed, often came from families with relatively lower socioeconomic status relative to other Palo Alto families) felt that the celebration of difference and freedom of expression at Sanders was, in a sense, a marketing ploy. The contradiction between an obligation to display one's talents and passions and one's individual extracurricular activities and quirks and a desire to do so out of inspiration and passion created, for some, a kind of trap. Eric, the student described above who drew on the Korean child laborers for an economics assignment, put it this way: "[At Sanders] it's the selling of nonconformity—sort of like, 'Let's all be different together,' you know? That's what I notice a lot."

Parents' Entrapment

One evening toward the end of my fieldwork I attended a meeting of the Parent-Teacher-Student Association (PTSA) at Sanders. The topic of the evening was "Stress and Your Teenager." An audience of about twenty mothers and one father—all white except for one Asian—sat in folding chairs, listening to the opening remarks of the interim high school principal, Ms. S., in which she described new homework, testing, and grading policies that were being developed to reduce student stress including an upcoming "homework holiday" which Ms. S. had brokered with teachers for spring break. The mothers cheered loudly.

Ms. S. then introduced the evening's speaker, a well-known and respected psychologist for adolescents and a parenting coach with thirty years' experience. The speaker, Naomi, a casually dressed, suntanned white woman in her forties or early fifties, assumed a deferential tone with her audience, looking down demurely when discussing the delicate subject of the overstressed children of the parents present and speaking softly in a calm and thoughtful manner. Naomi calibrated her talk to the high educational levels and general worldliness of the audience; no attempt was made to avoid psychological or academic-sounding terminology in her explanations of processes like the developmental mandates of adolescence. With her audience paying rapt attention, the speaker declared that their children were part of "the first over-programmed generation." Such children suffer intense pressure to get into college, she noted, adding that "there is a fine line between being happy and succeeding" in an "affluent culture" that values "making money" and "being high-achieving."

Mothers began to raise their hands. One claimed that only a third of Sanders children were taking AP classes, and complained that others must endure the "pain of the AP model." Another woman brought up a "lack of enjoyment," commenting that "school for my kid is something to get through." The speaker recommended a book, *Doing School,* about the phenomenon of the joyless, grinding atmosphere in local schools. She suggested delicately that it might be hard for parents to say, "I care more about what you are learning than what you are doing."

At this point in the discussion, a mother pointed out that "kids in this community get stress from peers," and another asked what to do "if your kid is staying up working until two and three in the morning seven nights a week." "Research shows," Naomi informed the parents, "that adolescents who engage in 'real stuff'—hiking, doing sports, volunteering—have lower stress levels." "But," a woman protested, "playing sports is not just about playing sports! It's about getting ready to play sports at the college level!" Parents murmured in agreement. The psychologist suggested that one strategy might be for the kids to skip practice from time to time. The parents chuckled derisively at this impossibility. "Colleges are complaining that they are getting kids who arrive as freshmen already burnt out from high school," the psychologist warned. The atmosphere in the room became subdued when a mother opined bitterly that young people who do not take AP courses or who do not shine or excel at Sanders "feel like scum."

Parents had come to this event motivated to seek help for their overstressed teenagers, and yet, when confronted with strategies for addressing stress and providing "balance," they expressed a sense of the impossibility of their children not competing. As the meeting progressed, parents met each suggestion with sarcasm. They seemed to feel stymied, aware of the competition their children faced but at the same time of the psychic burdens created by that competition.

As this PTSA meeting illustrates, parents were worried about the stress their children were experiencing and were eager to hear solutions. Attaching a negative moral valence to the competitive "culture" of the area, parents told stories about other, more competitive and histrionic parents, noting the effects of such attitudes on friends of their children who seemed to be struggling under the weight of parental expectations regarding grades or the caliber of a child's talent in a particular area.

In fact, parents' musings about children and childhood highlighted ambiguities and conflicts about child rearing that arose in the process of negotiating the competitive environment their families inhabited. Many parents informed me that their children's stress began long before they were in high school, and they criticized other parents in the community for over-scheduling their children. A venture capitalist with children in private school said,

I don't know if you saw the stress poll at [. . .]? I see [the pressure to succeed] in the lack of spontaneous play among [younger] kids. There are so many activities. I coach baseball, but the only time these kids play baseball is when they are with me as manager out on the field. They don't come home after school and say, "Let's go in the back yard and play." Now, some of them do, but not a lot, because they have violin lessons, they have soccer, and they have tons of homework, and they are exhausted from doing this all week. Now is that good or bad? I wish I had violin lessons. But I think kids are suffering from being made to be adults.

Lunching with me at a Palo Alto café, Alice Frost described mothers she knew through her children's elementary school whom she claimed had had their children take piano lessons for ten years so they would become concert pianists. After-school soccer, she noted, had been divided into a lower and a more competitive tier—one group "wasn't good enough," she said. Some mothers, moreover, encouraged their children to drop activities at which they did not excel so they might have more time to perfect their stronger skills. As another mother put it, "Soccer, ballet, swim team, the neighbor's five year old is doing stuff. It's crazy, and it's what's socially expected . . . by the other mothers on the street, in the school. It's a rat race."

Of course, no one I met during my fieldwork at Sanders and in Palo Alto admitted to being the prime agent of their child's stress, but the existence of a parental discourse criticizing other, pushier parents was significant. Such criticism revealed the anxiety and ambivalence that parents felt about children's stress and their own role in it. In turn, they sought to overcome this anxiety by creating boundaries of unacceptable pushiness marked by sharing stories of parental excess. At times the racialized figure of the gruelingly strict and high-pressure Chinese parent served this purpose. Occasionally I listened to stories about the demands that Chinese parents placed on their children. "Chinese parents"[15] were represented as the most stress-inducing parents of all. Although I don't dispute, for example, one teacher's observation of Chinese students crumbling under stress from home or working so hard that they "burn out" halfway through the semester, one effect of this discourse was to project guilt about the "rat race" atmosphere onto Chinese community members when, in fact parents, the school, and the community were all complicit in creating a high-stress atmosphere for high school students.

According to faculty and staff at Sanders and on the school board, many parents put extreme pressure on both their children and the school system. One member of the school board for the Palo Alto school district described to me, with some measure of critical and amused distance, the ferocious competition to get into Advanced Placement courses. Parents, he explained dryly, sometimes became hysterical over their child's bad grades or being rejected for an AP course. He described urgent phone calls in which board members were asked to negotiate with the school on behalf of parents worried about their children's low grades or assigned class level. Over coffee with a vice president of a major tech firm who had made a lot of money from stock options during the boom—and who mentioned being brought up on the East Coast and trained in engineering—I asked how he and his wife, who had hired a private college tutor for their senior daughter, felt about academic success. "A's are better then B's," he half-joked, explaining that parents are freaked out because they see you need an A average to get into UCSB [UC, Santa Barbara]."

The prevalence of students with a "504 plan," which gives students the right to take un-timed standardized tests based on the diagnosis of a learning disability such as dyslexia, offers evidence of a parental preoccupation with student performance. Such diagnoses, in fact, abounded. A number of students at Sanders mentioned that they were diagnosed with attention deficit disorder (ADD) or attention deficit hyperactivity disorder (ADHD)[16] and were subsequently medicated with drugs such as Ritalin after their parents had become alarmed by their school performances or a perceived inability to concentrate. A school counselor on campus reported receiving approximately twenty calls per school year from parents of Sanders youth—typically male youth, she noted—demanding diagnostic tests for ADD and ADHD. In these cases teachers were given a questionnaire to fill out about the students' behavior in class and their academic performance, and, depending on the responses, students were referred to a physician.

Alice Frost explained the feelings of many parents trying to balance student performance and stress: "It's hard, you want your kids to do well." A pastor of an evangelical church in Palo Alto where, according to the pastor, most adult congregants were high-tech professionals, described the following dilemma:

One of the things that Palo Alto and this area does is just put enormous pressure to perform. You hear sixth graders talking and worrying that they are not going to get into Harvard. Parents sleeping out three nights in a row to get your unborn child signed up for some nursery school. I mean, it's crazy . . . [in the voice of a hypothetical congregant] "Everybody else at school is giving their ninth graders prep courses for the SATs, and I don't want to put my kids through that, and yet, on the other hand, if I don't, they will fall behind." I think kids live with that. I think the community does that to them, and then there's, if you're Christian, you should be able to say, 'Gosh, let's not get sucked into this completely, there's more to life than academic competition . . . but it's a real battle.

A Fear of Slipping

In post-millennium Palo Alto, young people and their parents felt so intensely pressured to succeed that each generation suffered a kind of entrapment. Young people confronted a pressure to succeed that encouraged them to cultivate strategies of competitiveness that, in turn, engendered a social environment defined by values and aspirations that often appeared contradictory to my informants and also to me. Thus students like Katherine sought to cultivate themselves and define their authenticity through career aspirations and individual tastes while simultaneously struggling to measure up to social and academic standards that conflicted with ideals of self-cultivation through freedom of expression and creative exploration. And yet that authenticity—which represented one's means of empowerment, one's ethos of creative exploration and freedom of expression, one's passions, and one's originality—was effectively co-opted: Katherine and her classmates were, in fact, encouraged to represent themselves and perform in ways that marketed their authenticity as well as their "well-roundedness" in order to gain "an edge" in the competitive economy of youthful potential. Hence there was no getting away from the pressure to excel, save refusing to compete altogether. For some students, especially those, like Eric, who came from more economically struggling or socially marginal families, the obligation to market one's originality and authenticity amounted to a form of social and moral entrapment of which they were well aware.

Parents also experienced a similar kind of entrapment; they felt the psychic and physical burden of stress their children faced and yet feared that their children might fall behind. In interviews, parents sometimes worried aloud about how their children would ultimately support themselves, and almost always expressed the hope that their children would be "comfortable" and not have to live with financial anxiety in adulthood. As the mother of one Sanders senior put it, "Well, I guess there's always the being-able-to-make-a-living thing. I guess [mentions a student's name] and her friends just automatically assume that they aren't going to be able to afford living in Palo Alto." A few parents joked about the prospect of children moving back into the family home after college. These anxieties resulted in a moral dilemma about what it meant to do right by one's children. What social and historical forces contributed to the forms of social entrapment embroiling Sanders students and their parents? What made the desire to compete so intense and the specter of failure so unthinkable?

Time and time again among middle-class Valleyites, I heard the phrase: "We're in a bubble here." In fact, the meaning of this was ambiguous. In one sense, the "bubble" referred to artificially high stock valuations associated with e-commerce during the late 1990s. But for Sanders students and their families—some of whom had experienced recession related layoffs, others made rich by "cashing in" stock options before the crash, and still others fearing and awaiting layoffs—the idea of living in a bubble expressed more than the shock of rapid wealth accumulation.[17] It expressed fragility and vulnerability as well as an awareness and wistful desire to maintain one's position above the fray of a sliding economy in which middle-class and even upper-middle-class people lacking the silver bullet of stock options cashed in at the right time struggled to maintain social and economic position in a region where the number of high-paying jobs was diminishing while the cost of living remained high. Moreover, "the bubble" had strong temporal associations: one waited for a bubble to pop, worrying, meanwhile, about a fragile present inside the bubble and doubting the future outside it.

"The bubble"—as in the tech stock-market bubble—had, of course, already burst by the time I arrived in Silicon Valley in the fall of 2001.[18] Over the next eighteen months daily reckoning in local and national newspapers and economic reports told the story of a declining regional economy: average annual pay for Silicon Valley residents had declined in inflation adjusted terms from $81,700 in 2000 to $64,400 in 2003; commercial space vacancy rates had jumped in Santa Clara County from 4 percent to 22 percent during the same period, and, by July of 2003, the jobless rate of Santa Clara County had risen to 8.5 percent,[19] the worst local jobless rate in the county since 1983 (Murr and Ordonez 2003).[20]

There was frank talk about the situation among residents of Palo Alto and other middle-class Valley residents I spent time with. The pastor at the evangelical church I visited described weekly meetings where seventy to eighty men—mostly fathers—met to discuss their anxieties about possible layoffs, having either been laid off or feeling guilty about laying people off. Parents I interviewed recounted stories about family friends who had been forced to leave Silicon Valley after being laid off or who were barely managing to stay while looking for work. Some confided anxiety about job security. The school psychologist at Sanders reported that a large number of students had come to her office during the 2002–2003 school year reporting that a parent had been laid off and that the family was worried about having to move.[21]

Daily habits revealed how parents and their children registered and negotiated these anxieties. Sanders students' habits of comparing and measuring wealth, grades, and other markers of social and academic status including familial or personal stock portfolios echoed the habits of local adults. My conversations with most adults in Silicon Valley turned at some point to the rising or falling valuation of houses, of tech stocks, and of worried speculation about future valuations. Parents compared themselves to other fathers and mothers, noting Ivy League schools and graduate schools that neighbors attended, and commenting on the value of an acquaintance's house or the meteoric rise and dizzying fall of a friend's stock worth. They joked about the falling price of their own investments and the crassness of someone's "dot-com" new-money aesthetic and how it was ruining the block; jokes about McMansions and Taco Bell houses abounded. In fact, references to the habits and tastes of young, moneyed "dot.commers" served, like references to conformist, materialist masses at Sanders High School, as a means of demarcation through an implicit contrast. Likewise, when people compared perks, they sought to distinguish themselves. As one Sanders father put it:

> People [in Palo Alto] find ways to demonstrate wealth in tasteful, unostentatious ways. Cars are important . . . Los Altos Hills, Saratoga, Atherton [other affluent Valley cities] are more ostentatious. So it's 'What trip did you take?' Back-road bike trips, the Galapagos Islands to retrace the Beagle voyage, enlightenment and self-improvement. It's positive to show that you are curious about the world.

Positive references to wealth were conflated with moral attributes; adults often commented on the brilliance, risk-taking ethos, and innovative spirit—

and money—of local techno-entrepreneurs, a representation that implicitly served as a yardstick by which to measure oneself and one's peers.

Beyond the realm of everyday familial and social life, a public discourse that dominated the local media and cropped up in casual conversations in Palo Alto while I was in the field—about private funding of public schools—reveals the extent of local middle-class and affluent families' social and economic anxieties and the strategies they employed at the scale of the community to maintain privilege. During 2001–2002 Palo Alto was abuzz with a debate over private fund-raising for its public schools. Within the Palo Alto Unified School District (PAUSD), an argument had broken out between more affluent school-specific Parent Teacher Associations (PTAs). Whereas parents participating in PTAs in the town's northern section had, by dint of fund-raising expertise and social connections, been able to raise enough money to supplement their children's schools such that students received more individualized attention owing to the hiring of extra support staff and educational technology given an upgrade, other local PTAs, mostly located in the town's south section, were able to earn only one-third of the that which Palo Alto PTAs raised. The school board proposed that moneys raised through private fund-raising be centralized at the district level, thereby banning parents from raising money for their own children's schools. The issue reached a near hysterical pitch for some. As one local school board member put it, "This private fund-raising issue has been extremely destructive to our district. I kind of compare it to an insatiable appetite—nothing will ever be enough if we don't call a halt" (Berry 2002:3).Sanders parents with whom I spoke about the issue came down on both sides; some commented disparagingly about how parents in powerful PTAs conspicuously showed off their resources, whereas others agreed with one school board member who pronounced the proposed ban a celebration of "equitable mediocrity." These parents felt that those endowed with what the *San Jose Mercury*, in a story on the issue, referred to as an "innovative Silicon Valley ingenuity and work ethic [applied to] their hometown educational arena" should not be punished for their talents.

This local debate, which infuriated parents on both sides of the issue, revealed the extent to which parents were invested in creating competitive elementary and middle schools in a district already known for its exceptional public schools. It also made clear the depth of resentment some residents felt toward what they perceived as the selfishness of those with elite social and economic connections. Like the recent statewide debate about inequalities created as a result of the private educational foundations that arose in affluent districts since Proposition 13 was passed in 1978 (Suryaraman 2002:1B, 4B), the Palo Alto PTA debate offers a snapshot of a predominantly white, upper middle class struggling to maintain class privilege during an economic downturn and budget crisis that threatened to affect them in ways long familiar to lower-middle- and working-class Californians accustomed to the painful combination of long-term income stagnation and declines in state services in an increasingly expensive state (Zavella 2001).[22] Not surprisingly, in 2002, when the then governor Gray Davis proposed that Basic Aid school districts return their excess property tax revenues to the state, residents of Palo Alto strongly opposed the measure (*Palo Alto Daily News* 2003:50).

A well-off white Sanders father who was a vice president at a major tech firm with household name status commented on why parents were so worried about young people's performances and so involved in the schools:

> It's a much more competitive world. There are so many successful people here—very brilliant people—great doctors—there's a lot of pressure to have successful children in the same terms that they were successful . . . There won't be the same opportunities for our kids [as existed during Silicon Valley's recent boom]. This gold rush will not be back. In the 1980s there was Wall Street, but compared to high tech it was small. Globalization will reduce some of their opportunities.

Another father, with the prestigious position of General Counsel for the same corporation as the father quoted above, summed up the future in Silicon Valley as one in which high-tech jobs will ultimately migrate to India and other places: "[There will be] a basic loss of high-wage jobs here. It'll be service jobs and senior management positions."

These parents' comments reflected a long-term reality of shrinking job opportunities and increased competition among Silicon Valley's educated middle class that transcended the time horizon of the tech boom and bust but was nonetheless made more apparent by the bust. High-tech work requiring high skill levels, such as engineering and software positions, has for the past decade been migrating to China, India, and Ireland, among other locales (Bjorhus 2002:1A). The recent tech bust exacerbated this trend; smaller budgets and increased pressure for profits during the economic slowdown in Silicon Valley accelerated the rate of global outsourcing of highly skilled tech jobs, as companies looked for cheaper labor abroad in China, for example, where engineering wages range from four to eight dollars per hour (Forte 2003).[23]

As the recession began to take its toll on Silicon Valley's engineers, a controversy ensued about the place of highly educated immigrant workers in Silicon Valley that illustrates the sense of pressure and competition experienced by the region's highly educated, middle-class workers. The local media began running stories about whether H1-B visa holders, who many engineers noted were paid less, were receiving preferential treatment when it came to laying off engineers (Bjorhus 2002:1A, 10A). Unlike the ongoing, national debate about stock options, in which local middle- and upper-middle-class tech and industry-affiliated service professionals have typically allied themselves with local techno-entrepreneurial elites by decrying congressional proposals to force companies to count stock options as a normal business expense, the H1-B visa issue has led middle-class workers to side against both management and foreign workers in a region known for its celebration of diversity (Rivlin 2004:sec. 3, p. 1).

That opportunities to work in Silicon Valley's principal high-wage sectors were diminishing contributed to parents' generalized sense of concern about the future socioeconomic status and stability of their children, whether or not those children planned to pursue careers in the local high-tech economy. The cost of living in Silicon Valley—which was a frequent topic among middle-class Valleyites and Palo Altans I met and spent time with in the field—compounded worries about shrinking economic opportunity. Between 1990 and 1999 living in Silicon Valley became one-and-a-half times more expensive than the national average. Local housing prices were a prime culprit. Even though the median household income in Palo Alto rose from $55,333 to $90,377 during the boom, it failed to keep up with local median housing prices. Even in the midst of the downturn in 2002, only 26 percent of residents of Santa Clara County could afford a median-priced home in the county, up from 18 percent in 2000, a sharp contrast to the 56 percent national average for the same time period (JVSV Network 2003).

In fact, these local social and economic pressures reflect contemporary conditions for similarly educated professional middle-class families throughout the nation. As noted in a report of the Century Foundation cited in the *New York Times* (Herbert 2004), middle-class debt crisis and bankruptcy has grown as the costs of child care, medical care, education, energy, and housing rise in proportion to wages. However, Silicon Valley's established professional middle class is experiencing a concentrated version of the national situation; the higher local cost of living, the region's intensifying wealth polarization—which outstripped the nation's—during the 1990s (Benner

2002:213; JVSV Network 2003:19), and the techno-entrepreneurial success and affluence of local the new entrepreneurial elite heighten insecurity for many middle-class Valleyites.

Demographic transformation within the region and within the state's public educational system posed another source of anxiety, especially for local middle- and upper-middle-class whites. By 2000 no ethnic group was in a statistical majority in Santa Clara County or California. Asian American students comprised 39 percent of the school-aged populations of Santa Clara and San Mateo counties, and in 2000, in Santa Clara County, Asian American students were outperforming whites in terms of percentages of students eligible for the state and UC public educational system.[24] Moreover, the percentage of Asian Americans—who comprise 11 percent of California's population—that were admitted to the freshman class at UC, Berkeley jumped six percentage points to 45 percent between 1998 and 2001. Over the same period white admittance dropped one percentage point, to 29 percent (Steinberg 2003).[25]

Such statistics compounded the anxiety of local, white, middle-class families about the shifting racial composition of the regional information economy. By 2000, 53 percent of the Silicon Valley science and engineering workforce was foreign-born, and, of these, workers from India, China, and Taiwan were the most highly represented (Wadhwa et al. 2007). Moreover, the percentage of firms with Indian, Chinese, or Taiwanese founders had increased to 28 percent. For some white middle-class residents, such figures exacerbated the reality of highly skilled tech-industry jobs disappearing because of global outsourcing.

In Palo Alto these educational, demographic, and occupational realities fueled a racial discourse about local, highly educated, middle-class Asian families. At Sanders and in the community I heard descriptions of strict Chinese parents, joyless, competitive Chinese children, and overly intelligent Chinese youth snapping up all the spots in the UC system. Such talk was not limited to Palo Alto. A mother I met and interviewed in Saratoga, a similarly affluent town with a much larger Chinese population than that in Palo Alto, informed me that local whites referred to a neighborhood where many of Saratoga's Chinese families lived as the "Golden Triangle." As we sat in her expansive ranch home on a hill discussing tech moguls in the neighborhood and the pressure her children felt competing against Asian students at the local public school, her daughter, a senior, arrived home from school. Soon immersed in our conversation, her daughter volunteered that fellow white students joked that an A or B grade was an "Asian C."

In fact, this racial anxiety did not only manifest itself in jokes and gossip. Some white parents have taken their children out of the region's public school system, initiating a "new white flight" from the system in schools with increasing numbers of Asian students (Huang 2005). This practical strategy against a perceived threat of Asian competition can be understood as of a piece with legislative developments in the state of California and nationally. In California, in particular, discourses of entitlement to public goods and services have often been cast in racial terms, as the passing of California Propositions 187 (in 1994) and 209 (in 1996) attest.[26] In the state the retrenchment of long-term social services and cuts in public education have, since the anti-tax revolts of the 1970s, generated a tendency among white middle-class families to identify with discourses of limited entitlement.

These political, economic, and social forces have intensified the obligation to compete through forms of self-discipline and expression that demonstrate certain markers of self-cultivation—academic excellence, creativity, intellectual sophistication, and "well-roundedness." Moreover, these circumstances have encouraged young people to imitate the pragmatic stance of the region's high-tech professional class, for whom work and play are indistinguishable and diversity and maverick creativity are principally a means of competition. Such conditions have also fostered practices of exclusion and feelings of inadequacy, including habitually comparing wealth to academic status, feelings of disgust with "slackers," and disdain for "shallow" conformists and materialists.

The politics of race and strategies of demarcation and self-cultivation have everything to do with a "fear of slipping"—both out of the middle class and permanently away from the upper middle class, of stagnating as others, highly skilled immigrants, more brilliant and enterprising neighbors, those with larger and more secure portfolios, manage to remain, despite turbulent economic conditions, "comfortable" and even prosperous. The phrase, "fear of slipping," of course, recalls Barbara Ehrenreich's classic, *Fear of Falling: The Inner Life of the Middle Class* (1989). This comparison raises a question: Is the fear of slipping any different from the "fear of falling" that Ehrenreich wrote about? Ehrenreich chronicled the "frantic positioning" of a professional middle class afraid of losing its status. The middle-class world she described, of "yuppies" confronting an increasingly expensive world and futilely attempting to keep up with the wealthy through conspicuous consumption and the pleasure of work, may be thought of as a preamble to the present.

But there are differences between Ehrenreich's trenchant summation of an American middle class in the 1980s, and the middle class youth and parents we have met here, and these differences make clear the new tactics of class maintenance required in a new era of changing labor conditions for highly skilled, middle-class Americans. Such changes, wrought by the intensifying globalization of capital and labor, and the neoliberal ascendancy of public-sector retrenchment and privatization (Harvey 1996; Goode and Maskovsky 2001), have resulted in middle-class Americans' shrinking and disappearing benefits, job security, pensions, and other guarantors of middle-class stability, such as the steady increases in income nostalgically recalled by some of the local middle-class professionals whom I interviewed for this book.

With the benefit of hindsight, it is apparent that Ehrenreich presciently chronicled the beginning of this era. In the 1980s middle-class families feared falling out of a middle-class lifestyle. The burden, however, had not yet shifted so dramatically onto middle-class youth. In Ehrenreich's telling, white middle-class youth competed for status at the mall and via "sweet sixteen" parties. For young people at Sanders, the terrain of self-cultivation has expanded beyond the mall. Material status symbols are but one of many requirements of maintaining status in an upper middle class secure enough to withstand the economic and social risks—the overnight disappearance of retirement funds and jobs, private college costs exceeding $200,000, insurance companies frequently raising rates by large percentages—which define and sometimes destruct ordinary middle-class life in the contemporary United States. Although there still exists (often racialized) anxieties about "softness" that Ehrenreich described, now animated by the presence of middle-class Asian families in Silicon Valley, middle-class teenagers today, both consciously and unconsciously, self-craft, work, and play in an instrumentalized way like adults. The "sweet sixteen" party as status strategy has been replaced, then, by parties that, like the extreme sports networking events described at the outset of this book, test physical endurance, involve rituals of bodily risk showcasing fitness for competition, and broaden one's list of potential contacts.

In this project of self-demarcation and cultivation—if not in the particulars of parties that often occur while parents are away—parents are, of course, key players. Simply put, middle-class Valley residents have come to feel that the futures of their offspring are not only hanging by a thread but constitute an indispensable marker of middle-class status and privilege. Such sentiments have in turn engendered a parenting style aptly described as "concerted cultivation" (Lareau 2003). This style of parenting, which is a strategy of coping with the risks associated with slipping out of the middle class imperiled by a shrinking social wage, transforms communities' relationships with school districts, and dynamics between parents and children. A symptom of social and economic insecurity, "concerted cultivation" also depends on experiences of class and race privilege, of the everyday perks and structural benefits that come, quite literally, with the territory of a place like Palo Alto: access to private college counselors, private transportation, a cornucopia of activities through which to develop oneself, domestic service workers whose labor enables parents to focus on the particulars of children's school assignments and extracurricular activities, and, of course, a school district buffered from public-sector retrenchment.

This atmosphere of insecurity and privilege compels middle-class youth to demonstrate their exceptionalism on multiple fronts simultaneously, thereby gaining an "edge" in the college marketplace and warding off a descent out of middle-class privilege—a predicament for which, if Sanders students' views of slackers are any indication, they would most likely feel responsible.

Coda

What, overall, comprise the political effects of the Sanders students' strategies of self-cultivation and aspiration? The habit of talking about the brilliance and creativity of the student body and the production of the school's social space as a free atmosphere promoting creative exploration and self-realization shaped young people's aspirations, and framed their understanding of their place in the world as well as their assumptions about the social spaces they inhabited or imagined. These everyday discourses, practices, and special events—Principal A's commencement address serves as an example, as do students' career aspirations, which emphasized personal choice and interests as a sole consideration, or, for that matter, sexy clothing and expressions of sexuality—fostered a disposition of class entitlement among Sanders youth, and, as some Sanders staff suggested, their parents as well.

Students, faculty, and staff justified this sense of entitlement with historic and geographic references to Silicon Valley; like the Puritan colonists who argued that evidence of their productive use of the land justified their ownership of the land, student brilliance and local innovation served to explain and maintain the class status of students and their families. For families that felt themselves slipping behind, such a discursive tactic might serve to defend class position.

Thus students' feelings of class entitlement and hierarchy may solidify their position in relation to a globalized Silicon Valley society and economy. Indeed, this book's comparative exploration of students' modes of self-discipline and values at Morton and Sanders High Schools—representing disparate sectors of Silicon Valley's economy and society—suggests that educational processes resonate with social, political, and economic circumstances to reinforce existing class and ethnic hierarchies. Whereas, at Morton, students ultimately felt an obligation—which they framed as empowerment—to the community, at Sanders, students framed their aspirations in terms of self-fulfillment.

And yet the pressures that Sanders students and their families felt, as people living, learning, and working in a community reminded continually of entrepreneurial success and the value of competitiveness and simultaneously threatened by social and economic insecurity, encouraged young people to value freedom of expression, diversity, and the cultivation of an authentic self and to compete by marketing themselves as authentic, original, sophisticated youth. The result was an educational and community environment in which empowerment through self-cultivation could not be separated from competition; normative forms of self-expression were both empowering and entrapping. For some, the prospect of competing by marketing one's difference was unappealing, just as, for others, more obvious kinds of competition symbolized by racial hierarchies on campus or Tiffany's bracelets represented a kind of shallow conformity.

At the very least, these responses suggest a psychic toll upon Silicon Valley's middle-class youth. After spending time on the Sanders campus and interviewing young people there, I was left with the impression that, although young people at Sanders experienced intense friendships as at any high school, the hard work of appearing well-rounded, excelling in multiple areas, and displaying authenticity—in short, exhibiting a marketable flexibility—spawned for some a feeling of isolation and for many acute stress. In this sense Sanders students were genuinely at risk. As anthropologist Emily Martin has argued, the costs of learning to be, as sociologist Manuel Castells has put it, "prosperous in the post-industrial era," a goal that requires the cultivation of "creative selves and complex minds," should not be underestimated (Martin 1996:50).

Students' styles of aspiration management may also serve to heighten their sense of alienation toward a system that has created an imperative for young people to market themselves. Students I knew at Sanders experienced doubts about "the system" at the micro and macro levels; many, like Katherine, identified with a path that privileged personal exploration over the material, others experienced burnout, sometimes pointing out their own acts of self-marketing, and still others, like Rob, whose father was in some sense a casualty of the tech bust, questioned capitalism itself and its effect on high-tech Willy Lomans. While students' jokes signaling awareness of a complicit position within a global capitalist order may represent a means—however unconscious—through which to demonstrate one's own authenticity, one might also interpret the double-identity signaled through such humor as an expression of doubt and disaffection with a subject-position so in sync with the demands of the marketplace. Either way, the burdens for these young people were multiple and multiplying.

The Politics of Social Reproduction in Silicon Valley

"Every Youth a Start-up"

Education and Training in Silicon Valley

"The Challenge"

Right after I arrived in Silicon Valley during the fall of 2001 I witnessed a newly minted local "tradition," the annual "Sandhill Challenge," a soapbox derby sponsored by local high-tech firms to raise money for programs serving at-risk youth. At this event, teams of mostly male youth of diverse ethnic and class backgrounds raced homemade, aerodynamically designed vehicles down Silicon Valley's "Wall Street," Sandhill Road, competing in various speed and design categories.

In their futuristic, low-slung vehicles decorated with the logos of local high-tech firms, these young people embodied a local ethos of risk taking, competition, and creative problem solving in the service of technological innovation. The vehicles that they had made and were now commandeering down the slope of Sandhill Road represented months of collaboration and networking between young people, teachers, local corporations, and community-based organizations—practices that highly skilled tech workers and entrepreneurs often credit for their success. A visual symbol of the race's motto, "Every Youth a Start-up," the spectacle conveyed the potential of all young people, regardless of race, ethnicity, class, or gender, to transform and perhaps uplift themselves by becoming excited about technology. Essentially "The Challenge" was an instructive event intended to empower youth through exposure to the networking practices and values associated with professional-level membership in a globalized and prosperous information economy.

More broadly the event's participants served as emblems of democratic participation in a regional "information" society and economy beset with social and economic disparity. At the turn of the millennium, when, according to one locally ubiquitous statistic, Silicon Valley was producing "sixty-four millionaires a day," and titles like *Cyberselfish* (Barsook 1999) appeared in bookstores across the nation, events like "The Challenge" served as a symbolic counterweight to representations of local social inequality, presenting its corporate supporters as midwives of democracy and opportunity in Silicon Valley.

This observation is not meant to imply that the event was just for appearances or to question the motives of the event's sponsors. On the contrary, as I learned talking to people who were part of the region's high-tech managerial class and to nonprofit employees who had cultivated working relationships with them, many tech-industry elites and local middle-class tech professionals considered the global information economy an ideal vehicle through which to foster more socially, economically, and politically inclusive communities. In particular, they saw the problem of gaps in educational and professional achievement and technological access along lines of race, ethnicity, and income as one best solved through collaboration between the private techno-entrepreneurial sector and "the community."

As a charitable event that forged public-private connections and focused on providing low-income youth an opportunity to develop skills, innovate, and make social connections with engineers and other professionals working at local tech corporations, "The Challenge" exemplified a civic agenda focused upon the education and training of youth that emerged in Silicon Valley during the 1990s. Generally this regional effort, which was comprised of a range of unrelated and uncoordinated but similarly focused initiatives, targeted low-income youth, many of whom came from Latino and Asian immigrant families, and lived in neighborhoods like the one surrounding Morton High School in San Jose.[1]

By examining the political, economic, and social contexts of regional initiatives and discourse addressing the training and education of working-class youth in Silicon Valley, we can situate the Biotechnology Academy within a broader field of local sites of formal social reproduction focused on bridging the digital divide through educational enrichment and workforce preparation initiatives. Moreover, we can come to understand connections between the priorities and messages of a program such as the Academy, which provides career-oriented educational enrichment and training for underserved youth within the context of a public school, and a local dynamic of privatization that has become influential within nonprofit youth service organizations and public schools.

In the course of these efforts we will examine the particular educational priorities and skill emphases within workforce-oriented education and training programs for youth in Silicon Valley, and link them to a wider field of political and economic forces. Through attention to such priorities, and to perceptions of youth skills and skill deficits, in particular, we can gain a richer sense of the expectations and contradictions of schooling for Academy participants, and the conditions under which they forged aspirations. We can also observe a local political effect of such regional educational initiatives, including the Academy: the representation of low-income, at-risk Latino youth and public and nonprofit youth service institutions as subjects in need of corporate salvation.

Framing the Politics of Education and Training in Silicon Valley: Silicon Valley's "Digital Divide"

At the start of my preliminary fieldwork I was intrigued by the role that the high-tech community and public-interest groups associated with it had taken in disseminating information about professional and educational disparities in the Valley along race, ethnic, and class lines. The term "digital divide" was on the lips and websites of educators, nonprofit providers, journalists, and high-tech executives in Silicon Valley; a preferred shorthand for local occupational, educational, and economic inequality.

As I listened to representatives of large high-tech companies, employees at workforce development organizations, and local researchers discuss the digital divide, I noticed that almost everyone I spoke with brought up the organization Plugged-In, a technology-oriented community organization founded in 1992 in the town of East Palo Alto, a historically low-income but now gentrifying community adjacent to the high-rent "birthplace of Silicon Valley," Palo Alto. In fact, Plugged-In had played a key role in the national discourse around the digital divide promoted during the Clinton-Gore administration, serving as an organizational poster child for attempts to bridge the digital divide. High-tech managers and nonprofit employees alike commented on the success of Plugged In—an annual high-profile participant, incidentally, in the Sandhill Challenge—in empowering youth and community members by providing them access to and knowledge of technology, and in garnering local high-tech corporate support in the form of funds, technology, and mentorship.

By the mid-1990s the term "digital divide" was in wide circulation in the United States, partly because of the creation of a national network of Community Technology Centers (CTCs) to address the problem.[2] With the creation of new markets for Internet-related products locally and globally, the term became more pervasive and has often referred to disparities between the global North and South. In Silicon Valley, however, it connoted something much broader than a lack of technological access. In discussions I had with people involved in youth services and workforce development and with middle-class people in Silicon Valley, the digital divide was a shorthand gloss for the increasingly stark, intraregional socioeconomic disparity characterizing the region. If "Silicon Valley" was defined by the social, cultural, and economic practices of its high-tech sector, the "digital divide" referred to working-class people who lived and worked outside or at the margins of this amorphous "network." Moreover, the term was racially coded; people with whom I spoke in Silicon Valley used it to denote the occupational and educational circumstances of working-class people of color, including Latinos, Pacific Islanders, African Americans, and some Southeast Asians in low-income areas of Silicon Valley. Obliquely, then, the digital divide conveyed regional structural inequalities along racial, ethnic, and class lines as well as a lack of technological access.

During the 1990s a high-profile organization in Silicon Valley called Joint Venture: Silicon Valley Network, a self-described and industry-funded "civic incubator for Silicon Valley" comprised of business, community and education leaders concerned with the regional economic and social development and sustainability, became a prominent vehicle for public discourse and action around the digital divide, a topic that had already been raised by high-tech corporations, community advocates, local scholars, and journalists investigating the persistent disparity in occupational opportunities in Silicon Valley (see, for example, Angwin and Castaneda 1998). Joint Venture explicitly defined the "digital divide" in terms of three kinds of deficits: an educational attainment gap along racial and ethnic lines; a locally under-skilled workforce unprepared to perform local, desirable "New Economy" jobs; and a lack of technological access.

By the end of the 1990s Joint Venture had designed a campaign to bridge the digital divide. In the mid-1990s the organization had engaged in a "visioning project," Silicon Valley 2010, surveying two thousand Valley residents from business, government, education, and Silicon Valley's various communities. This process resulted in Joint Venture identifying seventeen "regional goals" (publicized in 1998) under four subheadings: Innovative Economy, Livable Environment, Inclusive Society, and Regional Stewardship. In 2000, just before the initial market slide that heralded the tech bust, Joint Venture announced a new initiative, SV-CAN (Silicon Valley Civic Action Network). Funded by a $900,000 two-year grant from the David and

Lucile Packard Foundation, SV-CAN was focused upon ensuring that the seventeen regional goals of 2010, many of which had to do with promoting an inclusive society, were met.[3]

SV-CAN continued the Joint Venture practice of holding large forums and focus groups throughout Silicon Valley, events my contact at Joint Venture described in baroque corporate style as "a cozy community forum of doers." In the spring of 2000 SV-CAN held a forum examining the "growing digital divide" in Silicon Valley. It was held at the symbolically significant Mexican Heritage Plaza in East San Jose, a historically Latino and low-income area of San Jose, and the discussion focused on disparities along ethnic lines in workforce participation, education, and access to technology. At the time Joint Venture was concerned with galvanizing Silicon Valley's high-tech corporate community to address issues of workforce preparedness, educational reform, and technological access. Specifically it intended to bridge the digital divide through the promotion of civic and corporate involvement in schools, after-school programs, and the creation of CTCs. It also started Web portals to coordinate a network of tech-savvy volunteers drawn from Silicon Valley's high-tech private sector, and to provide low-income, post–high school youth with opportunities to gain technological skills, a project implemented in conjunction with the North Valley Santa Clara County employment office.

Ultimately Joint Venture was unable to garner sufficient corporate support for its digital divide initiative. According to many I spoke with, this lack of success was the result of various factors. These included the tech bust; the fact that the well-connected former CEO of Joint Venture had turned over her position to Ruben Barrales, a man whose connections to the Bush administration exceeded his connections to high-tech corporate leadership in Silicon Valley;[4] the development by major tech corporations such as HP, IBM, Applied Materials, Intel, and Agilent of "in-house" community educational programs during the 1990s; and an apparent corporate ambivalence about the term "digital divide," which some considered too negative and class and racially divisive.

The failure of Joint Venture's particular initiative aside, speakers at public forums on the digital divide attended by local tech industry representatives, educators, community advocates, public officials, and representatives of the consulting firm, A. T. Kearney, which produced workforce reports for Joint Venture, argued that the region's digital divide was a major impediment to solving the problem of the regional high-tech "workforce gap," a labor gap within the high-tech industry that included unfilled positions and workers recruited from outside the Bay Area. In its 2002 Workforce Study, Joint Venture reported that the local high-tech sector's workforce gap was still costing the regional high-tech industry between two to three billion dollars per year even well into the downturn during 2001 (Joint Venture 2002).[5] The deleterious effect of this workforce gap on the highly competitive local high-tech industry was a common source of discussion during interviews I conducted in the field in 2000 as well as in 2001 and 2002. A representative of a powerful, regional high-tech trade association described corporate concern about local education and professional achievement gaps in the following way:

> We were in the middle of the big boom years, and with all of these companies growing so quickly, everyone was looking at their workforces–a lot of employees being brought from out of the area and out of the country. So companies started to say we've got to grow our workforce locally.

Corporate discourse about the workforce gap, along with an industry-fueled talk about regional inclusiveness to be fostered through corporate citizenship, resulted in the dissemination of statistics and qualitative data about social inequality in Silicon Valley. During the boom and into the subsequent downturn, Joint Venture was the prime conduit for such information, producing reports and annual indexes demonstrating that regionwide gaps in educational and professional attainment by race and class had, in fact, become a major barrier to creating a much-needed "homegrown" workforce.

Disparity along racial and ethnic lines was highlighted in these reports. For instance, the *2002 Workforce Study* revealed that only 53 percent of Hispanic students in Santa Clara County planned to attend a four-year college compared to 75 percent of Asian high school students and 69 percent of white students (JVSV Network 2002). Moreover, only 23 percent of Hispanic students in the county met UC/CSU entrance requirements in 2000 compared to 66 percent of Asian students and 47 percent of white students (Joint Venture 2000).

Joint Venture reports also stressed income disparity as a threat to Silicon Valley's social fabric. In 2000 Joint Venture's widely disseminated annual index revealed that while real per capita income increased by 32 percent in Santa Clara County during the 1990s (compared to 13% for the nation), the household income of the county's bottom 20 percent remained below 1992 earnings at the millennium. In fact, other sources reframed this disparity in starker terms; as already noted in chapter 1, the ratio of annual income of the top one hundred executives to the average production worker rose from 42:1 to 956:1 by 2000 (Benner 2002:213).[6]

At an event at Microsoft's Silicon Valley campus[7] hosted in the fall of 2000 by Joint Venture: Silicon Valley Network, the Teacher Quality Collaboratory, and a Joint Venture subgroup, 21st Century Education Initiative, various corporate speakers and educators explored in detail the politics of economic and educational inequality along racial lines in Silicon Valley. One education professor from Stanford University argued that a national emphasis on testing in public schools, a hallmark of "results-oriented" federal educational policy, denigrated the quality of education. An African American Microsoft executive introduced a discussion of test score gaps between white and African American students by recounting his childhood in the segregated South. After asking audience members to raise their hands if they had read W. E. B. Du Bois, the executive went on to compare Jim Crow Mississippi to contemporary Silicon Valley in terms of educational inequalities and the loss of opportunities suffered by low-income youth of color. The professor then gave a long PowerPoint talk, explicating the problem of the workforce gap and the link to failing public schools in California, Silicon Valley, and the nation—schools that fell into the camp of the "factory model" of schooling as opposed to an idealized "twenty-first-century" model. "We have to recruit in Southeast Asia because we aren't educating people," she explained. Rattling off statistics on California state funding for prisons as opposed to schools, she highlighted structural inequalities inherent in the public educational system, and argued that a national politics and economics of school reform had led to a punitive over-dependence upon test scores that ultimately raise drop-out rates. Ultimately she made a case for combating the achievement gap and reversing the drop-out rate by investing in teacher training and technology.

Collectively reports such as the annual *JVSV Index* and Joint Venture's community forums, and events such as the one at Microsoft, raised awareness of social inequality in Silicon Valley. The facts about local inequalities presented in such reports and forums, however, did not serve as a rationale for a strong, state-supported public educational system; instead, they supported an argument for a private-sector role in education and workforce preparation. For example, at the Microsoft talk, the Stanford professor ended her presentation by touting a charter school in San Jose for its pedagogical practices emphasizing "lifelong learning" and "technology all the time," and encouraging venture capitalists and high-tech entrepreneurs to join the project of "reinventing" local schools. Likewise, Joint Venture's dissemination of information about the achievement gap in low-income areas of the Valley, the percentage of Latinos in managerial positions in high-tech firms, and the fact of high-tech workforce recruitment in South and East Asia served to demonstrate the need for high-tech expertise and private-sector funds to compensate for an anachronistic state unable to provide for its citizens.

For example, Joint Venture's "2002 Workforce Report" drew upon statistics to create an argument for a private sector role in education and training. It revealed that eighth and eleventh graders of *all* socioeconomic backgrounds exhibited a lack of interest in technology and technological careers. At the well-attended regional public forum focused on this report that I attended in the fall of 2002, young people's lack of interest in technological innovation was the basis for a rallying cry for industry to take a more active role in education. The atmosphere at this meeting was somewhat forced; speeches by panelists about the need to excite "youth" for work in the local high-tech economy rang hollow, given that the local tech economy was, at the time, in a nose-dive. Nonetheless, like the discursive strategy of glossing social inequality in terms of a digital divide, facts and figures about skill deficits, achievement gaps, and a lack of interest in technology among youth served the purpose of linking the solution to these problems to the expertise and support of local high-tech corporations.

Reinventing Education and
Workforce Development in Silicon Valley

Such regional public discourse during the 1990s reflected the neoliberal ideas of private-sector solutions to social problems and private-sector reform of inadequate public services. In public discussion in which the local tech industry played a significant role, the region's public school system, in particular, was presented as ineffective, wasteful, and anachronistic, inherently unable to keep up with changing skill demands without outside intervention. Public discussion around this theme helped to distill a regional, corporate-supported agenda around public education and workforce development during the 1990s, when regionally based industry trade associations—such as the Silicon Valley Manufacturing Group (SVMG) and the American Electronics Association (AEA)—as well as public-private coalitions such as the Joint Venture Silicon Valley Network and Smart Valley (both founded in the wake of the early 1990s recession)—increasingly focused their attention upon local education and workforce development. In 1992, for example, Joint Venture identified education as its highest priority (Smart Valley 1998:63).

These organizations shared a notion of "reinventing" education through various means. For example, during the early and mid-1990s Smart Valley and Joint Venture—whose boards included the CEOs of major Silicon Valley companies—sought to transform local school systems in accordance with the local tech sector's organizational practices and use of technology. They also envisioned transforming teacher and student skills in accordance with the workforce needs of local industry. The Silicon Valley Manufacturing Group, a powerful regional trade association concerned with economic and policy issues,[8] regional groups like Workforce Silicon Valley (WSV), a publicly and privately funded organization founded with the help of SVMG, and individual corporate-community programs at major firms initiated the penetration of private-sector initiatives and ideas into public schools and educational nonprofit settings.[9]

"Organizational Effectiveness": "Results" and Technological Access

In 1993 high-tech business leaders, under the auspices of the newly founded Joint Venture and the offshoot trade association, Smart Valley, joined with local educators to begin work on Challenge 2000, a corporate-funded, regionwide initiative to "spark an educational renaissance" designed to enable "students to be successful and productive citizens in the 21st century." Challenge 2000 worked directly with schools to develop and refine K-12 standards and to link elementary and high school curricula, an effort that the deputy superintendent of East Side Union High School District, a San Jose district with a large, low-income Latino and Asian population, told me was highly successful in the area of science. Challenge 2000 also worked with schools to develop a new set of measurements of student performance as well as new school organizational policies, requirements, and technical guidance (Smart Valley 1998).

In particular, Joint Venture's 21st Century Education Initiative, a component of Challenge 2000 with a $24 million dollar budget,[10] thanks to the CEOs on Joint Venture's Board of Directors (including Lew Platt, the CEO of Hewlett-Packard at the time), was specifically concerned with reinventing how child performance was measured. The notion of creating effective ways to gather fine-tuned data—"results," in business-speak—was prioritized by Joint Venture's Board of Directors. Joint Venture wanted schools to measure a "vertical slice" of a given school's population, such that the progress or lack thereof of children in the bottom 25 percent would be scrutinized as opposed to the overall student performance in a school. Hence, in focusing on generating better documentation of the achievement gap in order to address it in a substantive way, the Board imported a private-sector practice of generating documentable "results" in the context of the region's public schools.[11]

At the same time that these initiatives were being established, members of Smart Valley were concerned with the technological transformation of various public and commercial sectors in Silicon Valley. Originally a "flagship initiative" of Joint Venture, its founding mission was to "create a region that has both the technological infrastructure and the collective ability to use it for maximum benefit." As a former Smart Valley employee explained it: "Some prominent local CEOs from large companies such as Applied Materials came together and said, 'We're Silicon Valley. We should be modeling how to use and bring technology into the community.'" In keeping with this goal, Smart Valley designed five initiatives to provide Internet access to local government, health-care, community, and educational organizations. In the realm of education Smart Valley, through its Smart Schools Initiative, worked to integrate technology into classrooms and school administrative practice as well as to create online school communities. This democratically oriented regional project fostered new public-private linkages; a key outcome of the Smart Schools Initiative was the creation of local private-sector school partnerships (English-Lueck 2002; Smart Valley 1998; private communication).

Smart Valley's plan to integrate technology into local schools was hastened when, in 1995, President Bill Clinton announced that 30 percent of California's schools would be "wired" within a year. According to a former Smart Valley employee, the notion of a kind of "digital barn-raising" based upon a "grassroots" effort in which volunteers would "wire" schools was enormously appealing to some local high-tech CEOS as well as to Clinton himself, who, according to the former Smart Valley employee, was at the time in communication with local business leaders such as John Gage of Sun Microsystems. To meet this goal, Smart Valley organized a series of "Net Days," which resulted in the wiring of 10,500 classrooms in 425 schools within eighteen months between 1996 and 1998. Funded largely by Apple, Cisco Systems, Sun Microsystems, and Intel (English-Lueck 2002), three Net Days resulted in 85 percent of local schools acquiring high-speed Internet access during this time (Smart Valley 1998).

Teacher Practice

The collaborative movement to "reinvent" local schools also sought to redress a perceived lack of knowledge of high-tech industry and its skill requirements on the part of teachers. According to a former Joint Venture employee affiliated with the 21st Century project, Joint Venture's 21st Century Education Initiative sought to transform teacher practice by "[funding] a bunch of teachers to learn organizational effectiveness from [local] cor-, porations." Teachers learned "team skills" and received curriculum training focused upon "best practices" and pedagogies aligned with the daily realities of the high-tech corporate workplace. Technological training was also a major component of Joint Venture's partnership with local schools.

Joint Venture's focus upon teacher skills dovetailed with efforts of other local industry-affiliated groups concerned with the quality of regional education in relation to workforce preparedness for local industry. For example, a well-established nonprofit called Industry Initiatives in Science and Math Education (IISME), founded by eminent local executives and scientific educators in 1984 after the publication of the federal report, *A Nation at Risk*, runs a summer internship program for K-12 teachers within local high-tech companies. As an Applied Materials supervisor of an IISME internee told me, "It's good for them [the teachers] to see the real world, how industry works" in a work environment concerned with "hands-on technology making."

Although the tech bust had weakened corporate support for the program—IISME's teacher intern program shrunk from 150 placements to 80 in the 2002–2003 academic year—the program was nonetheless championed by the influential regional trade association, Silicon Valley Manufacturing Group (SVMG). [12] Primarily focused on issues other than education, such as energy policy and its effect upon local industry since its founding in 1977, SVMG had reassessed its goals in the early and mid-1990s, identifying education as a chief priority in light of the high-tech industry's workforce gap and the educational problems facing the region, state, and nation.

Soliciting input from local school superintendents, SVMG decided to assist in the recruitment, retention, and training of teachers. As the director put it, "Private companies have trouble recruiting and retaining employees, so you know, maybe we've got some skill sets that can be helpful on this issue." SVMG was thus involved, via the training of local teachers, in the transformation of local education to reflect high-tech industry needs and in strengthening private-sector linkages to the public school system. For example, one initiative involved institutionalizing and legitimizing the incorporation of high-tech corporate know-how into the educational system by creating education transfer plans for teachers participating in IISME's program so that they would receive National Board Certification after apprenticing at local corporations.

In addition, Workforce Silicon Valley (WSV),[13] the program that SVMG helped found,[14] was instrumental in linking local schools and corporations in order to cultivate workforce skills suitable for high-tech industry in high

school and junior college students. One strategy in play was to familiarize teachers with the information technology (IT) industry by giving them
opportunities to visit and work for a limited period of time in "high-perfor-
mance" firms in Silicon Valley.

Evidence of such a bond could be seen within the Biotechnology Academy. Although the Academy's coordinator, Chris, did not participate in
IISME's program, she actively maintained her relationships with various
corporate representatives at local biotechnology firms. She visited corporate campuses, conveyed to students how particular corporations focused on
innovation, and she became familiar with the kinds of skills and expectations that corporations had for incoming technician-level employees. And
although Workforce Silicon Valley had little direct input at the Academy,
something Chris complained about, the science teacher within the Academy who taught a course that trained students in entry-level lab skills and
concepts for the biotechnology industry had aligned his curriculum with the
needs of the industry.

Addressing Youth Skills

The public-private focus on teacher skills in Silicon Valley during the
1990s cannot, of course, be separated from an emergent local focus on youth
skills during the same period. According to virtually everyone with whom I
spoke about educational issues in Silicon Valley, curriculum and pedagogy
designed for youth attending Silicon Valley's public schools and supplemental after-school programs—often targeting areas with larger percentages of
low-income Latino, African American, and Asian youth—constituted a central aim of local educational reform efforts during the 1990s.

In addition to efforts to expand technological access for low-income
youth, programs in public schools and nonprofits were often specifically
designed to address the structural issue of low-income young people lacking access to the "culture" of high tech, meaning access to its social networks, knowledge of what high-tech firms and their various kinds of workers do, and awareness of the social environment of high-tech workplaces
(social capital). Moreover, such programs sought to address a perceived
lack of awareness of and enthusiasm or passion for high-tech innovation
and entrepreneurship. For example, School-to-Career programs like the
Biotech Academy at Morton emphasized interdisciplinary project-based
learning assignments that required students to gain knowledge of the
biotech industry, think about biotechnological themes and debates while

developing teamwork skills, learn to solve problems, and develop relationships with industry mentors. As teachers and corporate supporters of Biotech told me, the process of presenting ideas in group projects, attending events with corporate mentors, holding industry internships, and learning about the world-transformative power of technology was designed to foster not just the social skills appropriate to a high-tech corporate workplace, but an abiding enthusiasm for the process of innovation and high-tech industry entrepreneurial skills.

The objectives of Morton's Biotechnology Academy, which WSV counted as part of its network of School-to-Career programs, loosely adhered to the curricula and pedagogy of WSV's programs for public high-school students. WSV's system of "Learning Collaboratives" involved WSV staff, educators, and industry representatives, and emphasized "project-based learning," oriented to the needs of Silicon Valley, that focused on real-world problems over set periods of time. The program entailed participation in work-based learning experiences in local industry in order to flexibly prepare the students for high-skill positions in local industry at the entry level (post–high school) or post-college or graduate professional level.

The influence of such high-tech oriented School-to-Career programs in Silicon Valley is relatively wide. WSV's Learning Collaboratives link industry to schools in School-to-Career programs in fifty-seven public high schools primarily located in the southern half of Santa Clara County, the less affluent region where Morton is located, and where, according to the WSV program director, school parent-teacher associations are less likely to balk at programs designed for students who may or may not attend four-year colleges.

Moreover, a number of in-house corporate educational programs—Intel's "Digital Clubhouses," for example—as well as a number of independent, private, foundation, and publicly funded nonprofit programs in Silicon Valley emerged during the 1990s that also reflected this goal of promoting techno-entrepreneurial skills and generating enthusiasm and motivation for technological innovation and pursuing a career within the local high-tech workforce. While in the field, I attended the launching of an SBC Telecommunications-funded program to train East San Jose's Latino youth to transform graffiti-writing skills into computer skills and a graphic design business, and visited BUILD, a two-year program sponsoring East Palo Alto youth to participate in youth-run business "incubators" supported by local model venture capitalists who served as role models and mentors. I also visited a new teen-run entrepreneurial program at Plugged-In that focused on creating a graphic design business to cater to local companies.

During the 1990s, then, the private sector gained considerable influence in setting the curricular goals, designing pedagogical practices, training teachers, and assessing student and teacher performance. Public connections to the local tech private sector developed as corporate representatives fanned out to public school campuses, or as youth attended corporate programs at "digital clubhouses" or in-house education departments. Taken together, such programs and initiatives facilitated the increased involvement of the local private sector within the public educational system and civic life.

Such private-sector influence was evident within Morton's School-to-Career, state-funded Biotechnology Academy when I conducted research there. Through its coordinator's relationship to industry representatives, school-industry events, field trips to particular corporations, oversight of the Academy by its steering committee, mentor relationships with students, donations of technological products, and, of course, through funding, the private sector played a significant role within the Academy, one that, in neo-liberal fashion, rendered its teachers beholden to private-sector educational priorities and administrative techniques, and its students subject to the goal of cultivating marketable skills for tech industry work above other skill objectives, such as the acquisition of critical analytical skills for participation in a democratic society. As we have seen, tech-sector educational priorities clashed with other educational and disciplinary priorities at Morton, such as school performance measures that threatened Morton with the withdrawal of funds, and surveillance policies related to gang prevention that clashed with the Academy's purported emphasis on creative problem solving and an inquiry-oriented learning environment. Nonetheless, private-sector messages about marketable skills and a curricula that encouraged technology were both central in students' formal educational experiences and career-oriented exposure, providing them with a sense of a corporate world beyond their neighborhood, a knowledge of which skills were desirable in that world, and, most of all, a model of personal success that might potentially influence their aspirations.

In sum, corporate involvement and investment in programs like Morton's Biotechnology Academy profoundly shaped public schools and non-profit programs just as it influenced public understanding of the problem and solutions to the local digital divide. It engendered a new dynamic of accountability for schools, and prioritized new skill objectives, values, and models of success for youth. But corporate involvement in educational programs, events, and forums had another substantive political effect, namely, the representation of corporate solutions to problems of social and educational inequality as superior to public programs. Forums like the Micro-soft event highlighted inequality and programs like the Biotech Academy at Morton or the SBC Telecommunications techno-entrepreneurial after-school program served youth, but they also appropriated for the private sector the right to influence and manage the public good of education and training. Collectively we can read these effects as expressions of a neolib-eral orientation toward education and, more broadly, toward the gover-nance of public institutions and individuals. The question remains, how-ever, why did this occur in the 1990s?

Global Motivations for Social and Educational Reform

Industry provided two main explanations for its push to reinvent schools and transform young people's skills during the 1990s: a bottom-line concern about the regional workforce gap and a desire to foster social and economic inclusion in Silicon Valley. Although I am not suggesting that these explana-tions were entirely false, or that particular schools and communities did not benefit from specific programs funded or supported by the private sector, the broader political-economic context surrounding the movement to reinvent education and workforce development in Silicon Valley during the 1990s reveals more complex motivations. The explanation based on a gap in the workforce, for example, evades the issue of how state regulation of Internet-related commerce in the United States created new market conditions for Silicon Valley companies that focused on the digital divide and education more worthwhile for corporations.

The Effect of the E-rate Law

The Joint Venture and Smart Valley emphasis upon networking the schools can be understood in relation to this political-economic shift. The Net Day initiative seeding the Internet into schools was perfectly timed to coincide with the federal government's implementation of nationwide uni-versal access funding under the Federal Communications Commission's E-rate Telecommunication Act of 1996. Spearheaded by Al Gore, "E-rate," as it was called by the high-tech and nonprofit employees with whom I spoke, made "universal access" funds—derived from phone bill taxes—available to a broader range of companies. This meant an allotment of $2.2 billion of fed-eral money per year to the technological industry to provide telecommuni-cations and networking equipment to schools. The E-rate Act also rendered schools with poorer student populations—those in which 50 percent or more of students were eligible for reduced-price lunches—eligible for a 90 percent discount on telecommunications and networking equipment.[15]

The high-profile act of good corporate citizens helping to bring schools into the twenty-first century served the interests of many high-tech firms, especially those benefiting from the E-rate legislation. The Internet infrastructure company, 3-Com, where I attended a Job Shadow Day, is one example. At 3-Com I interviewed Jim Fast, an older, white, community-relations consultant who had worked at the company since 1988 and, before that, at HP for twelve years. Jim explained that, as of 2001, approximately one-third of 3-Com's revenue had come from products sold to schools, a number indicative of both the centrality of the school market to 3-Com's profit as well as the toll of the recession on other areas of the corporation's business. 3-Com began selling equipment to schools around the time of the E-rate legislation and, in 1998, began to donate network curriculum designed for students, teachers, and nonprofits using 3-Com's products. Corporate links to the political establishment in Washington, D.C., facilitated the school market. Jim commented on the political alliances that 3-Com has formed in this process:

> The White House annual Conference of Mayors offers 3-Com a spot—they give out grants–100K Urban Challenge grants. Mayors go to the White House—Clinton loved this event. It's like fifty or sixty mayors and it's invitation only and it benefits tech companies greatly—3-Com networks and then builds relationships and gets their products into schools and after-school programs.

As Jim pointed out, network curriculum constantly shifts, and schools must constantly buy new products so as not to become obsolete:

> If schools don't make use of technology they won't buy more and then the market stops, so companies like Intel and 3-Com have a vested interest in the technology being utilized and well understood. You can cloak that in terms of the digital divide or community concern, but it's really that.

My foreknowledge of this fact made me acutely aware of the content of the Job Shadow day I attended in early 2002 at the 3-Com campus.[16] Before an audience of mostly Vietnamese and some Latino students and a few teachers and student aides Jim gave a PowerPoint discussion of 3-Com's mission: "to connect consumers and commercial organizations to information and services in more innovative, simple, and reliable ways than any other networking company."

"Our strategy," Jim informed everyone, "is to make it simple. We make remarkable things happen effortlessly. We're about a $1.5 billion company, and one-third of that is product revenue we sell to schools." He then presented a slide show and description of 3-Com products, at one point asking students who had a computer at home to raise their hands (almost all hands went up). This query segued neatly into a home networking solutions pitch, which the students received somewhat blankly.

In our interview, Jim was quite frank about the extent to which local high-tech corporate investment in schools and programs for youth was altruistic. In his words: "Our motives, like Cisco's, are less pure." As an example, he told me of a recent $500 million grant offered to the Santa Clara County Office of Education (SCCOE) by Intel and HP to educate teachers about technology. Because SCCOE used both Macs and PCs, however, it turned the grant down, as Intel and HP would only be teaching PC material. "Intel," he opined, "was trying to grow their market by offering only PC material." Although some corporate representatives readily discussed the importance of corporate citizenship to corporations maintaining their image, and educational philanthropy in particular to the long-term project of producing a "homegrown workforce," Jim Fast spoke of Applied Materials, which donates technology to schools in San Jose and Austin, where its workforce lives, despite having no product to sell to schools. Most people I spoke to about the corporate role in bridging the digital divide agreed with former Smart Valley employee, Jane Bell: "There's no altruism, and that includes HP."

Jane started noticing that, during the mid-1990s, high-tech corporations were focusing their philanthropic efforts on mathematics and science and on the K-12 curriculum. She noted, too, that most corporations' philanthropy centered on the latter, providing hardware and software to schools, "because they get one and a half times the cost of manufacturing in tax write-offs."[17] An active observer of Silicon Valley's nonprofit sector, Jane also pointed out that, since the mid-1990s, grants to local nonprofits from local high-tech corporations had become less diversified. The focus switched to "e-inclusion." "This is now what HP is all about in terms of its philanthropy," Jane commented. "HP's definition of the digital divide is e-inclusion, and their focus now is on rural areas and low-income areas."

A founding director of IISME noted a similar shift in the organization of large Silicon Valley companies: "In the mid-1980s there was no K-12 education manager at any large company, and now, within large companies, it's very common; HP, Intel, [and] IBM have someone called an education manager or an outreach director." Hence, the intensification during the 1990s of educational and workforce development initiatives and civic attention to the digital divide in Silicon Valley can be linked to the subsidization of the tech industry by the federal government, which in turn can be understood as a response that reflects the new economic conditions of a globalized technological industry.[18] This does not invalidate the argument made by those in Silicon Valley that the regional information economy requires a tech-savvy, homegrown workforce; rather, it demonstrates that public discussion of this problem legitimated the creation of the school market.

The Marketing of Regional "Culture"

The discourse surrounding the digital divide and the need to reinvent education and training can also be understood as the product of political and economic imperatives other than the much-discussed workforce gap. Understanding this additional motivation involves exploring the broader civic discourse that flourished in Silicon Valley during the boom of the late 1990s and continued into the bust.

While Joint Venture was campaigning to bridge the region's digital divide, it was also focusing on a number of other issues ranging from the region's housing crisis to problems of transportation and regional environmental degradation. The organization's Vision Leadership Team—which included the Santa Clara County supervisor and the chairman and publisher of the *San Jose Mercury News* as co-chairs, as well as leaders from local high-tech corporations and the Packard Foundation, presidents of local universities, leading bureaucrats and judges from Santa Clara and San Mateo counties, and the presidents of prominent nonprofit groups concerned with housing and the environment—sought opinions from experts and the community to put together "Silicon Valley 2010: A Regional Framework for Growing Together." Its collective "2010 Vision," stated the following: "We will use our innovative, entrepreneurial spirit to create a strong foundation for regional stewardship, so future generations can enjoy Silicon Valley's broad prosperity, healthy and attractive environment, and inclusive communities."

Just as Palo Alto parents invoked a local "culture" of competition and achievement to describe the conditions at Sanders High School, local civic discourse about a range of issues, from the need to promote a more active artistic and cultural environment in Silicon Valley to the environment, typically invoked a regional, techno-entrepreneurial "spirit" or "culture."[19] Despite the region's economic expansion during the boom, the sustainability of regional growth was, in the view of those affiliated with industry, in peril because of challenges to the quality of life. A *Mercury News* article, taking stock of Silicon Valley's successes and failures during the 1990s, warned that,

> despite a decade of competition from other technology regions in the country, [during which] Silicon Valley's industries and institutions steadily increased their share of technological advances . . . measured by the number of patents awarded . . . housing has become more expensive, traffic congestion remains intractable, and some disturbing trends are developing in education (Sylvester 2002:4E).

The unmentioned threat in this article was the fear of Silicon Valley losing out to another high-tech region, one with better schools and a better quality of life.

The expansion of community relations and education departments in Silicon Valley during the 1990s can also be seen in relation to corporate anxiety about quality-of-life issues. Former Smart Valley employee Jane Bell, quoted above, said that, in addition to the need to cultivate a workforce and the potential profit to be garnered by expanding into the realm of educational support, companies "want the community to be more attractive to workers; to the extent that they focus on homelessness, it's to get the homeless off the streets and make the community more attractive."

Collectively such corporate discourse about a regional spirit of innovation and civic campaigns for affordable housing or against a digital divide represent a defense of "territorial interests," a classic pattern of interregional competition under conditions of global capitalism as regions struggle to maintain growth and attract capital within a global network of regions (Smith 1999:153).

Regional civic discourse and the proliferation of initiatives focused on a local digital divide can thus be understood in terms of a local corporate strategy to protect and sustain growth in the face of intensifying global competition. In Silicon Valley in the 1990s the creation of new markets with federal assistance, via educational products and corporate involvement in public educational reform, and the defense of elite interests via civic engagements focused on improving regional quality of life for a professional, middle-class workforce comprised elements of this strategy.

What Is Missing in Our Youth?
"Soft Skills" and the Desire for Tech Innovation

With the dimensions of and motivations behind a regional effort to transform education and training for the youth of Silicon Valley, particularly low-income youth in mind, we can now consider in more depth the content of youth programming and the perceived problems of young people's preparedness for the workforce. In local news articles about the region's digital divide, and in conversations with high-tech and community leaders, school and public officials, and nonprofit program directors involved in workforce development for teachers and youth, I noticed a particular discourse around the need for youth, particularly those from low-income, immigrant families, to cultivate a certain set of skills. Although a Latino program director for the City of San Jose's Youth Services Division told me, "You ain't done nothin' if the kids don't have computers [at school]," technological access itself was, in fact, just one aspect of young people's workforce preparedness that seemed to concern people. "What is the most critical skill to have?" I asked David Smith, a white Applied Materials mentor for IISME's teacher-training program. "The network relationship," he answered. "Industries are horizontally organized. Information sharing is critical within the company." Rose Pritchard, a veteran in the field of industry-related educational reform and the director of IISME, put it this way, when I asked her whether corporate needs had shifted over the course of a few decades: "The focus twenty years ago was on technical skills more purely, and now the public discourse is more focused on the 'soft skills'—good communication, teamwork, flexibility, and lifelong learning."

Most high-tech industry people I interviewed ticked off this same list of soft skills. In relation to flexibility, teamwork, and lifelong learning, public discourse about what young people needed to succeed in the regional high-tech economy, and what schools and youth service programs should encourage, focused on another, more interior and affective quality: enthusiasm and passion for the vocation of techno-entrepreneurship and innovation.

As I learned conducting interviews and attending public forums about youth skills and educational priorities, the perception that this affective deficit existed among young people was widespread among high-tech industry representatives, and it ranked high among concerns related to the building of a competitive, high-tech workforce during the boom and even into the subsequent bust. In fact, this deficit discourse was particularly focused on low-income Latino youth, and it was framed as a critique of local schools and programs for youth unconnected to high-tech industry. As SVMG's Tim Burr put it, by the mid-1990s, "there was a sense that schools were not preparing students well, and . . . that students didn't understand high-tech in a way that they would become interested in it as a career option. Not a sense on the part of kids about what people in high tech actually do."

Eric Benhamou, former member of President Clinton's task force on technology, former CEO of 3-Com, and chairman of the board of 3-Com when I conducted my research, emphasized this issue of desire and enthusiasm in Joint Venture's 2002 Workforce Report:

> It has been my experience that the desire to get connected should not be taken for granted. Even if access exists and is affordable, even if skills exist and can be taught readily, even if relevant content is available, an individual can still refuse to get connected if the desire has not been stimulated or if other psychological or philosophical inhibitions are in the way.

This lack of desire for technology or for work related to technological innovation on the part of young people in fact constituted the subject of a Workforce Silicon Valley survey and was also a major theme in Joint Venture's Workforce Report. WSV's survey, conducted at their annual Student Leadership Conference, which I attended in 2002, revealed that local young people generally think about and engage in technology in more immediate ways—by taking apart computers or playing video games.

This was a problem that Workforce Silicon Valley's Sue Feld had thought about at length. As a former assistant to the public policy director responsible for global workforce development projects at Semiconductor Equipment and Materials International (SEMI), an industry association representing companies that make the equipment used by companies that manufacture computers, Sue had interviewed older SEMI member executives in order to get their input before developing SEMI's outreach programs to teachers and students as part of a new workforce development program. Many of the engineers and executives with whom she spoke recalled their own training during the Cold War era, and their sense of a larger purpose at that time. As Sue expressed it:

> I don't know whether the space race inspired people to use technology as a tool to solve wider spanning problems. I do think it got people's attention as a unifying cultural event that spoke to people of many different concerns, such as technical, political, and artistic. Because the space race was easy to visualize for everyone, and because it was primarily a positive

thing (except for some concerns about Russia's military capabilities), it got people's attention, and they went forward to use it in their various pursuits. Maybe because the space race didn't solve a horrible problem, but created a new challenge, it seemed positive. I believe that all Americans were united in wanting to explore space. This is in comparison to today, when genetic breakthroughs are needed to cure diseases (many people have conflicting emotions about genetic work) or biotech is needed to make computers even smarter (some people are scared of computers as it is).

What was lacking, Sue felt, was a convincing "meta-narrative" to attach young people in a deeper way to technological innovation and entrepreneurship.

A Shift in Ideas about Skills

This regional discourse concerning the deficits of local youth—particularly low-income, immigrant youth— reflects certain notions of skill grounded in contemporary ideas about education and training in the United States. Dr. H., Morton High School's principal, described shifts he has observed in his thirty-year history at the school:

> [Morton] used to have auto-shop, metal shop, wood shop, electronics shop—there was a shift to teaching about the sophisticated workplace. . . . Now for auto-shop you need to read a scope, not just use a wrench. Auto mechanics need to know how to use complicated technologies . . . so there's more theoretical higher learning skills that a person needs now.

In this educational paradigm, technology is simply a tool and not an end in itself. Our conversation turned to Biotech's School-to-Career program and school-to-career programs in general. Dr. H. observed that "School-to-Careers is about preparing [students] with . . . critical thinking skills. [This has been a] huge shift over the last ten, fifteen, twenty years." Dr. H. commented on the role of "smaller learning communities" in facilitating the acquisition of these deeper social and intellectual skills: "Kids learn better in smaller groups. Biotech is a good example. A common goal, a team of teachers, accountability, time to network; it makes it more intimate."

Dr. H's focus on the intimacy of the learning environment subtly reveals something more: an emphasis upon the *attitude* students have toward learning the required social and intellectual or cognitive skills. While interviewing the program manager at Workforce Silicon Valley, she handed me a booklet, *New Work Habits for the Next Millennium* (1999) by Price Pritchett of the consulting firm Pritchett and Associates. On page 2 of this booklet, under the heading "Think Differently, See Differently," the author describes the contemporary world of work: "The biggest career challenges are *perceptual . . . not technical.* Not even skills-based."

In another section, "Migrate to the Fourth Level of Change," Pritchett outlines a hierarchy of attitudes toward change. Whereas at the first, second, and third levels of change people are condemned to cope, adjust, or exploit change to their own advantage, at the fourth level people achieve "a possibilities mentality":

> When you're operating at level four, you're fired up by your work. You move with initiative, imagination, and a true sense of urgency . . . The mind-set at the fourth level of change is one of purpose, adventure, optimism, and faith. Here we invest ourselves resourcefully in exploring, experimenting, and learning. We operate with a spirit of curiosity . . . a sense of mobility and pursuit . . . a hope for breakthroughs. We deliberately set forth to do things differently—to innovate—because we recognize [that] change is our most promising solution. . . . At level four we don't fight the future. We partner with the world of tomorrow and co-create change. Level four is the success zone. Migrate there, and you can meet the twenty-first century on its own terms.

As the above quotes make clear, in the contemporary period content is not the most important priority in the education and training of youth for the workforce; most important is the generation of deeper intellectual and social capacities that include the emotive dimension of desire or enthusiasm.

This emphasis on students' psychological disposition toward learning and the need to cultivate deeper cognitive and social skills that may be applied flexibly to different areas was pervasive within the region's workforce-oriented programs for youth. The Biotechnology Academy was no exception; via mentorship from high-tech professionals, participation in inspirational and sometimes spectacular events such as the ropes course, project-based learning curricula, visits to high-tech corporations, and immersion in the content of specific industries, it sought to address Morton students' presumed lack of engagement with technological innovation and careers and to cultivate soft skills. Activities and presentations that drew on the trope of the techno-pioneer, transforming "life as we know it," served, like the notion of "curing disease," as an element in program pedagogy designed to foster desire. Games to put students at ease, social events, and student film projects featuring clips of students engaged in Academy coursework set to pop music also sought to incite in students excitement about the topic of biotechnology and the possibility of gaining new skills and being exposed to a new world of innovation.

Simultaneously emotive engagement with the topic of biotechnology and with the very act of gaining skills was also encouraged within the Academy through students' exposure to models of economic and social success, symbolized by the grand corporate campuses and laboratories they visited on occasional fieldtrips, and personified by mentors whose clothes and cars and way of speaking denoted a more moneyed existence.

In fact, most of the programs that focused on the preparation of local—mostly less advantaged—youth for careers in high-tech industry centered on both the possibility of becoming wealthy through a high-tech career and the excitement of technological innovation. For example, at WSV's annual Student Leadership Conference, people with successful careers in industry as high-tech managers or engineers narrated to an audience of lower and middle income public high school students the story of their own ascendance from entry-level to managerial positions, emphasizing the content of their work and tales of sudden success while imploring the youth present to consider a high-tech career. In the conference hall, one floor above a sadly empty Santa Clara Convention Center job fair for engineers sparsely attended by company recruiters—only thirty-five people were present whereas the previous year, before the region had settled into a decided downturn, there had been three hundred attendees—students listened to a variety of panelists on "corporate values" and took part in focus groups designed to garner data on the lack of desire for high-tech careers among the region's youth.[20] Beth Johnson, a program director for WSV, reminded the young listeners: "You are a great asset to the Valley! We're trying to motivate you to build careers in the area this Valley is famous for. . . . Today is the tenth anniversary of the first Web page . . . people will be celebrating in the Valley today!"

Following one corporate testimony describing a white middle-class woman's rise through the ranks at HP and other local companies to become a general manager, a sharply dressed Vietnamese IT manager of a local bank bluntly tried to appeal to students' desire for material wealth by subtly representing high-tech careers as a dependable source of wealth: "Don't you want to have a nice house? Don't you want to be able to show your friends your new home?"

Other presentations I observed were also characterized by the inter-mingling of narratives about being on the frontier of new knowledge and technology—namely, being part of the future—and allusions to becoming rich. At a 3-Com Job Shadow Day, hosted by Workforce Silicon Valley and Junior Achievement, community relations manager Jim Fast, in addressing a roomful of Vietnamese, Latino, and Filipino eighth graders, described working at 3-Com as "being on the frontlines of a changing world," impressing upon them that the frontline was Silicon Valley. "This Valley is famous for companies with new ideas . . . it's almost like people coming to visit the zoo, but they're coming to see and learn how we do things in Silicon Valley." "You've heard of dot-coms?" he continued. "Well, we [at 3-Com] are the center of the networking industry." After a detour about the benefits of lifelong learning so important to industry, he went on to emphasize the economic perks of a high-tech career, telling his audience: "If you have good ideas, you can have a long productive career, and maybe make some money in the process. And who knows? A lot of people in this Valley like to retire early!"

"Soft Skills" and the Desire for Technological Innovation in Historical Context

Curricula and pedagogy that focuses on "soft skills" and desire has its roots in a broader political and economic context that emerged in force in the United States beginning in the 1980s and led to the articulation of an ideology focused on the training and education of the American "knowledge worker" for the globalized and competitive "knowledge economy."

Programs like Morton High School's School-to-Career Biotechnology Academy reflected skill imperatives in vogue during the Clinton administration, a period during which rhetoric and policy concerned with restructuring the U.S. society and economy in accordance with the needs of the globalized information economy, or "knowledge economy," was rampant. This ideology of skill is epitomized in the work of sociologist Manuel Castells, who outlined the requirements of work within an information society where "self-programmable labor" is infused with "the spirit of informationalism" and the former secretary of labor Robert Reich's definition of "symbolic analysts" who must flexibly identify problems, solve them, and broker relationships (cited in Robins and Webster 1999:76–78).

The federal government, together with private industry, was instrumental in disseminating these ideas. In 1983 the National Commission on Excellence in Education (under President Ronald Reagan) produced a report titled *A Nation at Risk*, which stated: "If only to keep and improve on the slim competitive edge we still retain in world markets, we must rededicate ourselves to the reform of the educational system for the benefit of all" (Spring 1986:23).

This report, which was mentioned in my conversations with nonprofit managers in the Valley a number of times, echoed other documents produced at the time in that it linked the country's economic health to the state of its school system (quoted in Spring 1986:23; see, too, Task Force on Education for Economic Growth 1983). In 1986 a Carnegie Forum report expanded upon this theme, suggesting that American public school bureaucracies were modeled on the factory era—a point emphasized by the Stanford professor at the Microsoft conference discussed earlier—and needed to be redesigned to reflect a knowledge economy instead of a mass production economy (ibid., 24–25).

Subsequently, under the Presidency of George Herbert Walker Bush, a report titled *The Secretary's Commission on Achieving Necessary Skills* was issued, in which it was argued that industry needed to take an active role in shaping the skills of the twenty-first-century worker. Listed in this document, produced jointly by the Labor and Education Departments of the first Bush administration, were provisions ultimately enacted by President Clinton under School-to-Career legislation in 1994. It also defined SCANS skills and practical competencies favored by industry. In contrast to older vocational models, the School to-Career program was designed to focus, as a program director for a Bay Area nonprofit School-to-Career advocacy group told me, on "fomenting interest in students" and flexibly gearing students toward any level within a given career that they might wish to attain.

Such reports were predicated on the notion of a failed educational system (Bartlett et al. 2002), a point made to me by the former IISME director. This underlying assumption acquired commonsensical status during the 1980s in the United States, along with the idea that the primary purpose of schooling was to serve economic interests rather than to increase social mobility or produce an informed citizenry, as John Dewey had contended in the early twentieth century (Aronowitz and Giroux 1993; Bartlett et al. 2002:6).[21]

This neoliberal orientation toward public education gained widespread acceptance among policy elites and the general public in the 1980s, in part because of the desire among the middle class, anxious about the economic instability at the time, to remain competitive in the workplace by means of up-to-date training. Instead of demanding the maintenance of state services and adopting a critical stance toward neoliberal reform, a threatened middle class responded to a manufactured crisis in public education that was well publicized by corporate elites, including Silicon Valley CEOs of IBM and Xerox (Bartlett et al. 2002:9).

In the 1990s, Silicon Valley business leaders were, of course, effective messengers of an ideology of skill focused on the need to redress school failure and build youth skills through an emphasis on global competitiveness, the needs of knowledge-based workplaces, and the value of techno-entrepreneurial capital, expertise, and priorities, often glossed as "regional culture." It resonated with their direct experience leading organizations that, during the 1990s, were effectively restructured, as global political-economic shifts intensified flows of capital and labor into and out of Silicon Valley, leading to more flexible work and employment patterns in the region (Benner 2002).[22] Moreover, this ideology of skill related to more immediate, local corporate interests and concerns engendered by global competition: the federally subsidized emergence of an education market for the tech industry during the 1990s and dynamics of interregional competition that gave rise to regional corporate involvement in a host of civic concerns.

In addition, we can also understand local private-sector investments in education and training in relation to a global pattern of disinvestments in social reproduction by capital and municipal and state government (Katz 2002:251). As geographer Cindi Katz has observed, not only has capital sought to cut costs by abandoning commitments to communities in the global North and seeking out cheap labor in the global South, but municipal, state, and provincial governments in the global North have simultaneously extended tax breaks to corporations in an attempt to combat capital's enhanced mobility, stave off capital flight, and attract new investments. This tactic of the state in response to an increasingly globalized capitalism has in turn reduced the tax base and placed the tax burden on individuals (Katz 2002:251). The passing of Proposition 13, a measure that vastly limited property tax revenue for public education and essentially gutted California's public educational system, such that stark inequalities emerged between, for example, the Morton and Sanders school districts, can be read as a backlash to this burden (ibid.).[23] Ultimately the profound effects of disinvestment in public education, in combination with pervasive neoliberal rhetoric framing the problem of public education in California as a problem with the system itself (and not, primarily, a problem related to its de-funding) have created an ideal climate for the advancement of private-sector interests; techno-entrepreneurial organizations count schools among their customers and represent themselves as filling a need engendered by a flawed educational system.

Regional "Culture" and the Promise of Youth "At Risk"

Collectively, then, the expansion of an education market, new kinds of work and new ideologies of skill, intensifying global competition, and a pattern of job loss, corporate tax breaks, and disinvestment in social reproduction in the United States have deepened educational inequalities and facilitated the increasing dominance of private-sector notions of skill and priorities within formal educational contexts in Silicon Valley. As we have seen, this regional politics of education and training has depended upon an ideology of regional "culture." Indeed, one can argue that, in Silicon Valley, discourses and initiatives focused on disseminating a regional "culture" to local youth have not only been instrumental in framing an argument for privatization but instead have comprised a governmental technique or, as I have expressed it, a "techno-entrepreneurial civilizing process." This "civilizing process" renders commonsensical—through local idiom—a set of values, priorities, and ways of being associated with neoliberalism. It treats youth perceived to be at risk as potentially delinquent and uncompetitive and yet simultaneously filled with potential for self-transformation. In this process, the problem of social and educational inequality is not attributed to capital's ongoing need for low-skilled labor within the regional information economy or to the increasingly contingent and insecure nature of employment in the region as employers restructure the conditions of employment to remain globally competitive (Benner 2002). Rather, the solutions to regional social and educational inequality lie in individual transformation; it is up to those at risk to acquire a new disposition toward work, new values, and new skills, and it is the job of educational institutions and their supporters to facilitate this process.

In essence, this political dynamic was in play within the Biotechnology Academy. In a public atmosphere of pervasive representations of Latino youth as unproductive, economically redundant, and even delinquent, Academy youth, whose fantasies of failure (e.g., getting pregnant, sitting on the couch, and watching daytime TV) signaled the haunting effect of such stereotypes, were subject to a process of self-transformation. Their professed desire to perform the kind of work that entailed monitoring at-risk communities suggests that they understood and accepted the obligation to present themselves as enhanced or improved and less at risk as a result of participation in the program. And, as we saw, the Academy's emphasis on the cultivation of traits associated with regional "culture"—appropriate communication, problem-solving, and networking skills for a professional corporate environment, the ability to be a "team player," and enthusiastic identification with the goal of technological innovation and private-sector individual advancement—comprised a sanctioned strategy of risk management that was emphasized during classroom and field-trip time over the course of a school year.

This project of self-transformation via exposure to regional "culture" was locally promoted through the dissemination of narratives about at-risk young persons of color who acquire new inspiration, motivation, social and intellectual capital, and problem-solving and networking skills by participating in programs such as those at the Academy. Reading local newspapers and corporate annual reports, I found narratives about local workforce-oriented programs designed to steer Silicon Valley's working-class youth of color—particularly Latinos—away from dead-end, low-paying jobs and toward bright, high-tech futures, to be common content. I also encountered stories about local youth profoundly transformed by exposure (via internships) to high-tech companies.

One such local newspaper article, "Program Sets At-Risk Youth on New Path," exemplified how news stories can reinforce the link between techno-entrepreneurship and the personal potential and self-esteem of low-income, at-risk youth. Focused on the launching of a new Youth Entrepreneurship Project sponsored by a well-known nonprofit organization in East San Jose, the Mexican American Community Services Agency (MACSA), as well as SBC Communications/Pacific Bell, Applied Materials, Cisco, and IBM, the article's introductory paragraphs read as follows:

> A year ago [student's name] was a high school dropout who'd served time for vandalism and didn't see a bright future for himself.
>
> But then he was introduced to computers through the Mexican American Community Services Street Reach Program. Now, the 18 year old envisions himself becoming one of the top guys at Adobe Systems Inc. or owning a small computer repair business.
>
> "The program was a step forward for me. I couldn't graduate or do well in school, but I was good at computers. That felt good," says [student's name] with a proud grin. (Bellantoni 2001)

This narrative, in fact, echoes that of many actual narratives constructed about Biotech students I met at Morton, whose personal circumstances were transformed into uplifting stories that I came across in mainstream media sources such as the *San Jose Mercury News*, the *Wall Street Journal*, and *Fortune*, as well as on well-regarded philanthropic websites. On a practical level, such narratives promoted the nonprofit programs, the public schools, and the high-tech companies that supported them, but they also served as instructive discourses of potential. Focused especially on Latino youth, a group whose at-risk status derives from Latinos' long-term position within a racial and economic order that has placed them at the bottom of the local labor hierarchy, first as industrial agricultural workers and then as service-economy workers (Pitti 2003; Zavella 1987; Zlolniski 2006), such narratives, like the programs they describe, were both normative and disciplinary; they celebrated the transformation of Latino youth according to the values of a regionally dominant high-tech professional and managerial class.

In Silicon Valley, then, the deployment of regional "culture" has been central to this educational politics of self-transformation and empowerment. But the underlying political project of shifting the burden for social inequality and risk onto individuals deemed at risk because of race, ethnicity, and socioeconomic status remains a common if not ubiquitous phenomenon in the United States. As scholars of neoliberalism have observed, with the state's shedding of responsibility for social welfare and services for its citizenry, there has been a fluorescence of "neoliberal" discourses and programs stressing empowerment and personal responsibility for poor and disenfranchised groups throughout the nation (Hyatt 2001; Goldstein 2001; Lyon-Callo 2000). As such, poor youth and others deemed at risk have been steered toward supplanting the state as managers of their own risk and potential (Kelly 2001; Rose 1996; Nybell, Shook, and Finn 2009).

The Cultivation of Institutions

At a meeting with Jonathan Vinh, a coordinator for a number of programs for youth within a large-scale, multidimensional neighborhood development project in East San Jose, I listened as he summed up the local nonprofit social services scene with some disgust:

> I hate this field. I think this is the most unethical field. There are such inappropriate uses of funding. . . . People are spending money and wasting it . . . [it's] dirty. Agencies are trying to stay alive; [there are] inflated bureaucracies . . . People are burning through money. There is too much overlap in services. People need to collaborate not just sharing dollars but also designing programs.

Although I cannot assess the merits of Jonathan's claims about the local nonprofit community or reasons he might have had for being personally disgruntled, the vigorousness of his distaste for waste, inefficiency, and corruption in the nonprofit realm of Silicon Valley was striking in that it represented a more virulent version of what I heard from others with whom I spoke about the state of Silicon Valley's nonprofit social services targeting youth and low-income families. At a similar exploratory interview with the local director of the Silicon Valley chapter of Junior Achievement, the conversation turned to the organization Plugged-In in East Palo Alto. Mary-Ellen, the director of Junior Achievement and a veteran manager of a number of local vocational programs over a period of twenty years, said with sudden disapproval: "EPA [East Palo Alto] scares me. I mean, they're throwing so much money at it. It's sort of like the sixties. People are so eager to throw money at a problem."

The belief that employees at nonprofit organizations providing social services did not understand or practice good organizational management and that the money they received might be wasted was not limited to nonprofit insiders. In a private interview at Agilent Technologies with Linda Berry, a steering committee member and corporate liaison to Morton High School's Biotechnology Academy, I heard a similar message. Linda and I sat in the sleek cafeteria at Agilent, sipping coffee and discussing how Agilent addressed Silicon Valley's digital divide. Soon into our conversation, Linda assumed a conspiratorial tone as we talked about Morton and other high schools that Agilent and HP had supported.[24] Deploring the "level of bureaucracy" and the "stick-in-the-mud, turf-war attitude" about sharing information and resources that Linda said she had observed at the school district level, she summed up her view of public schools. "They've been given everything, but don't want to use it! The high-tech community tries to help, but it doesn't work." For Linda, public school teachers were at the center of this problem. With irritation, she recalled a time three or four years earlier when HP had given laptops to a local school: "They went back to check on them nine months later and some of them were still in the boxes!" she exclaimed. "You can lead a horse to water, but you can't make it drink."

The image of computers sitting dormant in boxes, and teachers, as stubborn as horses, unwilling to unwrap them and plug them in, connotes wastefulness, obstinacy, laziness, and, at worst, corruption. What social forces have shaped these perceptions? On the national scale, public debate and policy concerned with the perceived perils of "big government" and wasteful social-service institutions—particularly for those that serve poor and minority groups, which have been dominant since Ronald Reagan's presidency—might be said to constitute a discursive backdrop to the attitudes about social-service nonprofits and public schools that I encountered during my fieldwork. One might also relate such public attitudes to nativist politics in California, where the nationwide public debate about wasteful government and needless expenditures has often been targeted against organizations and institutions serving Latino immigrants in particular (Zavella 2001; Chavez 2008).

In addition to these political dynamics, a series of local events that unfolded in Silicon Valley during the tech boom may also have reinforced notions of nonprofit and public-sector profligacy. While I was in the field, I often read newspaper articles and heard gossip about the corruption and inept bureaucratic management plaguing municipal governance within lower-income neighborhoods of the Valley. An endless succession of well-reported scandals concerning the City Council of the City of East Palo Alto and East San Jose's poorly performing Alum Rock School District serving low-income Latino students in East San Jose illustrate this point.[25] As a Palo Alto bureaucrat working for Representative Joe Simitian told me, "The attitude about Alum Rock [School District] is, 'why can't they get it together down there?'" In addition, the financial mismanagement, in 1999, of United Way of Silicon Valley, recounted in detail in the local media and related to me by many people I interviewed, also helped create an association in the local public imagination between mismanagement and ineptitude in the nonprofit sector (see, for example, Workman 2000).

But although these events and the perceptions about them may have helped shape attitudes like those of Mary Ellen, Beth Samson, or Jonathan Vinh, I suggest that a complementary process was at work. Media stories and public rumors about ineptitude and corruption in public-sector agencies and organizations such as United Way created a perception that reform was necessary, while the reforms themselves that emerged as a result of public-private "collaboration" over the digital divide also generated such moralizing public discourse. The remedy helped create the perception of an inadequacy.

Fixing Nonprofits and Public Schools: "Organizational Efficiency"

Beth Samson described Agilent's role in the nonprofit community:

We lend expertise [we help] nonprofits organize themselves . . . do they need to downsize? How can they "tailor" their programs? Let's prioritize, and then when things turn around we [the nonprofit organization and the company working collaboratively] can get back to also providing priorities five, six, seven, and eight.

In addition to promises of funding and technological support, a primary kind of support offered in the public-private relationships I encountered in the Valley involved helping local nonprofits to scale, cut, trim, and rationalize their organizations. People I interviewed whose jobs involved forging institutional relationships between the business and public and nonprofit sectors often characterized the public-private relationship as "collaborative," and they emphasized lessons in "organizational efficiency" as one of the benefits of maintaining relationships with the private sector. For example, at a meeting of the Silicon Valley YMCA and other nonprofit agencies contracting youth services for the City of San Jose, I asked a group of nonprofit directors about Silicon Valley's relationship to nonprofit organizations serving local youth. The YMCA's regional director responded, "HP and the Packard Foundation really have set the trend by funding organizational effectiveness. [They assist with] multiyear increment business plans for CBOS."

I again heard about "organizational effectiveness" in an interview with Elizabeth Williamson, the director of a local "venture philanthropy" group, SV2, which, as part of the Community Foundation for Silicon Valley, trains young and wealthy entrepreneurs to become active in local causes. Rather than just giving money, venture philanthropists become active in the organization. As Elizabeth explained it,

> A lot of these people [SV2 members] are young, high net worth. [They] have business and organizational efficiency skills they are dying to share with SV2-funded nonprofits. This amounts to tech support, board development, strategic planning—which involves issues like the timing of expansion, mission, strategy, goals, strengths, and weaknesses. . . . They help scale the organization . . . "Organizational effectiveness" is the buzzword everyone uses.

Representatives of local county and city agencies concerned with youth and workforce development issues also eagerly connected the local entrepreneurial practice of collaboration with the quest to eradicate duplication and promote efficiency within the public sector. As a San Jose bureaucrat told me, the city acts as the facilitator, pulling nonprofits together to create, "networks in ways that already exist in the business world." Another City of San Jose official commented that he wished that San Jose would "integrate some of Silicon Valley's entrepreneurial spirit" into its programs for jobless youth funded by the federal Workforce Investment Act.

Julie Samuels, a woman who worked on a number of youth-related projects for the North Valley Private Industry Council (NOVA-PIC), which is a county agency that works with private industry and county services to provide job training, administer welfare-to-work, help train laid-off workers, and convince employers to invest in upgrading the training of existing workers, pointed out the ideological and practical effects of private-sector ideas on the local public sector as a result of the application of the 2000 Workforce Investment Act (WIA) (replacing the earlier Job Training Partnership Act [JTPA]): "[With] JTPA, the federal labor department had more control. [With WIA] what is new is the federal appropriation of the discourse of collaboration and their advocacy of 'one-stoppism.'"

The term "collaboration," Julie noted, had been written into the federal Workforce Investment Act. At NOVA-PIC the principle of "one-stoppism" meant the creation of a network of interacting agencies that provide "one-stop shopping" for workers/consumers in search of both employment and social services.[26] In Santa Clara County people now seek alcohol treatment and employment services in the same building. As we talked I commented that this conception of "collaboration" seemed to be everywhere in the Silicon Valley model.

If multiyear business plans to maximize efficiency and to eradicate duplication through "networks" and "collaboration" constituted areas of private-sector intervention within the sphere of Silicon Valley's public and nonprofit social services, the production and documentation of "results" was also central to the project of fomenting organizational efficiency. The director of education and workforce development of the Silicon Valley Manufacturing Group put it this way:

> Today people are looking for measurable results that focus us in on what our efforts are going to be. There used to be a time when educators would ask for resources, just give us some money, but now SVMG and others wants to see some results, have some input, the responsibility is on educators as well to be able to show what the results are.

Joint Venture's Challenge 2000 program and its 21st Century Education Initiative, with their emphases on making schools more efficient through new systems of management and technology, reflect that organization's primary focus upon generating new ways to measure institutional progress and create accountability. As SVMG's education director observed, Joint Venture's emphasis on measurability, manifest in its quest to document and ameliorate the regional digital divide, contained a threat: "under the model that Joint Venture was trying to get people to adopt, if you could not measure that you were bridging the digital divide, then you should drop that program."

This emphasis on measurement and results has a temporal dimension; the "results" in question are to be proven within a given time frame. One effect, for example, of the annual *JVSV Index*, initiated in the mid-1990s, and its reports on the state of Silicon Valley's workforce and youth interest in technology careers, has been to make people mindful of the pace of the transformation of social-service and educational institutions in Silicon Valley. Even the organization's way of representing itself as a "catalyst" and an "incubator" of ideas announces a self-conscious modeling of a temporality derived from local management practices within the innovation-based global information economy (O'Riain 2000).

This temporality informed a Silicon Valley impatience to "fix" things quickly. Elizabeth Williams, director of the SV2 philanthropy group, summed up this tendency best as she described the young philanthropists she was working with during the tech boom: "They made their money very quickly, [it was] very immediate, it's 'I just made two billion taking a concept (and developing it into a profitable business) in a six- to eight-month period, why can't I fix people that quickly?"

Civic and corporate representations that contrasted slow, inefficient public- and nonprofit-sector workers and institutions to a fast-moving, efficient entrepreneurial way of getting things done suggest a moral hierarchy in which slowness is associated with laziness and lack of vision.

One effect of this moral hierarchy was on display at Morton. One morning I attended a meeting of the steering committee of the Biotechnology Academy. Present were four Academy seniors I knew; Chris, the Academy's coordinator; Joyce Gelby, the director of the Santa Clara County Biotechnology Education Program; and a few corporate representatives from companies supporting the Academy, including a man from Genentech and Beth Sampson from Agilent Technologies.

Chris launched the meeting with a report on the status of her efforts to extract funds owed to her from the district office. Seemingly annoyed and nervous, she asked for help from the corporate representatives present. She reminded them, in a pleading voice, that at work she had no time to go to the bathroom or to eat, that she arrived at 7:00 in the morning, left at 4:30, and worked on her vacations. Beth responded that the superintendent would be at a dinner she was attending the next night and that she would see what she could do.

Uncomfortably for Chris, and perhaps for the student representatives, the conversation turned to two other topics: the seniors' performance during their final PowerPoint presentations of lab experiments that morning at Biotech, which we all had observed—Joyce Gelby called them "far below the bar"—and Biotech's recent lack of presence at a prestigious regional science competition. With a discernable frown, Joyce pointed out that a student from a rival public high school (also serving a low-income community in East San Jose) had participated in the competition. This observation hung in the air for a moment, before Joyce pointed out that teachers at other schools arrive at school at 6:00 am and leave at 9:00 pm, an obvious reproach of Chris's defense of her dedication earlier in the conversation.

Beth then chimed in, visibly annoyed: "I'm perfectly willing to provide some cash for science projects, but I just don't want to make a donation *AND HAVE THE MONEY JUST SIT THERE.*" In the next few minutes, she reiterated the point three times, the phrase "just sit there," making it into each restatement.

Despite any anger she may have felt at this patronizing lecture, Chris quietly absorbed these reproaches, occasionally defending herself and her staff in a pleading tone. Even though she and the other Academy teachers managed a successful academic and extra-curricular program that ultimately resulted in a tremendous increase in the rate of four-year college acceptances in comparison to the general student population, Chris assumed a role publicly subservient to Beth's, while Beth assumed the role of "boss."

Despite any anger she may have felt at this patronizing lecture, Chris quietly absorbed these reproaches, occasionally defending herself and her staff in a pleading tone. Even though she and the other Academy teachers managed a successful academic and extra-curricular program that ultimately resulted in a tremendous increase in the rate of four-year college acceptances in comparison to the general student population, Chris assumed a role publicly subservient to Beth's, while Beth assumed the role of "boss."

Although this vignette surely does not represent the tenor of all public-private collaborations within Silicon Valley's public sphere, it does reveal how such relationships, despite civic rhetoric about nonprofit and private-sector organizations "learning from each other," have facilitated and reinforced a regional second-class status for nonprofit and public-sector workers such as teachers. At the Job Shadow Day I spent at 3-Com, I saw a tired, overworked public school teacher and a teacher's aide, both having had spent five hours on their feet shepherding their junior high school charges around 3-Com's grand and half-empty campus, lope cautiously toward a buffet table after every student had eaten a company-provided sandwich only to find that their own lunches had been overlooked. No one from the company approached to rectify the situation or even seemed to notice the teachers. Mr. Torres, the teacher, took a few cookies, while the aide settled for a bottle of water.

Practical Skeptics and Moral Critics

The ways in which low-income youth, educators, and nonprofit social-service providers in Silicon Valley have been produced as "subjects" in need of "fixing" may be understood as a form of disciplinary power (Foucault 1979). Trained on a particular category of youth and institutions, such power has locally involved both the articulation of a set of complaints about youth, public schools, and nonprofit organizations, and the implementation of a process of transforming youth and organizations through exposure to practices and values associated with the region's much-touted, high-tech corporate culture. However, these disciplinary effects are not absolute. Just as the discussion of the everyday experiences and modes of aspiration management among Morton's Biotech students revealed that contradictory ideologies and practices within the school and community environment, as well as experiences of social and economic exclusion, served to undermine the goal of aligning young people's aspirations with a career in industry, global and local political economic realities may undermine the goal of fostering enthusiasm for technological innovation and careers in local youth, or transforming the practices and strategies of teachers or nonprofit workers.

During my time in the field, I often came across nonprofit directors of youth programs and educators worried about declining corporate as well as state funding. In fact, looking back on my field notes, it strikes me that many of my conversations with the coordinator of the Academy focused on the threat of disappearing corporate funding because of the tech downturn. The Biotechnology Academy at Morton, IISME, and numerous school-company relationships I heard about while in Silicon Valley experienced a drop in the level of corporate support they had received as a result of the downturn. Ultimately I found that the downturn (which locals did not speak of as a recession during that academic year) undermined the "buy-in" of young people, teachers, and nonprofit service providers regarding the very projects and goals endorsed by Silicon Valley's high-tech industry and its collaborators.

For example, the consequences of the intensifying tech bust were not lost on the young people who attended events such as 3-Com's Job Shadow Day or Workforce Silicon Valley's Student Leadership Conference. While the students attending 3-Com's Job Shadow Day probably did not know that 3-Com had vastly reduced its global workforce since 2001,[27] their comments revealed an awareness of the extent to which people's fates were subject to the vicissitudes of the local tech economy. Over a lunch of sandwiches with 3-Com staffers from marketing and a group of giggling girls, an employee remarked to a student, "When you come next year—" but one of the girls interrupted him, and asked, with a laugh: "Will you still be here next year if we do come back?"

An exchange between youth and corporate representatives at a Student Leadership Conference hosted by Workforce Silicon Valley revealed a similar skepticism. In a room full of students from generally less affluent public schools in the region, questions appeared on the overhead projector: "Who comes to mind when you think of people who work in technology?" "Rich people!" one student blurted out. "Bill Gates!" said another. "People dominating small businesses!" a third wryly remarked. The next statement on the overhead projector was one for students to complete themselves: "The reason I would choose a career in technology is . . ." A student responded: "Technology is hard because once the economy is going down the tubes, it's like, 'Uh, You're fired! Sorry!'" The moderator of the focus group persisted: "That wouldn't happen in another field?" she asked. Another student rejoined: "Look at psychology. As long as humans have problems, you have a job!"

Adults I met working as teachers or nonprofit or public-service providers serving low-income Valley youth and their families expressed similarly skeptical, and even negative, viewpoints about the local tech private sector. With memories beyond the rapid move from boom to bust, such people, often advocates for Silicon Valley's Latino community, took a jaundiced view of corporate Silicon Valley's commitment to creating a more inclusive regional society.

In a series of three interviews Linda Martinez, a San Jose native and a longtime unionist and bureaucrat working for the City of San Jose's community development Strong Neighborhood Initiative, framed the history of corporate Silicon Valley's connection to the region's long-standing, working-class Latino population as one of sustained disinterest and lack of investment, and she disregarded claims that times had changed:

[In the 1970s] Silicon Valley was growing and the connection between Silicon Valley corporations and low-income youth and educational services just wasn't there. . . . Silicon Valley never became a partner with our education system . . . Let's start providing training in the high schools or in the junior highs to these youth because they're gonna be our future work-force . . . develop your future programmers, your future IT people, your future people that work on the hardware. And they still to this point haven't connected. Because what they do now is give us hardware. Well that's won-derful and dandy, but if you don't give us training in the community, what good is it. . . . How [is] it that I as an individual minority have the capacity to work for an HP, a Sun, but do I have the ability to move to a higher level at these companies, out of the entry level? . . . Worst of all: the importation of the labor force, the H1B visa people. Why don't they train our people?

When I brought up the efforts of Workforce Silicon Valley, Linda waved her hand dismissively, telling me, "Our people have never heard of it."

Community Relations liaisons at any of the big Silicon Valley tech firms might have also found a hard sell in Joy Fisher, a popular Biotechnology Academy teacher at Morton High School. As I interviewed Joy in a cramped office supply room after school one day, we talked about the corporate world of Silicon Valley. Describing Morton students' alienation from Silicon Val-ley industry and the worldview of its professionals, Joy contrasted the moral qualities of the students with people she knew in Silicon Valley's techno-entrepreneurial sector. Pointing out that she could never work in Silicon Val-ley herself, she commented, "People [Silicon Valley professionals] are self-absorbed. They're manipulative. Often times there's no integrity. [They are] too 'I've got to get from point A to point B.' Our kids aren't like that."

Despite the efforts of civic-minded corporate elites and positive press about companies donating time, expertise, and technology to cash-strapped public schools during the boom, I continued to come across people work-ing in social services who echoed Joy Fisher's sentiments about a morally challenged high-tech elite. Talking to Naomi Swift, the director of the Cor-nerstone Project, a youth development organization focused upon creating healthy environments for young people within communities and institu-tions serving youth throughout the region, I heard a similar description of the Valley: "Silicon Valley networks but doesn't connect," Naomi said. "The networking is all very self-interested. This region . . . [is] transient. There are many adults here to innovate, be part of Silicon Valley—so many people don't feel that they have a responsibility to the community."

These voices serve as counternarratives to the locally pervasive represen-tation of Silicon Valley's high-tech elite and its collaborators in public office and positions of community leadership as mending social rifts and saving

the futures of local youth through a dissemination of local high-tech expertise, social practices, and money. Based on experience and historical mem-
ory, such critical viewpoints arise out of contradictory political, social, and
economic conditions. Although in the past decade Silicon Valley elites have
engaged in marketing the local "culture," and sought, for reasons more or
less civic-minded, to transform local educational and social-service organizations as well as young people's aspirations and skills in accordance with the
priorities of a profit-oriented global information economy, corporate Silicon
Valley's civic agenda is contingent upon immediate economic forces that
compete with such long-term visionary plans. In turn, the goal of sustainability loses out to that of profit making. Such historical forces render the
techno-utopian vision of a democratically inclusive, capitalist information
society, where every youth can become a "start-up" just that: a vision.

5

A Fear of Slipping

A Cultural Politics of Class

Venture Trippers and the Ideal Worker/Self

In January 1997, as the tech boom gained momentum, a cover story in the *San Jose Mercury News* profiled the region's optimistic, polyglot newcomers. These recent migrants, the article informed its readers, had flocked to the area for a myriad of reasons: the jobs ("30,000 new ones in Santa Clara County alone in 1996"); the educational opportunities; the region's "laid-back attitude"; the temperate climate; and, perhaps most of all, "the area's high-tech mystique: that of a place where a single idea can spawn a new industry." A tech professional from Ecuador featured in the piece put it this way: "Americans don't think there is any limit, and Silicon Valley is very representative of that . . . there's an energy here, a confluence of ideas, money, and talent. There's just no other place I'd rather be right now" (Jung 1997).

Hype surrounding these newcomers persisted in the media throughout Silicon Valley's tech boom. Two years after this article appeared in the *Mercury News*, Po Bronson, local novelist and journalistic chronicler of Silicon Valley's business elite, rendered this "new breed" in enthusiastic detail in his best-selling nonfiction account of boom-time Silicon Valley, *The Nudist on the Lateshift*:

> They come for the tremendous opportunity, believing that in no other place in the world right now can one person accomplish so much with talent, initiative, and a good idea. It's a region where who you know and how much money you have has never been less relevant to success. They come because it does not matter that they are young or left college without a degree or have dark skin or speak with an accent. They come even if it is illegal to do so . . . They come to be a part of history, to build the technology that will reshape how people live and work five and ten years

from now . . . They are the new breed, Venture Trippers . . . It is a mad, fertile time. Working has become nothing less than a blood sport here in Superachieverland: people are motivated by the thrill of competition and the danger of losing, and every year the rules evolve to make it all happen more quickly, on higher margins, reaching ever more amazing sums . . . what they see ahead of them, if they stay where they are, is a working life that seems fundamentally and unavoidably boring . . . rather than choosing not to work hard, the Venture Trippers are taking the opposite approach from the Slackers. They're saying, If I'm going to have to make that trade-off, then hell, why the fuck not? I'm young, let's raise the stakes. Let's up the bet. Let's make it exciting. Let's put it all on black. (Bronson 1999:3–4)

With a tap of the keyboard, Bronson flattens the differences between illegal workers in Silicon Valley and young educated fortune seekers who fear boredom. The resulting representation is of a gambling technophile's meritocracy where connections are irrelevant and there is no elite other than that which naturally arises as people begin to reap the benefits of their own individual propensity for passionate creativity, risk taking, and hard work. The very title of Bronson's book, *The Nudist on the Lateshift* (1999), suggests a convention-defying, cerebral maverick, burning up with an all-night passion for code that makes even clothing an irritatingly conventional imposition. In the meritocratic fantasy perpetuated by Bronson's text, the "Venture Tripper" breed naturally trumps the "Slackers" and those satisfied with a boring, stable, nine-to-five existence.

Drawing upon an older regional archetype, that of the tech-obsessed engineer/entrepreneur with a good idea, Bronson's late-1990s representation of an emergent techno-entrepreneurial class that arose in Silicon Valley during the tech boom reflects new discourses of work and lifestyle associated with the concept of the "free agent" that emerged during the late 1990s. As Michael Lewis (2000) has argued, the grey-flannel–suited man of 1950s corporate America has been replaced by the "New Economy" "free agent," a possibly nose-ringed worker whose allegiance remains to her- or himself instead of a corporation. Lewis, writing just prior to the implosion of the tech boom and subsequent descent into recession, names Silicon Valley as the ultimate locale for the new "free agent" worker, a place where stock options trump company loyalty, and the hunt for brighter prospects has created a region of unmoored and, Lewis is careful to say, vulnerable, "job-hoppers" (Lewis 2000). Such "New Economy" employees refuse to take orders unless they agree with them or consider them advantageous in some way. Self-motivated risk takers, they labor to fulfill their own goals and passions rather than to satisfy the company's bottom line.

For such "free agents," leisure activities present new opportunities to define and showcase entrepreneurial talents and tendencies. The macho and thrill-seeking antics of Larry Ellison, CEO of the Silicon Valley–based firm Oracle, who, it has often been reported, favors yacht racing, womanizing, and piloting fighter jets in his spare time, epitomize the competitiveness, maverick taste, and addiction to risk taking valued in contemporary American entrepreneurship. Similarly, the popularity among Silicon Valley tech professionals of the annual "Burning Man" festival of art and invention in the Nevada desert during the late 1990s is another example of the playtime showcasing of an emergent entrepreneurial ideal. A *Forbes Magazine* account of Burning Man from 1999 celebrates these traits:

> A tattoo-covered man swings high above the Nevada desert, suspended by four large hooks in the skin of his back. He is one of 23,000 people hanging around on four square miles of prehistoric, desiccated lake-bed 100 miles north of Reno for the week-long Burning Man festival.
>
> They are engineers, software developers, executives, digital artists, lawyers, and professors. To say Silicon Valley's denizens work hard is an understatement. To say they play hard doesn't begin to approach what you see at Burning Man. They are here to play with fire and drugs, erect monstrous sculptures, dodge fireworks, defy heat exhaustion, march in spontaneous parades and dance to ear-pounding music. They are at the cyberculture's *de rigeur* power-networking retreat of the year.
>
> Jeffrey Bezos of Amazon.com is here. So are throngs of techies from America Online, Netscape, Yahoo, George Lucas' Industrial Light and Magic and dozens of weblets. The general rule of thumb is anything goes. (McHugh 1999:99–101)

Taken together, Bronson's representation of Silicon Valley's dot-com era newcomers, Lewis's free agents, and the "techies" who attend Burning Man demonstrate a way of being that was defined in Silicon Valley at the end of the twentieth century. Such personifications possess a representational power that shapes notions of place and self simultaneously. Conferring on Silicon Valley the status of "[a] frontier of limitless possibilities [that] beckon the bold . . . [where] the risk of failure is routinely, perhaps recklessly, shunted aside" (Kwan 2001), such depictions represent for the body politic the qualities of an emergent ideal working self, one endowed with psychological and intellectual traits well suited to the increasingly globalized and competitive context of the contemporary United States. Authors such as Po Bronson and David Kaplan, author of *The Silicon Boys* (1999), a book exploring the personalities and biographies of numerous Silicon Valley titans, have raised the profile of this mythic, often masculinized entrepreneurial figure.

Anthropologist Emily Martin's conceptualizations of a contemporary ideal American worker who is not only flexible and self-sustaining but possessed of a manic mood and style is relevant here. Building on her earlier ethnographic exploration of contemporary ideals of worker behavior and worker experience with increasingly insecure and "flexible" employment (Martin 1994), Martin's *Biopolar Expeditions* (2009) explores the increasing prevalence of representations of a "manic style" of being in popular culture and the contemporary American business world. The Silicon Valley characters in Bronson's *Nudist and the Lateshift*, portrayed as madcap, hyperactive, sleep-deprived geniuses,[1] reflect such a manic model of selfhood, a self that Martin suggests is increasingly celebrated in American public culture because it constitutes a valuable asset within the contemporary political-economic regime. Martin demonstrates, in particular, the relationship of a manic style of selfhood to the market, perceived in contemporary American society as irrational and hyperactive, and to the neoliberal workplace, which encourages in workers a kind of conformist, instrumentalized mania in order to meet market demands of productivity and competition (Martin 2009:277). This turn toward the manic, she maintains, represents a significant aspect of "the social and cultural world now inhabited by many middle-class Americans" (Martin 2000).

My own ethnographic observation of an established professional middle class in Silicon Valley during the tail end of the tech boom and its aftermath offers an opportunity to explore how such an ideal worker/self, placed in critical perspective by Martin and celebrated by authors like Po Bronson, actually figures in the world of middle-class America to which Martin refers. If the "new breed" of "Venture Tripper" might be said to represent an emergent star protagonist within a commonsensical social imaginary operating at the national if not global scale,[2] what function did this "free-agent" ideal serve within the local context of Silicon Valley during the economically volatile and socially polarizing period of the tech boom and its subsequent bust? Attention to local public discourse in the wake of the boom and conversations I had with established middle-class professionals in Silicon Valley led me to wonder about the extent to which Silicon Valley's established professional middle class had come to identify with this "New Economy" ideal self, and what the political and personal effects of such identification might be. Did exposure to this social imaginary naturalize a hegemonic hierarchy of people/workers in a region like Silicon Valley, financial and social successes serving as proof of having the correct, suitably entrepreneurial psychological makeup and intellectual traits, and economic struggle serving as evidence of individual or, in the case of marginalized or ethnic groups, cultural flaws? Did it lead the region's established, professional middle class to emulate a "free agent" orientation toward employment? Finally, how did the responses of middle-class professionals to this ideal, manifested in their collective mood, self-perceptions, and social judgments, affect the children of the region's established professional middle class, who were surely not immune to the attitudes of adults in their midst?

Adult Ambivalence toward a New Social Order

A key element of this investigation involves consideration of the effects of lived experience and social contradiction on the internalization of ideals of selfhood. The speech of established, professional middle-class adults—many of whom were parents of Sanders students—signaled ambivalence toward a techno-entrepreneurial ideal self; such people classified their own economic and social experience during the boom and that of acquaintances and friends in contradictory ways. Even as these affluent and middle-class parents, high school teachers, and tech professionals acknowledged chance and luck as factors in stock market success, in off-the-cuff comments along the lines of "X was at the right place at the right time" or "Y hit the jackpot," they often invoked a neighbor's or friend's penchant for hard work, risk taking, and a Silicon Valley-style competitive streak as an explanation for personal financial success.

And yet, despite the commonness of psychological and behavioral explanations for personal success, many of these people expressed moral disapproval of young techno-entrepreneurial professionals who had suddenly become wealthy during the tech boom, and waxed nostalgic for a pre–dot-com-boom Silicon Valley. People sensed that something was not quite fair or right about these newcomers' success, and that their presence signaled a new, and not necessarily favorable, social and economic order. The attitudes that Silicon Valley's established, older professional middle class exhibited toward the newcomer class of affluent young tech professionals amounted to a form of social critique that might potentially disrupt commonsense thinking about Silicon Valley as a place where success comes to those with the right entrepreneurial traits and values celebrating innovation and risk-taking.

Who comprised what I am calling this emergent "new entrepreneurial" middle class? I am borrowing the term from some of my interviewees, who used it as a shorthand for tech professionals, typically affluent, who identified with a "new entrepreneurial" business subculture. I include in this affluent middle-class category the "dot–commers": young people, often from California but not necessarily, who moved to Silicon Valley to work as technical or managerial staff at "dot-coms." I also place in this group high-status, tech-company elites who represent the business practices, values, and style of boom-time Silicon Valley. Many such residents of the Valley graduated from prestigious business or law schools, such as Stanford or Harvard, many were formally recruited, and many came as a result of their membership in informal, personal networks (fraternities, friends who worked for start-ups, etc.).

At the height of the boom and into its aftermath, these people rented office space, drove high-status SUVs, and frequented expensive restaurants. They purchased and built expensive houses in high-status areas of Silicon Valley that had long been home to an established, professional middle class, and they worked in start-up companies or in new, upper-level management positions in established firms. In contrast, established Valleyites tended to be long-term property owners and employees of local tech corporations and other kinds of organizations, from hospitals to Stanford University. As was revealed in off-hand comments and interviews, Silicon Valley's established professional middle class felt usurped by and irritated with this young, "new entrepreneurial" class; I heard complaints about stolen parking spaces and about neighborhood blocks and even city councils ruined by the presence of "dot-commers." And in middle-class Valley residents' descriptions of the sense of entitlement, material wealth, and networking prowess of the young "new entrepreneurial" class, I detected a degree of resentment.

But despite their irritation, and perhaps envy, toward these young entrepreneurially oriented newcomers, many middle-class people I encountered were sufficiently impressed by their hard-charging, competitive, and risk-taking style to measure themselves against them. And yet middle-class identification with a "new entrepreneurial" ideal, and willingness to read personal success as a measure of entrepreneurial character, was intermittent, compromised by social and economic pressures that Silicon Valley's established professional middle class confronted during the boom and its aftermath.

A news debate that dominated public discussion in Silicon Valley during the spring of 2002, over the proposed (and ultimately realized) HP-Compaq merger, offers an unlikely lens through which to approach the question of professional middle-class identification with a new entrepreneurial subject. By exploring public and private discourse about the merger, representations of HP's past and present corporate culture, and local professional middle-class responses to both the presence of a new, young, wealthy tech elite and a new entrepreneurial mode of corporate conduct, we can gain insight into the experience of mounting social and economic insecurity for Silicon Valley's established professional middle class and learn more about their responses to it. Moreover, we can illuminate in more depth the social and political context of the middle-class youth who attended Sanders High School, and link adults' responses to social, economic, and cultural transformation to young people's expressions of self-definition and self-cultivation.

"The HP Way"

The mythology of William Hewlett and David Packard, who founded Hewlett-Packard in a garage in Palo Alto in 1938, has served for sixty years as a symbol of Silicon Valley's innovative spirit and forward-looking attitude. The story of the birth of the company and its first product, cobbled together during long hours in the landmark garage on Addison Street, represents a kind of Christ-child manger, wherein two plucky and passionate engineers founded a corporate giant. The garage also symbolizes a meritocratic capitalism wherein ingenuity and vision are the key ingredients. As one columnist put it, "The myth of the garage reinforced the idea that everything doesn't have to come from the top . . . the idea behind it is that you can start up a company with such modest means and can grow it into something really great" ("'HP Way' Changed the Valley" 2002:11).

As news stories have rehashed over the years, Hewlett and Packard's collaboration in the garage also represents the birth of the collaborative corporate culture known as "the HP Way." "The HP Way" is not only a common phrase heard in discussions of Silicon Valley business practices; it has been immortalized in a book by Hewlett and Packard (1996), which was published at a time when, according to HP employees with whom I spoke, internal corporate practices representative of the HP Way, such as a lack of hierarchy and democratic participation within the company, were on the wane.[3]

Although I was aware of the lore about HP before arriving to conduct fieldwork in Silicon Valley, I first heard about the HP Way a few weeks after arriving in the field, when I met with a white middle-class Palo Alto woman,

Sharon Hughes, long active in the League of Women Voters, community issues, and local Democratic Party politics. Sharon provided me with an overview of "hot button" issues in Santa Clara County, from the effects on teachers of the astronomical price of housing to public and private initiatives on K-12 education. When education came up in our conversation, I asked Sharon about local private-sector efforts to address educational inequalities. She immediately brought up HP's central role, pointing out that HP's tentacles extended into the regional community far and wide, via the Hewlett Foundation, Packard Foundation, and Packard Children's Hospital Foundation. "There's a lot of Packard money around the Valley," Sharon laughed. She then assumed a more serious expression: "HP is in a category of its own . . . The two founders were very clear about doing good in the community for its own sake." Sharon, who had never worked at HP herself, recounted a story about how two HP employees had been assigned to come up with a marketing tag for HP in order to represent it as the best company in the world, and they came up with "HP for the world." Sharon uttered the tag with passion. "The HP Way has been for the community," she said.

Without my seeking information about it, the theme of HP's civic largesse was brought up repeatedly as I scouted around for the right educationally oriented program in which to initiate regular fieldwork. In conversations with nonprofit directors in East San Jose and East Palo Alto,[4] I heard about HP's contributions of both dollars and technical equipment for youth-related projects. For example, at the meeting of local directors of youth-oriented nonprofit organizations including the Santa Clara Valley YMCA, four directors at the table assessed HP's community contributions positively, after critically dissecting the lack of altruism of companies such as IBM and Dell, whose support came with strings and had tapered off during the downturn. In contrast, they praised HP for its long-term commitment to funding "organizational efficiency."

In sum, the recurrent message about the HP Way conveyed to me by nonprofit representatives and tech professionals both affiliated and unaffiliated with HP was its emphasis upon community values and the role of HP as a catalyst generating livable, sustainable communities. The sense was that the HP Way rendered community and corporate goals synonymous; as a veteran columnist for the *San Jose Mercury* put it, "Under the HP Way, profits and human values fueled each other" (Gillmor 2002:1F, 8F). Moreover, according to former and current employees, the HP Way was "democratic." As a longtime HP public-relations director featured in a local editorial explained: "The HP environment is such that if you have a question, you pick up the phone and call the best person who could answer, no matter how high up they are" ("'HP Way' Changed the Valley" 2002:11).

Such media narratives contradicted pervasive representations of the dotcom boom and its competitive environment of perpetual work, in which workers, typically unattached young men without family responsibilities, labored toward the goal of an IPO. Similarly, my informants' comments about the HP Way, with its emphasis on civic responsibility and family-oriented values aimed to protect the interests of the "HP family," seemed at odds with the much repeated story line about the Valley's boom-time, "free-agent" environment, personified by risk-taking CEOs and carefree dot-commers obsessed with IPOs and e-commerce without loyalty to a particular workplace.

This alternative narrative became especially politically charged during 2002 and 2003, when the prospect of an HP-Compaq merger was endlessly analyzed in the local and national business press, and references to the HP Way and its apparent demise constituted a daily topic for local and national business columnists covering the merger. In retrospect, attention to how the HP Way was discussed in the press, in casual conversation, and during more formal interviews I conducted about issues related to the digital divide revealed that representations of the HP Way constituted more than a rehashing of Silicon Valley lore for old times' sake; instead, they amounted to a cultural critique, a reworking, via public nostalgia, of Silicon Valley's past, and a critical assessment of its present and future. Discussion of the HP Way in the local press offered competing visions of a Silicon Valley "culture" as a series of emotionally and morally charged binary oppositions that revealed much about local middle-class experience of the tech boom and the subsequent bust.

The Merger

In the fall of 2001 articles about a proposed merger between HP and Compaq began to appear on the front pages (see, e.g., Poletti and Ackerman 2001:1A, 12A). Advocates of the merger—the brainchild of HP's CEO at the time, Carly Fiorina, nationally famous as the highest-level female CEO in the country (Poletti 2002a:1A, 17A)—argued that it would give HP/Compaq the dominant market share in the personal computer, server, and printer business in America. As such, advocates argued that, for the price of $25 billion to be paid by HP, the newly joined corporation would sell two out of every three personal computers sold in the United States, thereby competing effectively against Sun Microsystems and Dell Computer. In 2001, as tech stocks fell in value, HP's stock was no exception. Fiorina argued that such radical action was needed to make HP competitive again.

This view was controversial among HP stockholders and board members, HP employees, the general public who paid attention to tech industry news, and, most symbolic, the Hewlett and Packard families, who held 18 percent of HP shares (the rest was held by institutional investors and individual stockholders) (Poletti and Ackerman 2001:1A, 12A). Fiorina claimed to admire Compaq's culture, approving of its quick decision-making processes, willingness to take risks, and refusal to rely on the past, which she and others contrasted to HP's more conservative business style. In this vein, she advocated that HP concentrate to a greater extent on technology "services" as opposed to stock-in-trade products such as its printer business. In contrast, Walter Hewlett, HP board member and eldest son of HP co-founder William Hewlett, opposed the merger, arguing that it was too risky, costly, and time-consuming, that more money should be invested in HP's successful printer business, and that the employee-friendly "HP Way" style of management had resulted in HP becoming Silicon Valley's biggest company (Poletti 2002b: 1A).

As the merger fight gained momentum in early 2002, just prior to the shareholder vote that decided the issue, the battle became more acrimonious, in no small part because of Fiorina's reputation as a manager who had actively undermined the HP Way since her arrival at the company in 1999. In a break with HP's past practice of reassigning employees to other business units within HP instead of laying them off, Fiorina did not shy away from the layoffs as a cost-cutting strategy. She had already laid off seven thousand employees in 2001 and promised another fifteen thousand layoffs should the merger she advocated succeed. Moreover, she did not consult regularly or mingle with HP's rank and file, a point often mentioned in news accounts and recounted to me by current and former HP employees. This break with the non-hierarchical and employee-centered management style associated with the HP Way was extremely unpopular with many employees as well as with the star protagonist in the anti-merger fight, Walter Hewlett.

In the weeks leading up to the merger vote, pro- and anti-merger forces bombarded individual shareholders and institutional investors with propaganda in a way reminiscent of a national presidential campaign, spending tens of millions on public relations, advertisements, trips to meet with investors, and legal fees (Bergstein 2002:10). Meanwhile, the story of the closely contested merger fight remained an ongoing nationally important business story in the mainstream media, and made headlines daily in Silicon Valley newspapers such as the *Palo Alto Daily News,* the *San Jose Mercury News,* and the Bay Area's *San Francisco Chronicle.* The event was treated like a Hollywood spectacle, and speculation abounded concerning the possibility of unrest at the actual vote (ibid.). Ultimately the vote over the merger resulted in a victory for the pro-merger advocates led by Carly Fiorina. HP merged with Compaq, Walter Hewlett lost his battle, and the layoff that followed exceeded Fiorina's initial estimate of fifteen thousand (Fordahl 2002b:10).

Nostalgia for a Bygone Era

The fiercely contested merger fight generated strong emotions on both sides. How did those who opposed it represent HP, and Silicon Valley's past and present? Less than two months after the HP merger vote and a day or two after the final judicial decision on the vote—which had been contested by Walter Hewlett—David Packard, Packard heir and owner of the local Stanford Theater, a popular, old-fashioned Palo Alto movie house that plays such classics as *Bringing Up Baby* and *Singing in the Rain,* took out a front-page ad in the *Palo Alto Daily News* that stated "Hewlett Packard, 1938–2002, R.I.P." In the print under this funereal announcement, Packard wrote:

> The Hewlett Packard Company was founded in 1938 in a garage on Addison Street only a few blocks from where you are now standing. Back then, the Stanford Theater was showing brand new movies . . . You can still see the same movies at the Stanford Theater. Our audiences know that they are truly timeless.
>
> The HP Way touched many people's lives. Most of us expected that it would last forever—that it would prove as timeless as a Frank Capra movie. But those entrusted with the duty to safeguard it have exercised their legal right to make another choice. *Dura lex, sed lex.* The law is harsh, but it is the law . . .
>
> For the sake of the surviving employees, of course, I hope for a good outcome. But it is hard to imagine that their leaders can invent something better than what they left behind. (*Palo Alto Daily News* 2002)

Such nostalgia suffused all the postmortem accounts of the merger in the press. A columnist for the *San Francisco Chronicle* who had covered HP for more than twenty-five years waxed on about senior management's particular habit of chatting with employees in the cafeteria or over coffee carts, or Packard's practice of "MBWA," (Management by Walking Around). The tone in all these articles was reverent, reminding readers that Hewlett and Packard were men who genuinely favored a meritocratic and more democratic approach to doing business; that they were people who understood that an innovative idea might be born in the lunch line in the course of conversation with an inspired "average Joe" employee. Dan Gillmor, a prominent columnist who wrote at the time about the Silicon Valley business world for the *San Jose Mercury News*, contrasted the HP past and present:

> In general, Fiorina and her senior colleagues inside HP and on the board have acted in ways that the senior Hewlett and his partner, David Packard, might well have rejected. They put a final, poisoned stake into the HP Way, the principle that respect for people and communities is essential to a long-lasting, profitable enterprise. They ended a Silicon Valley era. (Gillmor 2002a:11A).

In a more pointedly nostalgic article, Gillmor excused Fiorina, arguing that the HP Way had in fact been a "victim of its times." Silicon Valley, he claimed, "grew up on the example of William Hewlett and David Packard. Theirs was an era when *actual* innovation, *honest* hard work and concern beyond one's own immediate sphere were core to the corporate mission" (Gillmor 2002b:1F; emphasis added).

References to the "old days" held great emotional weight for the half-dozen or so current and former HP employees with whom I was able to conduct in-depth interviews. Kevin Samuels, a white middle-aged man living in Saratoga—an extremely affluent town on the Valley's "West Side"—was a former HP financial manager who had decamped to Cisco Systems in October 2000 after twelve years at HP. At the time of our interview in the spring of 2003, shortly before the vote on the HP merger, Kevin was working in investment relations with Cisco's CEO and president John Chambers and executive management, keeping them apprised of changes in the financial markets.

Sitting with Kevin in his living room which was dominated by a wide-screen TV and wall-sized entertainment system, I asked him why he had left HP:

> It had been about a year since Carly Fiorina had come, and I was already sensing some changes in the culture—we called it the "HP Way." I truly

believed that HP was an incredibly special place to work, and I literally loved the company. [But] . . . I had this realization, or decision I should say, that as much as I really liked or loved HP and its culture, that it was not going to stay that way . . . [HP] was a very nurturing culture . . . It's almost like there's a sense of family in that there's um, the people—you know, that I remember from HP . . . family values were very important to them and they brought their family values into work . . . it was a very comfortable place to work . . . I've been at Cisco now for a couple of years, and it's nothing like it was at HP.

Kevin's notion of the HP Way as a nurturing environment for its employees, much as a stable and ideal family nurtures its offspring, recurred throughout my interviews with current and former HP employees. Other HP employees with whom I spoke listed the company practices of permitting employees flexible working hours and regular family events, including an annual corporate camping trip for families, as evidence of this aspect of the HP Way.

Listening to people recount their fond memories of HP, one could easily forget that the subject at hand was a corporate workplace and instead feel that one was listening to a nostalgic narration over a family photo album. Over lunch Burt Wallace, a fortyish, white father of two who was unhappily working at HP in the post-merger era, summed up his fond memories of the "old" HP:

The HP Way meant people valuing you as a person—they care about you as well as the output of your work. People considered you more than just the guy there to get the job done. There were celebrations. There were beer busts. Beer busts were huge. They've disappeared, by the way. Every two to three months, kegs of beer and burgers. . . . You'd be socializing for four hours. . . . There was an annual barbecue picnic at Little Basin where HP has land, and you'd bring your family and there'd be a carnival—they'd have a dunk tank and managers—you'd get a guy who was a VP and your kid would hit the little target with a baseball and knock the manager into the water. The manager would be perched on a little chair. There were games for kids and crafts and a baseball game would be in progress. People would talk about it for weeks before it happened. Like, "Are you going?" These social activities used to make you feel that you were part of something—more than just the contract mentality.

Skepticism about the Present

In contrast to these halcyon days, Burt described his current position at the post-boom, post-merger HP as one that did not particularly thrill him.

I used to enjoy my job . . . My expectations have changed. I have other ways, other outlets to enjoy myself; coaching my kids' teams, volunteering at their schools. In a way I feel like I am stamping out the fiftieth part in something so big and so complex. I have no idea what the big picture is [in the data storage division of HP]. No one person has the overall picture of how things work and I feel like I'm doing this little piece of the puzzle.

Taylorized work had disassociated Burt from his position, but he felt trapped—caught needing a salary and knowing he would not find a comparable one elsewhere, and worried, too, that he might be about to get fired.

Burt attributed his circumstances to the style of entrepreneurship that had overtaken HP, now a place where "people are expendable . . . the whole social aspect has just disappeared." The changes Burt described made nostalgia for the "HP Way" poignant to HP employees, retirees, and onlookers. Current and former employees like Burt and Kevin emphasized the new, more autocratic, and even heartless managerial style at HP. Kevin said: "She [Carly Fiorina] got tougher and less concerned for employees. She has to lay off six thousand people? She just, you know, without a heartbeat, she just lays off six thousand people."

Occasionally talk about the heartlessness and imperiousness of the new managerial style at HP verged on a critique of entrepreneurial ethics at the post-merger HP. Kevin thought the merger made sense economically, but he believed that it had occurred to buy Carly Fiorina time to protect her job. She was, he noted, "under fire from investors." To be sure, Kevin did not classify HP as a "corrupt" organization: "Enron, Worldcom were just so blatantly corrupt. That would never happen at HP—even the new HP," he noted. And yet Kevin's use of "even" in this offhand comment reveals that he understood that the "new" HP dwelled in a murkier ethical terrain than the "old" HP. When I pushed him on this point, he elaborated that the "[new HP is] less conservative, more of a risk taker, and willing to 'push the envelope' [of accepted and ethical entrepreneurial practice]."

Sandy Greene, a white HP manager who, unlike Kevin, had stayed on at HP post-merger, went further:

I think before the merger, HP employees thought we were squeaky clean; we have internal audits, we have external audits . . . Also the culture at HP, if you thought something bad was going on, you felt pretty comfortable reporting that. Now it's interesting, some of the people who work in financial feel like Compaq books are kind of scary . . . I read a Wall Street analysis that says people think Carly might be presenting the books to make earnings look better than they really are. You know you hear that and you think, just how easy is it to do this, and to pull the wool over people's eyes. . . . I think people are hopeful that these are isolated incidents but in your gut you're thinking, you know, WorldCom: this is a reputable company. Enron was reputable, thousands of employees. It could happen pretty much anywhere. Especially in these times . . . Carly's desire [is] to be number one, but at what cost? Bill Hewlett and Dave Packard were such ethical, incredible individuals that gave back to the company, their lifestyles were not that of the rich and famous, but normal people, and people thought nothing like that could happen at HP. Just normal people, and everyone felt proud. Now we've got this aggressive, wants-to-be-number-one CEO . . . she comes on board, she's not driving an ugly car, she buys new jets, she doesn't walk around the cafeteria and talk to people. It's like, "Who is this person?" She's actually leading the lifestyle of many other CEOs in the country, but we weren't used to that. And then when Mike Capellas left . . . they paid fifteen million dollars to someone that didn't do anything for five months.

For Sandy and many others, Carly Fiorina personified a new model of entrepreneurship that was ostentatious, appearance-driven, heartless, and probably corrupt, one in which employees were to be disposed of without a second thought in order to a meet a bottom line. In contrast to Fiorina's champions, who depicted her as a pioneering and visionary female CEO, a brilliant risk taker able to steer Silicon Valley's most venerable company toward new vistas of productivity, her detractors represented her merger proposal as rash, ill-advised, and heartless, and a sign of her greediness, often invoking the $55.5 million pay package for top executives that HP (and Fiorina) approved as part of the merger deal (Quinn 2002d:1A, 18A). As a result of these stories, Fiorina came to be associated with the new way of doing business in Silicon Valley.

In contrast, the anti-merger faction stressed Walter Hewlett's ties to the founders, his concern for the long-term viability of the company, his championing of the rights of individual stockholders, and his compassion toward HP's employees. At the time of the merger vote, local papers reported the cheers that welcomed Walter Hewlett as a "rock star" and champion of the "little guy" at Cupertino's Flint Center, where the voting took place.

During the run-up to the merger vote, Fiorina's camp retaliated, representing the "old HP Way"—and Walter Hewlett—as ineffectual, staid, and uncompetitive. In one HP-sponsored advertisement, Walter Hewlett was described as a "musician and academic with no real business experience," a tag frequently reiterated in press narrations of the bitterly personal merger fight (Fordahl 2002a:8). Even in articles praising Hewlett this representation stuck. After Hewlett lost the fight, one journalist wrote, "The maverick can safely return to his classical music pursuits and academic cloister knowing that he made a difference" (Quinn 2002b:1A).

These dueling representations of Walter Hewlett and Carly Fiorina, produced during the economic downturn, when public criticism of corporate business ethics in the wake of numerous corporate scandals surrounding corporations like Enron and WorldCom was at a high, were charged with local and national meaning. The HP merger fight was presented as a moral choice and sign of the times. A columnist for the local and popular *Palo Alto Daily News* presented Silicon Valley's moral choice, encompassed in the merger fight, in the voice of Bill Krause, an older, former "HP man." Krause framed the choice as the "old way of doing business vs. the new, hurry up and go public" way. He is quoted in the article as saying: "You get out of down-turns like this by innovating your way out, not financially engineering your way out" (Nolan 2002:24).

This local critique paralleled and intertwined with a national class discourse framed around the issue of corporate greed and corruption. Frequently the local press eulogized the "HP Way" in relation to the corporate corruption scandals at Enron, WorldCom, and Anderson Consulting. Lamenting the passing of the "HP Way" as something bygone but still a "valid template for Silicon Valley, for America, for capitalism," Dan Gillmor (2002b) lambasted a "current generation [that] has defined a new American system [in] . . . a time when corruption, greed, and hype took over our financial and political systems . . . Oh, we're hearing lots of loud talk about honesty for the moment," Gillmor continued, "but Enron and its scheming cohorts are disgraced only because they failed so spectacularly and ripped off so many average people. Microsoft, ever contemptuous of law and truth, is still widely admired." Gillmor went on to rail against campaign finance laws, political leaders who could be bought cheaply, accounting professionals, self-rewarding CEOs, and "ventriloquist-dummy securities analysts."

Thus the merger discourse was tinged with middle-class populism linking "New Economy" entrepreneurialism to shallowness, greed, and corruption.

Despite his position as board member and heir to the Hewlett fortune, Walter Hewlett was portrayed in the *San Jose Mercury News* as striking "a blow for corporate democracy" by contesting a corporate decision made without consideration for employees or shareholders (Herhold 2002:1C, 6C; see, too, Quinn 2002a:1A). Supporters of Hewlett against the merger were dubbed "fleas," pitted against pro-merger "elephants" (ibid.), a tag many, including HP employees who had traveled from France to protest the possible loss of their jobs, assumed proudly.

Local Discontent

Dan Gillmor's comment about *honest* hard work, *actual* innovation, and corporate leaders who care about the broader world and other people reflected a bitterness toward the "new entrepreneurial" way of doing business that was expressed in manifold ways by many educated, middle-class people I met who had had nothing to do with HP, from nonprofit professionals and older high-tech professionals to the parents of students at Sanders High School. Presenting an alternative vision to Po Bronson's dot-com–era celebration of "Venture Trippers," columnists such as Gillmor and some of the tech professionals I met invoked a tried-and-true regional tradition of *actual* technical innovation, often denigrating e-commerce as vapid and lacking a "real" product. Others, from service workers to teachers to tech professionals, complained about the shallowness, self-centeredness, and heartlessness of a new order manned by powerful, youthful, and extremely wealthy people who expected everything to be done quickly. For example, a socially conscious teacher I met at Sanders High School who previously had been a well-off venture capitalist—recalled the social transformation of the Valley during the boom:

> We saw it in people's egos, the way people were treated, the traffic, the pace, it was a sense of frenzy that was pretty unattractive. Everybody was getting rich, a lot of people were getting rich, but a lot of basic human courtesies were put by the side. So from that standpoint I'm glad the boom's over, because it has caused a lot of people to be humbled and I think this place is a better place to live as a result.

Ambivalence and hostility toward the dot-com invasion of Silicon Valley was, in fact, so on the minds of the local, professional middle class that it cropped up in conversations about unrelated topics. During one such conversation with Jim Fast, the older consultant and former HP and 3-Com employee who exposed me to 3-Com's efforts to deal with the digital divide, he could hardly contain his distaste. Like the director of the center for non-profit support who commented, in an interview, that "the dot-coms" had "changed the ethos" in Silicon Valley, Jim deplored the "start-up mentality" of the Valley's boom, describing it as a selfish state of mind wherein issues of community involvement and low-income people were "not part of the picture." He stated:

> The feeling [of the "start-up mentality"] is "We are here, we have a mission to build our products, and be successful, and we also provide jobs." You have multimillionaires in their twenties in the past few years, and then you also have United Way in Silicon Valley going bankrupt. You see the out-of-touch-ness with the United Way situation happening during the boom . . . This was the Internet culture in particular.

On another occasion, Jim sounded both incredulous and irritated at the audacity of young people, "the dot-commers" who, "fresh out of college, want a quick job for the summer resume—no experience!"

The sense of the dot-com era as a soul-crushing one in Silicon Valley's history was also manifest in numerous off-the-cuff descriptions and remarks about the lifestyle of the dot-commers. For instance, such a tone pervaded the account of interviewee Steve Martinez, a Chicano and former bar owner and event producer involved in San Jose's civic and social affairs. Steve recalled San Jose in the early and mid-1990s, prior to the doc-com era, as an idyllic time when "creative" people—"thirty-five-year-old urban punk-rock fans who are graphic designers, artisans, retail people"—lived in and social-ized in the city's downtown. He dated the change in clientele to 1997, when the local crowd had to move out because of real estate prices or, alternately, joined start-ups and hence had no leisure time to spend at bars or clubs. "We all lost our audience, rents went up, and there were no jobs outside the tech industry. People [the pre-boom clientele of the early and mid-1990s] moved to LA [Los Angeles] and New York City . . . The focus on the tech world just subsumed everyone." Steve ultimately was evicted and lost his bar; he then developed a business putting on corporate Christmas parties for tech firms, where, he said bitingly, "at midnight, people expect to be drunk and dancing to 'Brick House.'"

In a similar vein, longtime homeowners in Palo Alto, who had benefited from the local real-estate boom associated with the tech boom, complained to me of watching the aesthetic trial of "Taco Bells" and "McMansions" being put up by new, young, rich next-door neighbors, and they balked that all the parking spaces were being consumed by their new neighbors' SUVs. Similarly, they closely followed the emerging "hot issue" of preserving Palo Alto's historic houses, a backlash against the new construction that was erasing an older and less ostentatious architectural era.

A Cultural Politics of Class and Age

As Silicon Valley's established professional middle class watched their neighborhoods assume a new identity and saw their workplaces transformed by a new set of corporate values and imperatives while witnessing at close range the meteoric rise in fortune of an emergent, young "New Economy" business class, they pined for an alternative version of the Silicon Valley myth. The version of that myth that they had in mind was one in which "community" was part of the calculus of corporations; employees were not only not expendable, they were "family," and any quiet and unglamorous engineer with a good idea might revolutionize industry with, as Dan Gillmor (2002b) put it, "actual innovation and hard work." This nostalgia and cultural critique depended upon a mythologized Silicon Valley past in which hard work, entrepreneurial and scientific brilliance, and a willingness to take risks melded with the supposedly more humane values of this earlier time.

With its mourning for a more innocent time in the Valley's past, public discussion of the HP-Compaq merger battle comprised one idiom through which Silicon Valley's established professional middle class could express anxiety about the disappearance of a perceived social contract—albeit a private-sector one—aimed at predominantly white, educated, middle-class professionals. This social contract enshrined a morality and form of capitalist practice and lifestyle that my middle-class informants and the local media felt had perpetuated their own stability and engendered steady, rule-bound upward mobility. A few HP employees commented to me approvingly that "Bill and Dave" and their surrogates used to say that as an employee at HP one would not get rich overnight, but one could look forward to a lifetime of family-friendly financial security and steady gains in income as well as rewarding work.

As suggested by Michael Lewis's and Po Bronson's descriptions of the "free agent" worker and Jim Fast's bitter comment about "fresh out of college" kids expecting good jobs with "no experience," a bitterness about ageism informs this nostalgic "cultural politics of class" (Rouse 1995). The moral value that the press and people I spoke with placed on steadiness, experience, and quality innovation was aimed at the young rich, who were represented as shallow and lacking in ideas, experience, and taste; the locally ubiquitous dichotomy of the baby-faced dot-commer versus the older engineer or the hip, forty-something marketing guru Carly Fiorina versus graying, conservative Walter Hewlett symbolized the decline of an aged established professional middle class and its domination by a youthful, rapacious elite better suited to market competition.

Such age-related resentment was, in fact, based on a social and economic reality: older high-tech workers in Silicon Valley and the nation endured a disadvantage in the job market during both the tech boom and the subsequent downturn (Lardner 1998:39, 45; see also Steen 2002:1A, 14A). In fact, U.S. Equal Employment Opportunity Commission reports citing a sharp rise in age discrimination complaints among California workers in 2002, and a 17 percent jump nationally since 2007,[5] lend credence to recent mainstream press articles suggesting that "experience" has apparently become too closely associated with age, and employers fear older workers will be unwilling to work late hours, may demand more compensation, and may not exhibit flexibility and agility in learning new things.

"Plugging Along" and Existing "On the Edge"

Recollections I heard about the period of the tech boom conveyed not just ambivalence toward the boom but also feelings of insecurity and anxiety that underlay the class-sensitive cultural politics of nostalgia and resentment I have described. As Kevin, the former HP employee who moved to Cisco, described that period:

> There was a fear of being left behind . . . I felt stupid. I didn't get it . . . I still have that same feeling of how did it happen? How did the, you know, the irrationality just take hold? The pace was frenetic. All the people that I worked with, they were all very intelligent smart people. But I'm just very curious. How did it happen that, you know, even though I worked in the marketing side, I was involved in the selling of money, what I did was very financially driven, It was you know, in finance, they call it valuation theory, which is, you know, how do you value things? And there are, you know, tried and true methods for valuation that have been around for years and years. And all of those were just being thrown out the window. And the typical mantra at the time was, "Well, you know, this is a new age" kind

of thing—"the old models just don't work anymore" . . . and it's just funny, everybody bought into it. I mean, I didn't really buy into it, but I didn't object to it.

At this point in our interview, I said, "Well maybe also it was that it was so hyped, and there were so many reports in the media of people getting rich overnight." Kevin responded with passion to this suggestion, and described the feelings of HP employees such as himself during the boom:

> You're very right. There were stories about how everybody's getting rich. I remember one of the things that led up to me ultimately making the decision to go to Cisco, was that, there was an article in the *Merc* at that time that said one in eight Cisco employees was a millionaire. And you know, it's a big company. And I'm thinking, one in eight Cisco employees is a *millionaire* [said incredulously and dramatically]? Well, I'm not a millionaire here [at HP]! He laughs out loud. Yeah, there was a group-think that was going on, and I was definitely following it . . .
>
> I definitely felt [we were missing out]. There would be open comments about "We've missed the first wave of the Internet as a company. We've missed it." And we felt like companies like Sun Micro were integrated into the Web, the Internet boom, and companies like Cisco were leading the boom. Yeah, we definitely felt behind the curve, very much so.

Sandy Greene similarly described the mix of excitement, tension, and anxiety during the boom:

> At work it was kind of like an unreal period of time . . . It was like people you knew—the risk takers—were leaving a company like HP and they'd go work for some dot-com because of the stock options, and they were going to be millionaires in a year . . . A lot of people would talk about this—this is not real, this can't be true, things just don't happen like this. But it was happening! I actually knew someone who hit it big. You know, within a year he was a millionaire.

> E.D.: The people that you knew that struck it big, or had a jump in their personal finances, to what did they attribute that?
> S.G.: Being at the right place at the right time, and being willing to take a risk, you know, leaving a company they'd worked for fifteen years, they got out of the high-tech rat race and got in with a start-up. I have a friend who

was working for a start-up making medical equipment. Got a great offer and was promised the world, and the company supposedly had funding, and boom, things started diving, laid off, with nothing . . . she kept asking me to leave HP and come work for the start-up, and I kept saying, no, no, no, I've got a family . . .

E.D.: So was risk taking a high status thing to do?

S.G.: Oh yeah, people were flaunting it. There was a sense that you're gonna be left behind, that people that took the risk and they thought they were gonna make it big, they thought they were going to be retiring in five years, while the rest of us are sort of plugging away.

In the above exchange, Sandy tacks between recounting the boom as a period when people "hit it big" and a more jaundiced view, noting that the boom was short-lived and describing the circumstances of a friend who risked stability—and lost. This cautionary tale seemed to hold a moral for Sandy, validating her path after she had endured the social pressures of a moral hierarchy that placed "risk takers" in a higher status than people in her position, who were seen at the time as just "plugging away" or, as another employee put it, "conservative."

During 2003, when I spoke to these current and former HP employees, ambivalence toward the value of risk taking and anxiety about being seen as "plugging away" or "conservative," had been replaced with a straightforward yearning for security. Burt Wallace confided:

Nobody's safe. I call it the "Vietnam Syndrome," the idea that somewhere out there there's a bullet with your name on it. I worry about it sometimes . . . This is the most anxiety I've ever had. Things were bad in '84' and '89 and '91 [he refers here to cyclical economic downturns that have shaped Silicon Valley's tech sector], but this has been such a long time and you start to wonder if there's a structural change here . . . I worry that [my sons] won't be able to have as good a lifestyle as we have now, have the opportunities that we have.

Sandy Greene felt the same way. As we wound up our discussion, she said, "There was never the uncertainty that there is today. It just seems like the last two years, you just kind of feel like you're on the edge all the time."

What do these recollections of the boom and bust reveal? Silicon Valley's established professional middle class felt extremely ambivalent about the boom, and the "new entrepreneurial" orientation toward work and security. While critical of the era's mentality in hindsight, they recalled their own and others' excitement and enthusiasm for the culture of risk and the prospect of overnight wealth, as well as a feeling of being unable to keep up, stigmatized as "left behind," "plugging away," or "missing the boat." Such phrases convey a slowness and a lack of competitiveness and, by extension, a lack of productivity. They signal an awareness among these middle-class professionals of the stigma associated with desiring security and regular work hours, and, as such, they recall Emily Martin's point about the cultural link between an optimized mania (the opposite of measured stability) and productivity (2009:191). It is no wonder that HP employees vividly remembered their own self-perceptions and self-consciousness about how others saw them at the time; within the "new entrepreneurial" public culture, desire for stability and a tendency to be "conservative" in one's decision making were seen as character deficits that impeded productivity, competitiveness, and innovation.

Intergenerational Angst

How might we relate middle-class adult anxiety about being perceived as risk-averse and "behind the curve" to styles of self-definition and aspiration management among middle-class youth at Sanders High School? The figure of the slow worker, plugging away and unable to take advantage of opportunities, closely resembles that of the coming-of-age "slacker" who wastes time and doesn't do what is required to succeed. Both these figures embody middle-class insecurity and feelings of inadequacy in the face of an increasingly competitive environment. As we have seen, such insecurity has multiple causes. The presence of a young, new, and risk-inclined entrepreneurial elite changing the world of work and overturning old rules of corporate conduct to the disadvantage of the middle class has been made that much more unnerving by the globalization of highly skilled tech work, the consolidation of wealth by an elite at the national scale, shifting demographics and disinvestments in public education, and a rising cost of living that makes it difficult for many middle-class families to stay in Silicon Valley. These forces have put pressure on middle-class adults and youth alike to adapt to competitive conditions, whether the context is a highly regarded public high school or a corporate workplace in which the desire for stability has become a sign of weakness, slowness, and, implicitly, a lack of productive potential.

The Politics of Distraction

And yet, for middle-class adults, internalization of "new entrepreneurial" values, manifest in self-consciousness about a desire for stability and boom-time admiration for risk takers, did not preclude the figure of the new entrepreneur serving as an object of distrust. People I spoke with and press reports I read critiquing the new entrepreneurial class focused on the overwhelming and expanded power of high-tech elites to shape corporate and community outcomes that affected middle-class professionals. The local established professional middle class was acutely aware of the elite power behind contemporary social and economic transformations that have meant new bottom lines, a new expendability, a new politics of age and experience, and even a new consumerist aesthetic shaping everyday life in Silicon Valley. Thus, although the ideal worker-self dominating Silicon Valley's boom-time social imaginary shaped middle-class self-perceptions and prompted a tendency to measure one's actions and accomplishments against those of an emergent tech elite, an awareness and critique of broader, structural social and economic shifts beyond the level of the individual meant that interpretations of success and failure were not entirely personalized. Historical contingencies—shifts in market forces, entrepreneurial practices and values, and corporate corruption—competed with character traits as an explanation for current circumstances. People simultaneously identified with and dismissed the ideal style of conduct defining Silicon Valley's social imaginary.

These contradictory interpretations of events and experiences suggest cracks in the smooth façade of the Silicon Valley entrepreneurial myth; middle-class Valley adults whom I met remained faithful to a more nuanced and communitarian idea of self and place than that represented by Po Bronson or others writing hagiographic accounts of the traits of industry titans or young wealthy entrepreneurs. But despite awareness of larger structural issues that contradicted the myth of a techno-meritocracy, this story demonstrates that middle-class anxiety and frustrations often resulted in nostalgia and resentment that simply fueled everyday grudges against the lifestyle and ethos of younger professionals felt to be usurping an older, middle-class order. As such, nostalgia for an idealized Silicon Valley's past amounted to a distraction that dissuaded the region's middle-class professionals from consciously confronting the broader economic and political shifts that have caused their loss of privilege and security. In the long run, lamenting a loss of stability and accepting it as a relic of the past, and criticizing the lifestyle and priorities of an emergent class of elites, cannot offer the kinds of rewards that might be had, for example, by forging political alliances with people of diverse class, racial, and ethnic backgrounds to protect social and economic rights and privileges (e.g., pensions and high-quality public education) that are fast disappearing at the hands of an increasingly powerful elite.[6] Through such coalition building, Silicon Valley's middle class might find itself innovating its way toward a different future, one in which the state maintains a commitment to the social welfare of its subjects and mercurial corporate largesse does not serve as the only buffer against insecurity.[7]

Stymied: The Entrapment of Middle-Class Adults and Youth

This adult politics of nostalgia represents not just a distraction, but a sense of entrapment and political paralysis. Collectively, public and private accounts of the merger and the bygone era of the HP Way, and the self-assessments and boom-time recollections of HP workers and other middle-class residents, portray a group of people stymied by their circumstances, insecure about their ability to match the success of some in their midst, prone to understanding success and failure in terms of personal qualities, and striving to measure up. And yet simultaneously the established professional middle class that we have encountered was aware of the structural mechanisms behind its threatened social and economic status.

In this way they resembled some of their adolescent counterparts at Sanders High School. As we have seen, such youth feared becoming slackers, and strove to excel in multiple realms. And yet at times, conscious of their role in broader social and economic processes, students stepped back from their daily grind and, casting a critical eye, found the perpetual quest for academic and social status phony, shallow, and inauthentic. They especially took issue with the materialism—literally in the case of consumption habits and figuratively in the case of underlying motivations for good grades—inherent in the pressured quest for status. This critique of rampant materialism at Sanders echoes adult middle-class discourse about a shallow, profit-driven elite that spent too much money and had little regard for authentic innovation or the futures of middle class professionals. Indeed, for at least some Sanders students, the ideal of conduct opposing what they considered a "phony" materialism lay in cultivating oneself as a true "free agent," one whose desires were not purely market-driven—a trait that was also a virtue, one might note, for those who lamented the passing of the HP Way.

Recalling the stories of Sanders youth and reading them against those of the adults we have just encountered, we can appreciate the pitch of middle-class anxiety in Silicon Valley. Young people felt this collective mood of insecurity and entrapment and had, perhaps to a larger extent than their parents' generation, internalized the emergent competitive orientation. There was something of the "Venture Tripper" in students' passion for work, degree of self-discipline, and aspirations, and there was also a fear, like that experienced by local middle-class adults, of falling behind, of going nowhere as others raced ahead. And in their quest for authenticity, there was also an echo of adult ambivalence toward an idealized neoliberal subject whose aspirations, disposition, and style of self-discipline were so defined by the market.

IV

Conclusion

A Flexible Politics of Citizenship

Old Patterns, New Burdens, and
the Space of Contradiction

Although the aim of this book has not been to represent the familiar as exotic—a common effect of ethnographies of "home," and a difficult task when the place in question is as overexposed as Silicon Valley—this exploration of young people's aspirations and the surrounding politics of class and social reproduction in Silicon Valley calls into question now commonsensical representations of a regional "culture" and of the people that inhabit the region.

In the case of this ethnography, the familiar involves my own personal history, an experiential backdrop to this research that has made me particularly attuned to contradictions between the glossy surface of twenty-first-century Silicon Valley and the realities of living, working, learning, and coming of age there for working and middle-class families. Recognizing this experiential disjuncture has made me think of Silicon Valley's public culture as not just a meaningless mystification but as a politically productive social imaginary. Although superficial representations of a "successful" region and populace that define the dominant public culture of Silicon Valley do not adequately represent the social and symbolic milieu of the region for people inhabiting its discrete life-worlds, such "selective representations," and the disciplinary practices and attitudes that I have argued are associated with them, serve particular political functions.

The preceding pages have explored the ways in which morally charged representations of techno-entrepreneurial practices, values, and economic success have explicitly shaped the aspirations of some of the Valley's middle-class youth and provided a model of self-discipline and success for many others; affected formative experiences of educational pedagogy and discipline for low-income, at-risk youth; and served as the idiom through which particular public-service institutions and educational environments engage the pressure for neoliberal reforms. But, as we have seen among working- and middle-class people, experience with and exposure to the region's dominant public culture does not amount to a code of self-conduct and values to be simply imitated, admired, or envied; experiences of social and ideological contradictions may give rise to unpredictable forms of subject formation as well as skepticism toward elite accounts of the power of techno-entrepreneurship to transform lives and bank accounts.

This exploration of how working- and middle-class young people and adults in Silicon Valley negotiate both a dominant public culture and a fast-changing political-economic and social context began with the question of how the social and political spaces of school and community shape young people's aspirations, motivations, and actions. But linking the aspirations of young people to the local context has comprised only a part of this analytic project. I have also linked the milieus of school and community inhabited by the young people and adults who participated in my study to regional, national, and global political-economic conditions and ideological forces that have divided Silicon Valley communities and educational contexts hierarchically along lines of class, race, and ethnicity. In so doing, I have explored how such forces, which often contradict dominant representations of Silicon Valley and the people who live there, defined meanings associated with social inclusion and exclusion that, in turn, influenced the actions and aspirations of local youth and adults.

This analytical perspective is, perhaps, best summed up through example. I have interpreted jokes about citizenship at Morton High School, for instance, or critical commentary about the plague of conformity afflicting peers at Sanders High School, in relation to a variety of historical experiences and configurations of power. These include daily experiences of discipline at school and on the street related to the phenomenon of increased surveillance of youth of color within gentrifying urban environments (Davis 1990; Smith 1996; Cahill 2006; Lipman 2003; Brown 2003); the criminalization of youth in the urban United States (Lipman 2003; Nolan and Anyon 2004); the migration of working-class immigrants with little formal education from Mexico to Silicon Valley since the 1980s (Rouse 1992); the demonization of immigrants in the United States in the post-9/11, neoliberal era (Perez 2009; Chavez 2008); the mantle of parentally imposed economic and social responsibilities in both Valley communities where I conducted research; the erosion of middle-class Americans' status (Ehrenreich 1989; Heiman 2009); the effects of intensifying globalization on highly skilled tech workers (Hayes 1989; Benner 2002; Wadhwa et al. 2007); and the emergence of national and global discourses about at-risk youth in the 1980s and 1990s (Cieslik and Pollock 2002; Kelly 2001; Stephens 1992).

The processes of aspiration formation that comprise this book's central focus involve negotiation of these and other historical forces and experiences, many of which stem from the application of neoliberal ideas to policy making, as in the case of a national educational reform that took shape in the 1980s or the "revitalization" of San Jose, California, during the 1990s. Indeed, as we have seen, the models of personal success that my informants were exposed to and the policies that transformed young people's and adults' learning and working environments reflect the neoliberal priorities of individual responsibility and privatization. But as is made clear by the skeptical attitudes of Silicon Valley's public-school teachers and other social-service workers—or by the daily school experience for Biotechnology Academy students at Morton—ideological messages in tune with a neoliberal agenda may not be effective with audiences struggling with difficult political-economic and institutional conditions created as a result of neoliberal thinking and policy making, or with young people whose daily life experiences make particular ideals of success and values seem out of touch and meaningless, even selfish or phony.

This book has addressed the question of the extent to which affluent and low-income immigrant youth, as well as different class fractions of Silicon Valley's middle classes, from public-sector workers to established tech professionals, internalized, ignored, or rejected models of self-cultivation and norms of personal success to which they were exposed within schools and workplaces, and within the public culture and civic space of Silicon Valley. Thus far we have linked patterns of aspiration and the inscription and maintenance of class identities to dynamics of neoliberal governance and globalization in various ways. But by comparing the divergent educational contexts of Morton and Sanders high schools, as well as the patterns of aspiration, self-perception, and modes of self-discipline that we have encountered, we can place these school sites and student experiences within a common theoretical framework, one that links students' experiences of schooling and their strategies of aspiration management to a contemporary American process of citizenship formation. This dynamic of citizenship has reconfigured the state's relationship to its citizenry as the globalization of labor and capital has intensified (Mitchell 2003; Maurer and Perry 2003; Ong 1999; Gordon 1991). And as the case studies we have considered make clear, it has framed personal responsibility and success in strikingly different—and yet related—ways across lines of race, class, and ethnicity, and within divergent educational settings.

At the same time, in revisiting the educational contexts and aspirations of students in Morton's Biotech Academy and at Sanders, we can call into question the "success" of this flexible process of citizenship formation, which depends upon a form of neoliberal governmentality that would produce subjects completely oriented toward neoliberal values and priorities. Conversely, we can reject overly simplistic and romantic notions of "resistance" to such forms of subjectification and, drawing on earlier ethnographies of class identification through schooling and aspiration, place the everyday lives and aspirations of Morton and Sanders youth, and the political and economic realities they confront, in historical context.

Our exploration of patterns of subjectification and agency necessarily involves a consideration of the role of experiences of social and ideological contradictions in processes of subject formation, a theme that calls us back in this book's final pages to the broader social contexts of adults discussed in chapters 4 and 5, and to the power, and potential mutability, of the symbols of exclusion and belonging that loomed large in the lives of the youth and adults whose stories and circumstances are represented here (inevitably, given the subjective aspect of ethnography, in a partial way).

Differences within a Larger Commonality: Flexible Neoliberalism and Working- and Middle-Class High School Students in Silicon Valley

While the Biotech Academy at Morton High School ostensibly prepared Academy participants to seek careers in the field of biotechnology, this goal was, in fact, underscored by a more profound objective: to cultivate a desire to learn about science and technology and to learn the habits, attitudes, and social skills necessary to compete in the local information economy at various levels depending upon academic aptitude. The program sought to awaken in students a sense of new kinds of potential and an awareness of new paths, modeled by the mentors assigned to each student during the student's second (junior) year in the program.

The implication of this approach was that if students worked hard and assumed the right attitude—dressed for success, learned the subject matter, developed a genuine interest in local industry and in the "science of life," as many Biotech students learned to describe biotechnology—they might, in essence, improve themselves, effectively taking control of their own destinies and shaking the status of being at risk, a racialized and gendered identity associated with particular imaginings of academic, moral, and economic failure such as dropping out of school or attending "UC Evergreen," succumbing to the temptations of a morally questionable milieu and joining a gang or getting pregnant. Academy youth—and their parents, some of whom mentioned to me their concerns about malevolent influences and gangs in their San Jose neighborhood—were thus reminded of their own potential as free young people in the process of developing a new set of intellectual and social proclivities and aspirations to be exercised in a broader world beyond the realm of family and immediate neighborhood.

And yet, as we have seen, the students at Biotech were also subject to other forms of discipline and to an alternative educational ideology different from the program goals of the Academy. Despite celebrations of the students' diverse cultural backgrounds, and alongside a feeling of close-knit camaraderie fostered by both students and teachers affiliated with the Academy, its students learned that they were young people who required policing, strict discipline, and micro-management. This was made clear to them via the hall monitoring by their teachers, the school dress code, a campus emphasis on their own at-risk status, the presence of police looking for signs of delinquency on the route home from school, and a temporal and academic environment affected by the phenomenon of "teaching to the test." Following school rules and cultivating the skills and desires stressed in the Academy warded off an implicit threat, voiced in off-hand jokes and sarcastic quips, and whispered sometimes tearfully during an interview, of economic and social marginalization along predictable lines of race, class, and gender.

By contrast, Sanders High School seemed to exist in a parallel universe. Its students were encouraged to explore themselves and a cosmopolitan world in an atmosphere of relative freedom. This freedom, however, had a pragmatic purpose. As evinced in the valedictorian's address discussed earlier, Sanders students learned to cultivate individual passions and talents, and simultaneously to excel in a wide variety of areas. Moreover, they learned to display their excellence, the subtleties of their reasoning, and the deep passion that they brought to their pursuits. According to some students and parents with whom I spoke and my own observations on campus and during interviews, students who did not employ the freedom they were granted to excel academically and to cultivate at least one grand and authentic artistic, athletic, scientific, or social talent were relegated to the margins of the school community or, if not marginalized, "lost in the shuffle." To paraphrase one parent, "[Sanders] doesn't do average well."

The environments of Morton and Sanders were thus, in quite different ways, contradictory places both ideologically and in daily practice. Students in each school were confronted with conflicting expectations and were encouraged to cultivate attitudes and disciplines that often contradicted one another. And as examples of student self-perceptions and aspirations revealed, students within these disparate social and educational environments registered and responded to the contradictory forms of self-discipline and attitudes with which they were encouraged to identify in complex and often unanticipated ways.

As we saw, both seemingly contradictory forms of regulation to which Academy students were subject—the more overtly authoritarian discipline of the school at large and the Academy ideology focused on personal potential and enthusiasm for biotechnology and experimental thinking—reflected, in effect, the neoliberal objective of transforming students into managers of their own risk. And yet these students ultimately reinterpreted models of citizenship to which they were exposed in politically ambiguous ways. Their lack of engagement with Silicon Valley notions of success and individual advancement in favor of a deeply felt obligation to "give back" to the community or nation through careers as soldiers, social workers, teachers, or probation officers simultaneously represented an internalization of the policing of their communities and themselves that they had observed and experienced, an internalization of an obligation of personal responsibility for an at-risk status, and an alternatively more community-oriented and public-embracing vision of their futures than that offered by the Academy's techno-entrepreneurial curriculum.

In contrast, the Sanders school environment not only fostered a sense of class entitlement—in contrast to the sense of obligation to manage risk on the part of the Morton students—but encouraged students to prize, above all, authenticity and freedom of the self, values that were manifest in students' often quirky or precisely specified career aspirations. Unfortunately, as demonstrated by Sanders students' split loyalties and self-perceptions, social and economic circumstances meant that this freedom actually represented a form of regulation; self-expression was at once empowering and disciplining, as it was inextricably linked to socioeconomic pressure to market oneself as a certain kind of young person. Although some students seemed unfazed by this instrumentalization of freedom and authenticity, and seemed to enjoy their particular niche within the school's stylistically heterogeneous social landscape, others expressed alienation and resentment at the normative crafting of a creative and productive self calibrated in relation to an ideal of "well-rounded" excellence. Still others simply registered the stress of the demands placed on them by striving to be successful in these terms. Hard-won and outstanding grades, forms of self-medication, sleepless nights, worries about not being able to conform to expectations and at the same time feeling self-consciousness about doing just that (thus diluting one's authenticity), and the specter of a future at a second- or third-rate college made up part of the laundry list of daily anxieties and tasks for many Sanders students I met.

Understood comparatively, these ethnographic findings provoke multiple, valid interpretations. My data from both schools may be interpreted as simply ethnographic evidence of the reproduction of class and racial hierarchies that are central to contemporary capitalist formation within contemporary educational institutions. For example, evidence suggesting that working-class Latino youth at Morton experienced a more regulated and authoritarian environment and identified with careers involved in the policing of populations deemed at risk, or that middle-class and predominantly white and Asian youth at Sanders enjoyed an atmosphere of relative freedom that promoted dispositions toward individualism and creativity useful in managerial positions, supports the findings of many scholars who have argued that schooling reproduces inequalities of class and race necessary to capitalist formations (see, for example, Aronowitz 1973; Bowles and Gintis 1976; and Sieber 1976).

This observation begs the question of gender. Did schooling at Morton and Sanders reproduce inequalities of gender that serve contemporary capitalist formations? Student patterns of aspiration at both schools suggest that much has changed in terms of gender role norms in the past thirty years; young women in the Academy aspired to be probation officers and young men social workers, and young women at Sanders aspired to be physicists and engineers as well as filmmakers. However, traditional and "post-feminist" constructions of gender played a role in producing particular kinds of class and racial identification at Morton and Sanders, respectively. At Morton, constructions of risk were gendered as well as racialized (e.g., the stereotype of the pregnant Latina who drops out of high school), and at Sanders strategies of self-cultivation that played with a "New Economy" ideal of the risk taker implicitly expressed racial privilege[1] and were gendered as well, as sexiness represented one way to define oneself as a self-determining, free-thinking, "well-rounded" person (e.g., "she's smart, creative, going to Harvard, socially successful, *and* fearlessly sexy"). Thus one might say that, at Morton, racialized and traditional constructions of at-risk girlhood might have contributed to a desire among young women to prove their capacity to flexibly accommodate school rules and display reliability and the potential for productivity, whereas, at Sanders, a construction of women as both sexy and powerful resonated with individualist leadership qualities prized in the postindustrial elite managerial class. In other words, meanings of gender served the broader political and economic project of habituating workers and differentiating them to meet the labor demands of a hierarchical, competitive global economy.

More specifically, however, our focus on how students participated in reproducing social hierarchies through their attitudes and aspirations echoes a particular aspect of Paul Willis's (1977) argument in *Learning to Labor* concerning young people's interactive responses to school and community environments, and the ways in which they encourage forms of identification that effectively reproduce class hierarchy. In particular, Academy students' aspirations to pursue careers in public and community service, including military service, and their skepticism toward the goal of individual advancement within the region's tech private sector recalls an observation Willis makes about working-class "lads" coming of age in a Fordist industrial economy: their community-oriented identification and solidarity with one another and with a set of working-class values and beliefs (associations, for example, of manual work with manliness and manliness with whiteness), and their expressed disaffection for a pathway toward professional, middle-class employment.[2] Although the cultural values of Latino youth in Silicon Valley in no way resemble the "lads" identification with a racialized masculinity—after all, Academy students, occupying a racially stigmatized group in a postindustrial context, contended with a strikingly different political-economic regime, different experiences of social exclusion, and different disciplines and expectations—the fact of Academy students' lack of engagement with a middle-class ideology of individual advancement and their publicly oriented ethos highlights continuities between industrial-era and postindustrial processes of class identification and social reproduction.

This connection between 1970s industrial Britain and contemporary Silicon Valley is not, as the North American ethnographic record on schooling, urban environment, and social reproduction attests, a fluke. The phenomenon of alienation from the goal of individual advancement toward middle-class status and the related formation of an alternative sense of working-class collectivity are central themes in two hallmark ethnographies of social reproduction in a de-industrializing urban United States: Mercer Sullivan's *Getting Paid* (1989) and Jay MacLeod's *Ain't No Makin' It* (2009 [1987]). In Sullivan's *Getting Paid*, an ethnographic response to arguments about individual pathology and youth crime, working-class Latino, African American, and white youth engage in criminal activity and call it "getting paid," an ironic and bitter commentary on the inaccessibility of gainful employment for youth.[3] Indeed, "getting paid" is reflective of a larger pattern of negative reciprocity and strategic sharing shaped by political-economic conditions. Like sharing, which has served as an effective means of coping with scarcity among poor people, it constitutes a social practice that goes against the grain of the normative American ideal of individual advancement (e.g., Stack 1975, Susser 1982). MacLeod (2009 [1987]) makes a similar point: working-class white "hallway hangers" attending high school in a down-and-out northeastern city rebel against an ideology of individual advancement which labels them failures, preferring instead the camaraderie of peers who do not apply themselves in school, "hang out," often abusing drugs and alcohol, and define themselves via a virulent racism as well a hyper-macho masculinity.

In contrast to Latino youth in the Biotechnology Academy, Sullivan's text concerns youth crime in relation to structural conditions confronting Latino, African American, and white urban communities, and MacLeod's white "hallway hangers" do not expressly articulate a desire to serve the common good, to "give back." Nonetheless, reading these ethnographies and Paul Willis's *Learning to Labour* (1977) against my own findings in Silicon Valley, one might conclude that little has changed in the past thirty years in terms of the ways that experiences of social and economic exclusion promote arguably oppositional stances toward the premium placed upon individualized forms of advancement or, as mentioned earlier, the ways that young people engage school and community environments such that they actively reproduce class and racial hierarchies.

And yet reading these ethnographies together simultaneously highlights shifts that have occurred in the past thirty years in terms of the kinds of costs and risks to youth now associated with particular patterns of aspiration, and in terms of the relationship of youth, their communities and schools to contemporary processes of citizenship formation which, in turn, shape processes of social reproduction. This last shift points to a second interpretation of my data, one that concerns the neoliberal rationality of rule to which students are subject, and how it intersects with economic processes that have transformed the function of nation-states within the global economy. In accordance with the logic of neoliberalism, working and middle-class young people are now being encouraged within such state institutions as public schools to tailor themselves to the needs of the global economy and to assume the burden of risk for social and economic insecurities associated with intensifying competition and the disintegration of a social contract that once guaranteed working- and middle-class youth differential and unequal forms of stability and status.

As political theorists such as Nikolas Rose (1996) and Graham Burchell (1996) have argued (following Foucault's discussion of governmentality) and anthropologists such as Emily Martin (1994) and Aihwa Ong (1999) have ethnographically demonstrated, globalized and flexible regimes of accumulation have emerged in conjunction with new (neoliberal) rationalities of rule that, in the course of creating opportunities for the production of new (neoliberal) subjectivities, have transformed the state's relationship to its citizenry in numerous countries in the West. What is the goal of neoliberal governmentality? Burchell sums it up succinctly:

> The generalization of an "enterprise form" to all forms of conduct—to the conduct of organizations hitherto seen as being non-economic, to the conduct of government, and to the conduct of individuals themselves—constitutes the essential characteristic of this style of government: the promotion of an enterprise culture. (Burchell 1996:29)

The disciplining of individuals, as Nikolas Rose points out, is a central technique of this form of governance:

> The enhancement of the powers of the client as customer—consumer of health services, of education, of training, of transport—specifies the subjects of rule in a new way: as active individuals seeking to "enterprise themselves," to maximize their quality of life through choice, according their life a meaning and value to the extent that it can be rationalized as the outcome of the choices made. (Rose 1996:57)

These two observations make clear that neoliberal governance aims to ensure that the state's goals become synonymous with the individual's goals. This overlap assumes that individual citizens will play a more active role in state making, "enterprising" themselves in the name of personal freedom and freedom of choice (Rose 1999), and thereby assisting with the neoliberal state's emphasis on economizing wherever and whenever possible by shifting the burden for social and economic security onto individual citizens.

The public educational system in the United States has provided an ideal venue for encouraging forms of subjectivity that advance the interests of a neoliberal state that requires flexible workers who are wholly responsible for themselves as well as the interests of global capital.[4] For example, geographer

Katharyne Mitchell (2003) explores how, under conditions of neoliberalism, preoccupation with the competitive conditions of the global marketplace plays a key role in determining modes of subject formation in public schools in Canada, the United States, and the United Kingdom. Posing the question of how contemporary conditions of transnationalism shape processes of citizenship formation, Mitchell argues that school systems that once emphasized a tolerant multiculturalist ethos designed to unify diverse nations and promote a Fordist regime of accumulation worldwide now stress the creation of student-citizens who are "strategic cosmopolitans."[5] Forged within neoliberal school environments that emphasize a "more individuated, mobile and highly tracked, skills-based" educational experience, strategic cosmopolitans ideally learn to "excel in ever transforming situations of global competition, either as workers, managers, or entrepreneurs" (Mitchell 2003:387–388). Thus the strategic cosmopolitan is a flexible subject-position, a "globally oriented state subject" that can be adapted to suit the imperatives of a hierarchical global labor market that requires both workers and managers.

Mitchell frames her notion of the strategic cosmopolitan in relation to an earlier construction of the "multicultural self" within public schools in the West, a Fordist-era subject position which she argues has gradually become associated with the weakening of academic "excellence" within the public educational system in the United States that began during the 1980s and solidified with the increasing emphasis on accountability and "excellence" during the 1990s. This conflation of multiculturalism with failure, she suggests, has created an educational climate in the contemporary United States in which pedagogical emphasis on multiculturalism and an appreciation of difference and inequalities within society have come to be seen as holding children back. From this ideological perspective, low achievement can only be eradicated through the inculcation of certain normative "cultural values" of academic "excellence" that effectively ignore difference and downplay certain forms of democratic literacy, such as multiculturalism. The ideal subject-citizen/strategic cosmopolitan thus acquires skills and aspirations most in demand within the global economy; he or she does not waste time acquiring forms of democratic literacy that champions of neoliberal school reform view as actual impediments to acquiring the "complex skills" necessary for individual success in the global economy (Mitchell 2003:399) and that, one might imagine, could potentially engender demand for particular kinds of rights and services and forms of social equality guaranteed by a nation-state.

Mitchell's ideal argument about the creation of a strategic cosmopolitan citizen/subject within public schools in the West is particularly relevant because, whereas most, although not all (see Ong 1999, 2003, for example), arguments about neoliberal subject formation tend to focus on working-class subject formation,[6] the strategic cosmopolitan Mitchell describes might belong to the working class or middle class or even upper-middle class, depending upon the student body of the school and the particular needs of the hierarchical global labor market. This flexible conception of a contemporary ideal citizen-subject links the environments of Morton and Sanders to each other. Indeed, the data I collected about school environments and students' experiences and aspirations afford an opportunity to explore the relevance of Mitchell's schema in a Californian context, examining the extent to which—if at all—the flexible subject-citizen ideal Mitchell describes was promoted and, to varying extents, realized at each school site.

Morton, the Biotechnology Academy, and the "Strategic Cosmopolitan"

As we have seen, Morton's Biotechnology Academy sought to cultivate students' identification with the needs of the regional and global informational economy, particularly within the field of biotechnology. Moreover, students were ideally supposed to cultivate both skills and attitudes that would prepare them for work at a number of levels within a corporation specializing in biotechnology. Through mentorship, field trips, and visits to local corporate campuses, students were encouraged to learn to *desire* this kind of work and lifestyle, and to familiarize themselves with the SCANS skills needed to participate in the regional techno-entrepreneurial "culture" from which their own families were, in almost all cases, excluded. In other words, the basic message of the Biotechnology Academy was, as Mitchell suggests, to "just acquire these cultural values and skills [by acquiring the normative attitudes, and academic and social skills useful in the field of biotechnology and in techno-entrepreneurial organizations] . . . and you will meet with individual success within the globalized and competitive regional economy."

Furthermore, the program presented the acquisition of these skills and values—the act of becoming a strategic cosmopolitan—as a way out of the at-risk status saddling the mostly low-income, immigrant youth in the program. This emphasis was significant in that it shaped the kind of strategic cosmopolitan that Biotech students were encouraged to become. In traveling the great experiential distance between program, community, and family, students at Morton learned the primacy that their teachers, school administrators, and mentors placed on the capacity to assimilate and adapt to middle-class styles of communicating, learning, and aspiring, modeled within the Biotech Academy by the biotech professionals affiliated with the Academy, and by the teachers and staff at Morton. Within the Academy, students understood that, as at-risk youth, they were expected to assimilate and adapt to the (dominant) worldview emphasized within the Academy. This emphasis on assimilation, on a flexible remaking of one's presentation style, skills, mode of communication, and desires, does not suggest the kind of "global subject" that manages a Fortune 500 company. Rather, it suggests a lower-echelon strategic cosmopolitan, a worker whose sense of social debt might result in suitability for less autonomous, less mobile, less managerial and yet highly flexible work, or might make the military appealing on both an emotive and economic level.

What does the actual pattern of aspiration management we have observed for Academy students tell us about the applicability of Mitchell's strategic cosmopolitan schema to the Biotech Academy and to Morton High School? As noted, the career aspirations of Biotech students did not reflect an affinity for the specific strategic cosmopolitan model with which students were encouraged to identify in the Academy, namely, that of the flexible worker attuned to the needs of industry, who was enthusiastic about biotechnology and entrepreneurship and looked forward to individual advancement in the globalized information economy. To the contrary, the disciplined and highly regulated environment of the school and neighborhood, and experiences of social and economic exclusion as well as mentorship and concerned monitoring, reinforced students' identities as at-risk young people and encouraged a sense of obligation to society to manage their own risk and to display reliability. In turn, this sensibility was manifest in the pattern of aspiration and lack of interest in techno-entrepreneurial work and values that we observed in Academy students.

Two other aspects of Mitchell's strategic cosmopolitan schema are also relevant to the pattern of aspiration that we saw within the Academy. As mentioned, Mitchell argued that multiculturalism as a goal of American education has waned, replaced by a neoliberal model of competitive excellence in the era of No Child Left Behind. Citing the recent introduction of patriotism legislation in numerous states, and the reemergence around the country of the Pledge of Allegiance, she also suggests that a component of the new strategic cosmopolitanism is its emphasis on making patriotism a part of school practice. As Mitchell puts it,

The new strategic cosmopolitanism serves as a nodal agent in the expanding networks of the global economy. He or she is the new superior foot soldier of global capitalism . . . heretofore crucial narratives of global coherence [have been] supplanted by narratives of individual patriotism. (Mitchell 2003:400)

Contrary to Mitchell's representation of contemporary American public schools as places where an emphasis on multiculturalism has been supplanted by the neoliberal prioritization of "excellence" and competition, at Morton I found that an emphasis on multicultural selfhood and community coexisted with an emphasis on "excellence" and accountability, and preparing students for work within a twenty-first-century global economy. This multicultural ethos combined with experiences of bodily discipline signaling students' at-risk status and of mentorship and sustained attention from teachers to shape a lack of identification with techno-entrepreneurial work and the goal of individual advancement within the corporate world. Morton students learned that their ethnic identity was stigmatized but also that it was a personal asset, and a quality that made them part of the larger fabric of the community and nation. They understood Cesar Chavez, who was frequently evoked at the school, to be a *national* hero, a Mexican American leader and model citizen who contributed to and improved the larger U.S. society. Moreover, this multiculturalist nationalism intertwined with a school-wide emphasis on patriotism and nation, manifest in the daily Pledge of Allegiance and the spotlessly uniformed ROTC recruits dotting the campus on certain days of the week at lunchtime.[7] Hence, the atmosphere of multiculturalism along with an emphasis on patriotism at Morton encouraged students to celebrate their heritage but also to associate it with the nation and with national duty. At the same time, they learned that they should contribute to the larger society as flexible, competitively oriented workers.

Thus, within the contradictory contexts of the highly regulated environment of Morton and the techno-entrepreneurially oriented Academy, students learned to be strategic cosmopolitans primed to become flexible workers oriented toward the demands of global economic competition and to equate personal success with assimilation and personal responsibility for their own at-risk status. As we have seen, however, in rejecting the goal of assimilating to a dominant model of selfhood defined by techno-entrepreneurial success, and identifying with a more community-oriented ideal of selfhood, these young people reframed their experiences in ways that were at once significant and immediately empowering to them. Moreover, their pattern of aspiration was potentially politically significant; their positive associations with public and collective work for the benefit of the community—whether the community in question comprised the multicultural nation, the military, poor Latinos, or at-risk youth in need of services—and their awareness of race and class oppression disposed them toward a more communal vision of the purpose of social institutions and citizenship, a form of idealism that might encourage students to work to transform the institutions and communities in which they could ultimately work. In other words, students' aspirations at Morton not only reflected a politics of personal responsibility; they also reflected a politics of collective responsibility to a broader community.

At Sanders another kind of idealized citizen-subject was promoted, and this ideal, together with students' daily experiences of school and community, engendered a very different pattern of aspiration and self-definition.

Sanders and the Strategic Cosmopolitan

Whether sprawled on the campus lawn, engaged in classroom discussion, or standing on the graduation stage, Sanders students expressed themselves in bold ways. Moreover, as we saw, they applauded diversity of all kinds, whether the issue was ethnic diversity, sexual orientation, or the particular tastes of classmates different than themselves. This celebration of diversity also constituted a celebration of the global. Their cultural references, whether they were in the classroom making jokes about child labor and the Nike corporation or discussing summer vacations and career aspirations, were quintessentially cosmopolitan. At the same time, as we saw earlier, Sanders students' talk of free, creative expression and the free environment of the school was belied by their evident stress at having to work constantly (the lack of sleep, the need for weekend obliteration, and for some, the careful, productivity-oriented self-medication in which some recreationally indulged or were encouraged to take by parents worried about test scores and grades), the ways in which they transformed interests into competitive advantages, and complaints about their own and others' acts of conformity to the pressure to succeed academically and socially. Young people at Sanders delighted in the opportunity to explore themselves and the world, and to excel in their work and devotion to particular passions and at the same time felt compelled to market these same passions, to advertise their well-roundedness. Whether working or playing, they seemed to be almost always "on." Thus their actions and utterances were implicitly pragmatic.

This careful marketing of an authentic and productive self offers a stark example of the "entrepreneurialization" of the self that Rose and Burchell describe as a fundamental goal of neoliberal governmentality. Talk of the importance of "well-roundedness," then, resembled a well-meaning but guilty tic on the part of school administrators and parents, signaling their awareness that their young people had been denied self-fulfillment for its own sake and, instead, experienced self-fulfillment and the obligation to find a niche within a competitive global economy as one and the same thing.

Indeed, Sanders students' forms of self-discipline and self-expression expressly recall Mitchell's conception of strategic cosmopolitanism. But what particular kind of strategic cosmopolitan does a school like Sanders end up promoting? In conceptualizing the ideal neoliberal subject, the strategic cosmopolitan, Mitchell draws upon a recent essay by geographer Susan Roberts concerning the "truth effects" of discourses of globalization. Roberts explores how globalization discourses generally render places, institutions, and people in reactive terms in opposition to "global managers" and global corporations, subjects portrayed as "shapers of world space" (Roberts 2003:3). The playing field of the "global manager," a global state subject that Roberts tells us is in the process of being carefully defined and indeed idolized within American business schools and corporations, is the world (ibid.:4). He or she is a "supercapitalist, *unfettered by a sense of responsibility* [my emphasis]" who celebrates difference and diversity and avoids making non-strategic and provincial cultural gaffes. In the words of Thomas P. Gerrity, once a dean of the Wharton School,

> What is truly needed is broad-gauged leaders. These are individuals who can discuss the nuts and bolts of operations with an employee on the line and a few hours later talk corporate strategy with the board of directors. They can review European marketing plans over breakfast in Paris and hold their own with a product design team in Chicago over dinner. They have simultaneously mastered the art and the science, the detail and the big picture, the local culture and the global context. They are true "renaissance leaders." (Gerrity 1998; quoted in Roberts 2003:21)

This "key subject in the "discursive constellation of globalization" has particular qualities that are strikingly reminiscent of what I observed at Sanders High School (Roberts 2003:4). I am not claiming that Sanders students were being explicitly groomed for the position of "global manager" within global corporations (although a number of Sanders parents would surely welcome such an outcome). Nevertheless, the qualities of this ideal subject, an architect of reality who appears unfettered by responsibility but possesses enormous amounts of it, who displays global cosmopolitan knowledge and simultaneously precise expertise, and who celebrates diversity while working terribly hard and with great passion, profoundly resemble the qualities and the unfettered attitude that Sanders students displayed and strove to attain. Their pursuit of intellectual and creative passions, their use of physical space, and even the female students' cultivated "sexy" look that signaled not just attractiveness but daring, freedom, and self-determination all represent a style of self-presentation and self-discipline that create an external appearance and internal perception of personal freedom and a refusal, at once libertine and individualist, to adhere to someone else's rules.

Thus, in viewing Morton and Sanders through the lens of how each school shapes the production of citizens, it is clear that the different forms of strategic cosmopolitanism encouraged at each school reflect the flexibility of a school-based project of citizenship formation that, in order to suit the imperatives of a hierarchical global economy, encourages appropriate styles of self-cultivation and self-definition depending on context. The model of strategic cosmopolitanism accommodates equally well students' experiences of race and class privilege or disadvantage, and it can also assimilate divergent school and community environments shaped by dynamics of race, class, and ethnic segregation and inequality. This flexible politics of citizenship, in effect, shifts the burden for social and economic status and risk onto youth, whether the youth in question are low-income Latinos considered at risk or affluent white and Asian youth. In other words, these case studies provide evidence for the argument that public schooling is now a venue for the promotion of *responsible* citizenship, an expression of neoliberal governmentality that encourages youth, as malleable citizens-in-the-making and key national symbols of potentiality, to craft identities that are oriented toward the interests of global capital and that compensate for state disinvestments in aspects of social reproduction by privatizing responsibility for it. This political move is accomplished through the association of youth with risk in racially and class-specific ways; for Academy youth deemed at risk, risk is something that happens to you and that you are responsible for. In contrast, Sanders youth, who also confront social and economic risk but are not deemed at risk, have been socialized to think of risk as something that they have the capacity to control. For them, risk taking is often a strategic and sanctioned act.[8]

The project of promoting responsible citizenship seems to have been achieved at Morton and Sanders; students' strategies of aspiration management and their styles of self-definition reflect a politics of personal responsibility—at Morton, responsibility for both at-risk selves and a broader community, and at Sanders, responsibility for threatened personal and familial status. And yet students' self-perceptions and career aspirations at each school attest to the fact that the neoliberal goal of producing citizens who are enterprising in ways that suit the dictates of the global economy and facilitate the state's reduction of services and shedding of responsibility for risk—and see such acts of self-cultivation as self-enhancing—was achieved in unpredictable ways. As John Clarke, a scholar of social policy, has noted, "new subjects," Clarke contends, "do not always come when they are called. Indeed, they might not hear the call, they might not recognize themselves as its subject, or they might just answer back in a different voice" (Clarke 2003:211).

Resistance or Subjugation? The Politics of Aspiration

What are the political implications of the forms of responsible citizenship, manifest in students' aspirations and modes of self-definition, with which Morton and Sanders youth identified? In considering the ways in which both groups of young people drew upon various representations of themselves and models of success to frame their experience and aspirations, we can draw conclusions about the extent to which the patterns of aspiration management we saw in each school context represent expressions of resistance or subjugation. At the same time we will highlight the fact that subjective worlds often do not directly reflect objective conditions, as in the case of the Latino youth at Morton's Biotechnology Academy.[9]

Let us revisit the case of Armando, the Biotechnology Academy student whose enthusiastic decision to join the Marines we explored earlier. As suggested, Armando's preference for a career as a Marine and his rejection or at least deferral of interest in a career as a biotechnology professional can be read as a rejection of the private sector and, in particular, of the goal of individual personal advancement in favor of a more communal sense of obligation. Rather than viewing this rejection as an act of resistance, I interpreted it as a lack of engagement with the goal of individual advancement, and a lack of identification with the aspirations and style of conduct common to the professional classes of the regional information economy. Many Academy students were essentially indifferent to this strategy of risk management;

they could not relate to their corporate mentors, to the narratives of personal advancement that they heard from guest speakers, or to the goal of pursuing high-tech professional work. Those falling into this camp included students like Armando who, on the surface, expressed great enthusiasm for the program and for the study of biotechnology but did not envision taking the educational and professional steps to pursue such a career path. Such students did not overtly resist the paradigm of selfhood represented by the Silicon Valley professionals with which they were encouraged to identify; they either did not recognize themselves in it or were simply drawn to more compelling options.

And why did Armando find the Marines to be a compelling choice? In addition to the economic benefits of the Marine Corps as a way to attend college, we can recall that Armando described his decision as one that would afford him the psychological fortitude and confidence to make it in the broader world. He said he wanted to join the Marines to experience an ordeal that would build his self-confidence and his skills, and he linked this goal to the benefit of not ending up like members of his family and community, whom he spoke of with a mixture of love and distaste. Put another way, Armando sought to ward off the potentially contagious at-risk status of his brothers and the economic precariousness of his family and simultaneously prepare for work in the global economy by shoring up his confidence and participating in what he understood to be a larger, common good.

In sum, Armando framed his identification with the Marine Corps in terms that stand in sharp contrast to a key element of a neoliberal ethos: the superiority of the private sector (in this case, a much mythologized regional information economy private sector that he was encouraged to embrace within the Academy). And yet he equated self-fulfillment with personal responsibility for his own at-risk status and his successful participation within the globalized and competitive labor market.

Armando's explanation suggests that it would be inaccurate to represent his chosen path as an act of resistance (against the grain of private-sector ideals) or as an example of passive subjugation in the face of economic need. Students like Armando learned two strategies of assuming responsibility for an at-risk status within Morton and the Biotech Academy. They mimicked the language of self-help and self-fulfillment as well as the narratives of personal potential that they heard in the Academy while at the same time identifying as at-risk youth in need of authoritarian discipline and accepting the associated obligation to society and their own immediate community to police themselves and others considered at risk. Moreover, some explained their career aspirations in terms of a Civil Rights–era idiom of uplift, drawing upon history lessons learned in social studies classes and their own observations of parents working multiple jobs, marginalized from the dominant society. Recall, for example, Armando's vivid recollections of his parents' oppression as workers performing back-breaking labor, Katreena's explicit mention of the Civil Rights movement, and other Biotech students' comments about helping their own at-risk, low-income, Latino community by "giving back" in some way.

In this process of expressing and rationalizing their aspirations, Morton students were, in effect, inventing new possibilities for themselves in relation to forms of discipline and oppressive representations of themselves that shaped their everyday experiences and self-perceptions. The reference to civil rights and allusions to the hardships of poor people of color are significant: drawing upon aspects of Morton's environment and everyday experience as people marginalized in relation to the dominant society, these young people's definition of themselves as connected—and indebted—to a larger community reframed experiences of stigmatization and thereby addressed a lack of confidence owing partly to daily disciplines and stigma associated with being at risk, experiences of racism, and their families' socioeconomic status. Such acts of self-definition also afforded students a sense of autonomy from a dominant society from which they felt marginalized, while augmenting their self-confidence and reframing their experience in terms of their own choosing. These students were aware of the perils associated with a lack of confidence; not surprisingly, given the neoliberal emphasis on self-improvement and self-transformation in institutions serving poor people (Goldstein 2001, Lyon-Callo 2000), self-esteem was a key concept stressed in school, especially for girls (Latina young women I knew in the Academy were summoned from class weekly to attend a group designed to boost their self-esteem). Students in Morton's Biotech Academy ultimately accommodated the expectation they encountered in school to assume responsibility for their own at-risk status by signaling their ability to transcend social, economic risk and insecurity through acts of self-discipline and aspiration, and the assumption of particular values and skills. At the same time they envisioned and articulated futures for themselves that satisfied immediate personal and psychological needs. Moreover, the prospect of a future in which they would "give back" provided for some a meaningful sense that one day they would be able to meet the obligation they felt toward their own disenfranchised community.[10]

Such gratifications, however, represent a subjective negotiation of objective conditions. For regardless of how Academy students perceived themselves, the realization of their aspirations will very possibly recapitulate familiar patterns of social reproduction; by opting out of the professional, private-sector information economy workforce from the start, such youth stand to compound extant dynamics of racial and class-based social exclusion. In contrast, by maintaining their style of self-cultivation and pursuing their aspirations, middle-class youth may likely acquire professional employment either within the local tech sector or within other professional and creative service-sector industries.

Further, the aspiration to "give back" will, if realized through the acquisition of public-sector careers in the "helping professions," police work, or military service, collide with new political, social, and economic realities to expose youth to new kinds of risks and burdens. Key elements of the current social and economic context that shape the aspirations of Academy youth include the pervasive presence of military recruiters and a large ROTC presence at Morton, a phenomenon linked to the new imperial ventures of the early twenty-first century, and the narrowing of opportunities for poor youth of color (Perez 2008, 2009); the persistent exclusion of Latinos from professional-level work in a globalized, innovation-oriented regional information economy (Pitti 2003) and their increasing presence within an expanding low-wage, service-sector economy with little opportunity for either security or advancement; a school system subject to federal accountability rules (as dictated by the 2001 No Child Left Behind Act) and increasingly influenced by private-sector money and ideas; a gentrifying urban/regional landscape in which intense surveillance of youth of color takes place in a broader context of prison expansion (Gilmore 2007); and a national and state context that, at times, demonizes Latino immigrants.[11] Significantly, these conditions exist in a political climate defined by the politics of personal responsibility[12] and disinvestments in social reproduction, which, as Cindi Katz (2002) has pointed out, have occurred globally in the last thirty years.[13] They determine the impact of the choices young people make as they attempt to realize their aspirations.

To sum up the situation for Academy youth coming of age in post-millennial, postindustrial Silicon Valley, not only was there no factory to follow one's father into—as there was for Willis's "lads," who grew up in a traditionally industrial English Midlands city of the 1970s, a place with relatively low unemployment where national and multinational corporations provided most factory work (Willis 1977:5), there existed new forms of discipline and expectations associated with a contemporary neoliberal paradigm of personal responsibility and discipline, and an atmosphere of intensifying authoritarianism and anti-immigrant sentiment consistent with neoconservative governing principles (Maskovsky and Susser 2009). The political atmosphere confronting Academy youth—at the micro level at school and, more broadly, within the state of California and the nation—recalls Gina Perez's (2008, 2009) recent analysis of Latino young people's experience of ROTC programs in Chicago. As Perez points out, for the poor Latino youth she interviewed, ROTC, one of the few federally funded programs providing opportunities for educational advancement for poor youth in a national context of social services cutbacks, made students feel respected and responsible, a "vehicle for inclusion" in a moment of "nativist hostility" (Perez 2009:43).

In reality, such historical conditions not only shape aspirations, they combine with them in ways that might entail increased economic and social risks for youth, not to mention outright danger. I refer here to students' professed interest in employment monitoring at-risk communities (promoting community security but within the context of a country that disproportionately incarcerates working-class communities of color), teaching in public schools or working as a social worker (occupations currently subject to massive layoffs and state budget cuts in California), and military service overseas in a context of escalating American militarism and authoritarianism in the post–9/11 era (Steinmetz 2003). With respect to this last possibility, it is notable that military service comprises one strategy of "responsibilization" for an "at-risk" status that is steadily available to poor youth. Thus, one might view Academy youths' own acts of interpretation and aspiration management as forms of identification that exposed them to new risks and promoted extant patterns of social reproduction but that also neutralized experiences of inequality and engendered a sense of collective identity and a publicly oriented ethos that strikingly contrasted with the dominant, local public culture. Indeed, as we observed earlier, it suggests the possibility that young people who want to "give back" through public service may eventually act to reframe the purpose and practice of public-service institutions in ways that benefit disenfranchised and marginalized groups within the society—a situation that, at the very least, suggests innovative and potentially transformative responses to subjugating forces.

As for Sanders students, how might we read the political implications of their pattern of aspiration? Did they define themselves and their futures in ways that were, at least to some extent, autonomous from the expectations of school and community? As we saw, they faced pressures from competing desires to be authentic, passionate individuals and to excel and "fit in," thereby ensuring successful futures. Their pattern of judging their own and others' actions and styles as either conformist and "trying too hard" (materialistic) or nonconformist and authentic signaled the existential tension they felt as a result of social and economic pressure to "stand out" and excel socially and economically while cultivating a creatively, intellectually, and socially self-fulfilling existence. The fear of conforming or being too materialistic was thus simultaneously a fear of not maintaining status or "making it," and a fear of not fulfilling an obligation to one's inner, authentic, individualized self. Not surprisingly, students tended to represent their own family backgrounds or passions as "marginal" (and thus more authentic) in some way; such evidence of marginality signaled a fear of being excluded and at the same time served as a kind of selling point.

In sum, the act of learning to market oneself corresponded to an intensified awareness of an "inner" state, resulting in a kind of double-consciousness among students. As we saw earlier, the young people I met at Sanders reported experiencing this tension—and revealed signs of this dual consciousness—to varying degrees, and the career aspirations, self-perceptions, and judgments of others that they expressed indicated a range of possible outcomes in adulthood. Indeed, a few, especially those from less elite socioeconomic backgrounds, seemed hyper-aware of the perils of conformity and cognizant of the marketing of a fake authenticity to serve the conformist goal of accruing social and economic status. Recall, for example, Eric's sarcastic humor about his fellow students: "Let's all be different together." Or the recognition by Evelyn, the stage tech, that the school administration offered little encouragement for kinds of authentic talent that were not competitively displayed and her admiration for the artist friend who exhibited little desire to play the game of using her artistic talent to get into a good college. Hence one might suggest that students like Eric and Evelyn rebelled against the fusing of personal self-fulfillment with the aims of the global marketplace. While internalizing the value placed on authenticity, they rejected the pragmatic, market orientation of the strategic cosmopolitan, preferring instead a more countercultural style of cosmopolitanism.

Evelyn's and Eric's attitudes, which constitute a kind of rebellion against the normative pressures of school and community, did not, however, represent the general pattern of self—and school—perception that I observed at Sanders. More often than not I witnessed the paradoxical reality of students who delighted in the environment of free expression at the school, and who expressed aspirations defined by creative or intellectual passions, but who privately talked of stress, exhaustion, burnout, and private tutors; recalled peers whose parents/ lobbied for an ADD or ADHD status to ensure better test scores; and told tales of "working and playing hard" that sounded more like "working and working hard."

Students' ways of representing themselves, and their performative moments inside and outside class, also signaled the psychic toll of the pressures they faced to excel academically and socially to ensure a status similar to that of their families or, in some cases, better. To watch Sanders students in class was at times like watching an overly self-conscious actor on stage, aware of his or her performance, anticipating the response of the viewer, and calibrating the performance accordingly. The nuanced and at times self-deprecating comments of students (Q: "Where did your father go to school?" A: "Nowhere significant.") seemed designed to prove to an audience of classmates or to me during an interview or perhaps most of all to themselves that they had mastered the art of nuance and subtlety and calculated self-deprecation, that they understood the ideological contradictions inherent in their school environment and the intricacies of the vast and diverse world and their relative place in it. Such displays, like talk of grades or one's family's economic status, seemed at once a show of sophistication and a sign of a paralyzing hyper–self-awareness, as well as a signal of anxiety.

In sum, students at Sanders seemed to be perpetually enacting strategies of self-marketing in order to remain competitive in the eyes of peers, family members, the community, and the out-of-sight but all-powerful college admissions staffs. Their moments of invention seemed often to be co-opted as a result of the pressures confronting them.

In light of my findings at Sanders, it is worth reconsidering the structural critiques of social reproduction through education that were made in the 1960s and 1970s, as the experience of these students indicates a shift in the educational circumstances and experience of middle-class youth. Initially, in describing my data about middle-class youth to people while still in the field, I seemed essentially to be echoing the now commonsensical observations of scholars of social reproduction and schooling who demonstrated the differential tracking of middle- and working-class children, and the tendency of public school systems to promote greater creativity and freedom among middle-class children. However, the pressure to self-market and the manifestations of that pressure among youth I met at Sanders—a social phenomenon notably absent in earlier accounts of the school as a vehicle of social reproduction—suggest that middle-class youth in the contemporary United States must contend with much more than the benefits of a public educational system that encourages them to explore their individuality and creativity, with the implicit aim of developing the leadership skills that facilitate the acquisition of high-status managerial positions. Although the encouragement of creativity and a focus on the self, as opposed to obeying orders, have remained the norm for such youth just as they were in the 1970s (Sieber 1976), this process of subject formation now entails a new urgency and competitiveness. It involves the highly pragmatic construction of unique, individualized identities that represent a marketable excellence and authenticity in order to compete—a form of self-crafting that occupies youth and outstrips by far the consumption strategies and exercise regimens of the adult yuppies so trenchantly described in Ehrenreich's *Fear of Falling* (1989).

Indeed, the work of self-cultivation required for the construction of such a self reflects the kind of perpetual effort and display of passion that, as Emily Martin (2009) has suggested, characterizes the manic style of an emergent ideal subject that is shaping middle-class subjectivity in the contemporary United States and, as we have seen, overshadowing adult middle-class self-perceptions in Silicon Valley. Although many of these young people relished their school life and flourished in an atmosphere devoted to free expression, the task of cultivating themselves, ironically, colonized their "downtime." It encouraged a preponderance of psychic tolls, from depression to a kind of insecure and self-deprecating second-guessing of the self. These effects offer evidence of the burden of assuming personal responsibility for profound and rapid social and economic change.

Such consequences imply, moreover, that the current experience of increased economic vulnerability among relatively privileged people has, if anything, intensified the kind of "hyper-vigilance" that has gradually been transforming the experience of middle-class childhood in the United States since the 1970s (Katz 2001). The cultural project of marketing young people's identities into various niches, which involves the careful performances on the part of the young described above, can be understood as of a piece with the emergence of new technologies of child surveillance (Katz 2001, 2008). Such hyper-vigilance, from "nanny cams" trained on the very young to college counselors helping high school students concoct marketable identities for colleges and ultimately for a secure place within the global economy, reflects the reality that, in order to maintain middle-class status, new forms of self and household regulation are required as opposed to engaging with the broader society via a social contract at the nation-state level (Katz 2004:2–4). Put simply, for the established, professional middle class, getting and staying ahead involves the construction of more and more narrowly specified identities that require ever greater degrees of self-monitoring. In its retreat into private interiors, this strategy of social reproduction mirrors the transformation of the private space of the home into a mini-state of surveillance monitoring every action of the privileged young (Katz 2001, 2008).

This phenomenon of hyper-vigilance transforming the coming of age of affluent and educated, professional middle-class Americans places in perspective the tendency among Sanders students to doubt themselves and to be self-deprecating, as evinced in their speech patterns and their carefully nuanced self-representations crafted during hours of both work and play. Are Sanders students youthful exemplars of the psychic effects of a politics of hyper-vigilance? And, if so, what are the long-term effects of such a form of governance?

The Space of Contradiction

As is evident from our reading of Sanders and Morton students' responses to the kinds of citizen-subjects they were encouraged to become, even though conditions at each school clearly reinforced class hierarchies and entitlements, Morton students felt comfortable managing their aspirations in ways that drew selectively upon the contradictory ideals of conduct to which they were exposed. They articulated futures for themselves that revealed a sense of autonomy from at least some of the expectations of the local and dominant public culture with which they were encouraged to identify, even if the distance they achieved was partly motivated by a lack of confidence stemming from experiences of social and economic marginalization and stigmatizing forms of discipline at school and within the neighborhood. Ironically, despite inequalities of race, class, and ethnicity, the stigma of being labeled "at risk," and the far more regulated school environment, the comments and actions of Academy students generally suggested that they felt less hemmed in by ideals of success in their midst, less compromised, and less haunted by self-doubt, self-deprecation, and self-criticism than Sanders students did. Also unlike Sanders students, the students at Morton's Academy appeared to enjoy a sense of autonomy and a lack of anxiety or self-consciousness about their aspirations.

In contrast, despite the relatively free environment at Sanders and the pleasure students there felt over their particular passions and the freedoms they enjoyed, Sanders students expressed a greater sense of social entrapment.[14] They were also less able than Morton students to reframe feelings of doubt or insecurity in the process of thinking through their future paths in life. How might this be explained?

The answer lies in the degree and kind of social contradictions each group of young people experienced. Biotech students at Morton had to reconcile conflicting approaches to the neoliberal imperative of personalized risk management. They also had to negotiate an experiential disjuncture between family life and school. Thus every day they juggled contradictory ways of looking at the world. These contradictions and the students' identity as at-risk youth from an at-risk community afforded them a kind of critical distance and communal identity: teachers did not necessarily agree with parents; the pedagogy stressing personal improvement through exposure to techno-entrepreneurial practices, themes, and values of creative exploration and innovation might be contradicted ten minutes later by the highly regulated school environment; and both overt and more subtle forms of discipline emphasized their "otherness" and identity outside the dominant society.

Sanders students' families and the community at large, in contrast, echoed values and practices encouraged within the school environment. Thus most students' daily home and school environments were not in contradiction with each other; these students therefore lacked an external vantage point from which to view their own situations; they simply felt social and economic pressure to achieve the same kinds of distinctions from all directions. And, as we saw, those who felt less entrapped or were more conscious of their entrapment—perhaps a first step toward an authentic personal freedom more detached from the "strategic cosmopolitan" subject position—tended to be those whose families occupied more economically and socially marginal positions within the community. Moreover, the emphasis on authentic individuality to which students were subject discouraged a collective oppositional identity. Paradoxically this rendered even marginality, like the display of an authentic self, a selling point. Thus the contradiction with which some students struggled, between a marketized, conformist self and an authentic, un-sellable self, was an *individualized* one; and the personal entrapment students felt as a result of the pressure to craft an identity that advertised uniqueness as a kind of brand was more pervasive.

To sum up, the contradictions each group of students experienced—between a conceived reality and a lived one defined by conflicting ideals of success and conduct, the realities of the tech boom and bust, the retrenchment and privatization of the public sector according to the dictates of neoliberal governance, the historical pathologization and increasingly authoritarian regulation of at-risk youth and low-income Latino immigrants, and the erosion of middle-class social and economic security—affected how they saw themselves and their circumstances, how they disciplined themselves, the aspirations they cultivated, and their perceptions of a dominant public culture. However, the degree to which experiences of contradiction shaped people's self-perceptions, modes of self-discipline, and aspirations depended on how powerful their fear was of social exclusion, a power enhanced, perhaps, by having much social and economic status to lose.

The patterns of subjectification and agency I observed among not just young people in Morton's Biotechnology Academy and at Sanders but also among the teachers, the nonprofit and public-sector workers, and the established middle-class professionals (mostly affiliated with tech organizations such as HP) support this claim. Like the students in Morton's Academy, who regarded the world of their tech professional mentors with ambivalence, if not indifference, some teachers and community advocates were also unable to reconcile their own experience with private-sector Silicon Valley and the reality of bust-related funding cuts and empty corporate parking lots with the hype they heard from well-intentioned corporate representatives about the power of the regional information economy to rectify social and economic divisions.

On one of my final days of fieldwork, I spoke to a youth organizer and cofounder of *De-Bug: The Voice of the Young and Temporary*, a progressive, youth-oriented Web magazine and activist group in Silicon Valley. In our discussion, he framed the experience of marginalization that he observed among young people during the boom in terms of the disjuncture between the experience of low-wage Valley workers and elite representation of the region:

> People wanted to be part of the image, even if the image didn't want them. During the day they'd be at the warehouse [working], wearing nice clothes, driving a nice car, living with their cousin. People wanted to be associated with the wave . . . I see these cats, knowing they make eight dollars an hour, driving these souped-up cars [laughs] . . . Indian men—South Asian men would come to the warehouse at six in the morning as if they were second to Bill Gates, in a suit and tie, nice dress shoes.

The contradictions that people such as this youth organizer have witnessed have, not surprisingly, encouraged them to be skeptical about the civilizing mission of social and educational reform shaping the public sphere of Silicon Valley. The same youth organizer sarcastically represented attitudes about the digital divide during Silicon Valley's boom: "At that time, the digital divide was conceptualized as computers: 'if you can just get computers in the ghetto, it'll be all right.'"

In contrast, the threat of a loss of status and social exclusion caused Sanders students and established middle-class professionals alike to compare themselves relentlessly to a hegemonic ideal of the "successful" citizen-subject, resent the imposition of the ideal as a norm, or simply try to conform to it. As we have seen, both middle-class adults and youth experienced a sense of entrapment that, for youth, shaped both processes of aspiration formation and, for adults, engendered what we have argued was an ineffectual political response to eroding security. Strikingly, as was the case with Sanders students, those adults who occupied more marginal positions within the Valley's middle strata—the would-be opera singer who saw his father as Willy Loman, the former HP worker and Silicon Valley "dropout"— seemed less constrained by social and economic pressures and therefore less identified with an elite citizen-subject ideal.

The Avoidance of Foregone Conclusions

As the ethnographic stories recounted in this book demonstrate, fantasies and realities of social exclusion and privilege, and experiences of social belonging, shape the divergent cultural politics of class upon which the making of neoliberal subjects depends. Such a politics depends on the emotive meanings attached to certain neighborhoods, to a father's history as an immigrant doing back-breaking work, to a teacher monitoring students walking out of school at the end of the day or logging extra hours to help students prepare for a test, or to a daughter's acceptance at an Ivy League school. They depend on the horror that some attach to the prospect of attending community college, and the sense of security and status associated with a public-sector job working with at-risk teenagers when you were once considered at risk yourself.[15]

One effect of such fears and reassurances is that they re-inscribe moral constructions of "middle class" and "underclass" in ways that provoke anxiety and preclude broad social allegiances that transcend class, race, and ethnicity. At the same time symbols of exclusion, security, and status can, like assurances that begin to ring hollow, lose their meaning or take on new meaning in response to shifting material and political circumstances, and experiences of heightened social contradiction. At such times, the imagining of and mobilization for an alternative politics becomes possible. What might such a scenario mean for Latino youth deemed to be at risk at schools such as Morton? Conditions of contradiction, mounting inequality, and collective social exclusion might provoke a youth-led disruption of the notion of being at risk, one that de-stigmatizes the label and re-values it, or uses it to begin a discussion about what the label masks.[16] Such a re-signification of the meaning of "at-risk youth" might serve as a starting point for collective identification and action focused, for example, on orienting schools more to the needs of youth as opposed to defining the needs of young people in accordance with the demands of the market or the imperatives of a state in the process of shedding responsibility for the social well-being and security of its citizenry. Likewise, middle-class youth and their families, experiencing intensifying economic insecurity and hardship, may, as "lived" reality increasingly diverges from a conceived ideal of success, reassess the value of particular status symbols as they become more and more unaffordable. Alternatively, such youth may become unwilling to bear the intensifying personal costs of trying to guarantee that increasingly elusive goal: social and economic security. Worsening economic circumstances, in no short supply at the time of this writing, can paradoxically work to create such political spaces. In such a situation, "responsible citizenship" might come to mean public—not privatized—responsibility for social reproduction, a political-economic shift that would result in schools and communities quite unlike those described in this book, and patterns of youth aspiration less likely to reproduce familiar inequalities than those we have just explored. In grasping these political possibilities, we must acknowledge the effects of lived experience on processes of citizenship formation, a dynamic that, in its very unpredictability, precludes forgone conclusions.

Notes

CHAPTER 1. PHANTOMS OF SUCCESS

1. The start-up, during the late 1990s, of the American business magazine *Fast Company* offers evidence of the ascendance of this new entrepreneurial ideal subject. Similarly, popular accounts of the personal traits and lifestyles of famous techno-entrepreneurs have helped to delineate this subject. See, for example, Leibovich and Saffo 2002.

2. Charles Taylor, quoted in Crapanzano 2004:7, describes a "social imaginary" as a "shared reality diffused through stories, legends, and popular images."

3. See Findlay 1993 for an analysis of the underlying ideological tensions manifest in Silicon Valley's built environment.

4. I am indebted here to earlier critiques of a globalizing information society and economy. For example, in Castells' analysis of the informational city as a "space of flows," the very concept of a "space of flows" can easily elide social conflict (Castells 1996, Susser 1996). I am also reminded of Susan Roberts' argument (2003) that most depictions of globalization—as, for example, a series of flows—are oddly agent-less. Against this tendency, Roberts argues that the figure of "global manager" constitutes the supreme subject of globalization.

5. My line of inquiry here is in a sense similar to the focus of Fisher and Downey (2006) on new subjectivities and "socialities" produced in relation to the "New Economy."

6. I use the term "working class" to refer to people who perform generally low-wage service or production work in Silicon Valley. Throughout this text I refer to three different middle-class fractions. I simply use the term "middle class," however, when the differentiation between class fractions is not relevant.

7. Two other scholars have recently explored the topic of youth in Silicon Valley. Amy Best (2006) examines car culture as a medium for cultural expression among San Jose youth, and Chicano/a youth in particular. Shalini Shankar (2008) looks at youth identities and notions of success as this book does, but she focuses on Desi teen culture and the formation of a class-diverse Desi diasporic community in the region.

8. I understand that racial and ethnic identities are critical to relations of power and domination. In terms of whiteness, a privileged racial category, I do not generally specify the ethnic background of white students, that is, Italian American or Irish American.

9. In Silicon Valley immigrants from some parts of Asia such as China, Taiwan, and India are well represented in the highly skilled labor force, whereas other ethnic groups such as Cambodians and Vietnamese are more represented in lower-status positions.

10. I interpret "social reproduction" to mean everyday practices that sustain and differentiate relations of production (Bourdieu and Passeron 1990). Such practices—which

may occur in formal and institutional as well as informal contexts such as family and social life—reinforce and normalize hierarchies of difference. As geographer Cindi Katz (2002:250) has put it, social reproduction includes "the fleshy, open-ended stuff of everyday life as much as a set of structured practices that unfold in tension with social reproduction."

11. My understanding of processes of class identification draws from Pierre Bourdieu, who throughout his work emphasizes the symbolic and stylistic as well as the material and structural in his conception of class (Bourdieu 1987; Aronowitz 2003).

12. Household income refers to all wages, investments, Social Security, and welfare payments for all people in the household (JVSV Network 2003:19)).

13. 6. Benner cites the California Employment Development Department, Labor Market Information Division 2001.

14. Although the official poverty rate in Silicon Valley, defined nationally as $18,000 for a family of four, hovered around 7 percent, this number does not reflect the number of people having severe economic difficulties because of the local cost of living (JVSV Network 2003:20).

15. These figures were compiled from census data for the 2003 *Joint Venture Silicon Valley Index* (JVSV Network 2003). Moreover, the *Index* points out that these numbers vary widely by ethnicity.

16. What I was seeing was well documented; during the tech boom, a survey of thirty-three local Valley high-tech firms had revealed that African Americans and Latinos were strikingly underrepresented on local staffs of these firms (accounting for 4 and 7 percent of the workforce, respectively). Moreover, when represented, African Americans and Latinos were much less likely than whites to hold managerial jobs (Angwin and Castaneda 1998).

17. A substantial body of work examines the relationship of Silicon Valley's tech-based economy to local environmental problems and labor conditions (Pellow and Park 2002; Pitti 2003; Siegel 1985; Sonnenfeld 1993; and Zloniski 1994, 2006) and to household and family forms (Stacey 1990).

18. Local educators and corporate representatives concerned with preparing local youth for high-tech jobs pinpointed the end of the 1990s as a time when the term "digital divide" gained widespread currency in Silicon Valley (despite its earlier emergence at the beginning of the 1990s) and assumed central importance in local civic discourse.

19. As Sharon Stephens (1992:13) has pointed out, not only is there "a growing consciousness of children *at risk* . . . there is also a growing sense of children themselves as *the risk.*"

20. I thank Vincent Crapanzano for suggesting this term.

21. With this conception in mind, Foucault sought to distill the characteristics of the "art of government" in the early modern period, a time of incipient liberalism beginning in the eighteenth century, and in the post–World War II emergence of neoliberal governance (Gordon 1991).

22. As Levinson, Foley, and Holland (1996:15) point out, people forge social identities within multiple and sometimes contradictory contexts.

23. As I discuss in chapters 2 and 3, however, young people's career aspirations were not gendered in traditional ways.

24. The general website is at http://www.sanjoseca.gov/planning/Census/dstprofiles.asp. I do not indicate the specific council district's Web page in order to obscure the school's location.

25. The income ceiling for a family of four to qualify for the reduced-price lunch was, at the time of my research, $33,485, according to 2002 federal poverty guidelines (*Federal Register* 2002:8934).

26. See chapter 2 for a more complete description, including results of a survey I conducted at the school for which students reported their parents' occupations.

27. In 2009 Palo Alto's population was 64,484. Data available at http://www.cityofpalo-alto.org/knowzone/labor_negotiations/facts_and_figures.asp. Provided by California Department of Finance.

28. Fact sheet for school district website.

29. See below for more information on the differences between the two school districts where I conducted my fieldwork. I do not name the districts in order to protect the privacy of participants in the study.

30. I carefully avoided mentioning the actual high schools by name, although I shared the name of their districts when it came up in conversation.

31. Available at http://www.pbs.org/merrow/tv/ftw/prop13.html.

32. "Fast facts" of the school district website.

33. Such yearly targets are measured by the *Academic Performance Index* (*API*), a rank that is based on results from yearly achievement tests including the Stanford Achievement Test, 9th ed.; the California Standards Test; and the California High School Exit Exam. In 2003 the Stanford Achievement Test was replaced by the California Achievement Test (California Department of Education 2002–2003). Notably Morton has met its API goal for the past four years (school district website).

34. Available at http://www.ed-data.k12.ca.us.

35. State budget constraints in 2002–2003 resulted in the decision to cut the $120 per student based on the average daily attendance. Lawmakers argued that other state funding from categorical programs such as special education satisfied the constitutional requirement of "basic aid." Moreover, Basic Aid Districts were allowed to keep their excess property taxes (http://www.edsource.org/glo.cfm).

CHAPTER 2. MANAGING "AT-RISK" SELVES AND "GIVING BACK"

1. All the names of students and adults in this chapter, unless famous public figures, are pseudonyms.

2. The school district in San Jose in which Morton High School is located currently (2008–2009) serves 26,259 students. The ethnic makeup of the district is as follows: Hispanic, 48.0 percent; Asian, 27.4percent; white, 10.1 percent; Filipino, 8.9 percent; African American, 4.0 percent; and smaller percentages of Native American and Pacific Islander students (District Profile, California Department of Education). Notably, since the time of research, white presence in the district has decreased; in 2002 whites accounted for 25.2 percent of the city council district population (http://www.sanjo-seca.gov/planning/census/dstprofiles). Note, the precise district of the school has been obscured to protect the anonymity of the school.

3. The school principal believed that underreporting occurred because some families were unwilling to provide information regarding their eligibility for reduced-price lunches and also because of the school's high transience rate. The state average at the time of my research was 35 percent for reduced-price lunches, and 47 percent

for reduced-price and free lunches. It is notable that the number of students state-wide receiving reduced-price and free lunches climbed from 47 percent to 53 percent between 2002 and 2009, with the greatest percentage jump occurring during the recent recession of 2009. Eligibility for both free and reduced-price lunches is based on federal poverty guidelines (http://www.cde.ca.gov/ds/sh/cw/filesafdc.asp).

4. For the 2002–2003 school year the income ceiling for a family of four for this grant was $31,950; for a family of six or more, the ceiling was $38,610 (California Department of Education 2002–2003).

5. This finding corroborates scholarship about insecure, flexible working conditions in Silicon Valley. See, for example, Chris Benner 2002 for a discussion of flexible employment within Silicon Valley's information economy, and Judith Stacey 1990 on the effects of unstable employment on the region's workers and their families.

6. I handed out a questionnaire in four government and social studies classes. Of eighty-one students surveyed during 2002, eighteen reported at least one currently unemployed parent, including homemakers. Some students reported parents working in "electronics assembly" or "electronics" or construction, but the majority of students reported that at least one parent performed a service-sector job, such as secretarial work, medical and dental assisting, landscaping, maintenance, security, customer service, technician, and food service positions such as cook, waitress, housekeeper, cafeteria worker, and caterer. A few Filipino American and Vietnamese American students reported that their parents were electrical engineers or had attained managerial positions. Some Latino parents owned landscaping businesses.

7. Census data for the San Jose Council District in which Morton High School is located indicate that 60 percent of the population own their own homes and 40 percent rent their homes. Data available at http://www.sanjoseca.gov/planning/Census/dstprofiles.asp). In addition, the local press has documented the common phenomenon of shared housing in low-income San Jose (see, e.g., Oanh 2002). Many Latino Academy students described living in crowded living conditions, and a few resided in garages.

8. During the 1998–1999 school year Morton had 2,189 students compared to 1,905 during 2002–2003. Morton's principal pointed out that, on school transfer forms, families often state that they are going to Turlock, Stockton, Sacramento, or Modesto—all San Joaquin Valley towns with cheaper housing than San Jose, where the median monthly rent in 2002 was $1,410 (City of San Jose, Office of Economic Development, 2002) compared to a median gross rent in the state of $747. In 2003 the median price of a single-family residence was $510,000 (Santa Clara County Association of Realtors 2003).

9. One father expressed frustration at having to ask his sixteen-year-old daughter, a student at Biotech, to read and explain a monthly mortgage statement to him. As it happened, the daughter refused initially, telling him that she was "too busy."

10. A great limitation of this study is that the experience of Vietnamese American students at Morton is discussed only peripherally. No Vietnamese parents consented to my interviewing their children, despite my friendly relations with a few Vietnamese American students. Many Vietnamese parents, moreover, did not speak English and I spoke no Vietnamese. See Zhou and Bankston 1999 for a discussion of refugee experiences, school experiences, and "selective Americanization" among youth; and Centrie 2004 for an ethnographic discussion of young Vietnamese Americans' positive identification with school as a source of freedom.

11. Some mothers declined interviews, saying they were too busy, and others failed to keep appointments. Still others, however, invited me into their homes, shared stories of their children and Morton, and asked me questions about my impressions of the school.

12. SCANS skills refers to the Secretary's Commission on Achieving Necessary Skills and dates back to 1983, when the Department of Labor and the Department of Education issued a report, titled "A Nation at Risk," arguing that industry needed to take a more active role in shaping "the twenty-first-century worker." This report divided learning objectives into "basic skills" and "competencies" based on research that examined national job trends.

13. On a symbolic and practical level, a key class barrier to such communication is, of course, students' grammar and style of speaking English.

14. The organization was made up of a network of corporate advisers, teachers, and education policy makers working to facilitate interest in biotechnology and skills among high school students.

15. Agilent's project was designed to sharpen "leadership skills" through community service, and to promote knowledge of biotechnology, local industry, and scientific methods among youth. According to Agilent's 2001 *Annual Report*, the Agilent After School hands-on science program was launched worldwide in 2001. Five hundred Agilent employee volunteers worked with twenty-eight thousand children worldwide through this program.

16. A Genentech liaison to the Biotech Academy made it clear that the corporation aimed to facilitate students' pursuit of advanced studies in biotechnology.

17. See Davis 2007 for an excellent journalistic discussion of the recruitment of non-citizen Latino youth in the Silicon Valley area and elsewhere across the nation (available at http://www.metroactive.com/metro/09.19.07/news-0738.html).

18. Perez (2006) refers to a statement made by John MacLaurin, Deputy Assistant Secretary of the Army for Human Resources; cited in Berkowitz 2003.

19. For an exploration of the Vietnamese refugee experience, see Freeman 1989.

20. Armando reported that his parents send remittances to Mexico periodically to support his grandmother and aunt in Michoacán.

21. Although the war in Iraq was gaining momentum that spring, Armando was only somewhat aware that he would most likely be deployed there and face combat conditions. The subsequent fall, when I was still conducting fieldwork at Morton, I inquired about Armando's whereabouts and was told that he had completed training at Camp Pendleton in California and was headed for Iraq. Despite my inquiries among his peers and former teachers the following year, I was unable to confirm his deployment.

22. Indeed, this desire to serve the greater good recalls David Graeber's (2007) argument that a pervasive desire among people, particularly within market-driven societies, to behave altruistically, and the fact that, as barriers to class mobility have become more impenetrable, military service has become one of the only ways for poor youth to satisfy their wish to do something "noble." This book attempts to understand working-class Latino students' altruistic aspirations in relation to emotively charged, daily experiences of school and community that include, but are not limited to, dynamics of social exclusion.

23. In a questionnaire I administered to eighty-one Biotech Academy students, students were asked to list the top three careers they found most interesting. Latino students' responses varied considerably in contrast to a pattern that emerged during interviews and in casual conversations. This may have been the result, in part, of the different contexts, the

wording of the question in each context, or indecision because of the age of informants. Most important to my argument, however, is the manner in which Latino students—and a few Asian students—articulated and explained their interest in public-service careers.

24. Many Biotech Academy students had participated in a pharmacy externship program during their sophomore year, and some Asian students with whom I spoke reported having a friend or family member who was a pharmacist.

25. Career choice changed to protect the student's identity.

26. Amy Best (2006) recounts a young Mexican American woman's aspiration to be a probation officer, a choice that Best links to the desire for secure employment.

27. While I conducted my research at Morton, the school received a $90,000 grant from Johnson & Johnson to begin a Nursing Academy to address the shortage of nurses in California. The Nursing Academy, like the Biotech Academy, was to be run out of the Medical Magnet program.

28. Notably, with the exception of nursing and military service, both male and female students expressed interest in these careers.

29. This estimate was provided by the school's ROTC director. The director also reported that, during the 2002–2003 school year, three hundred students participated in the school's ROTC program. The ethnic breakdown of the ROTC program reflected the school's demographics proportionally.

30. After three years of accelerated growth, Silicon Valley lost 127,000 jobs between the first quarter of 2001 and the second quarter of 2002 (JVSV Network 2003).

31. In her work about ROTC in Chicago, Gina Perez (2006, 2008, 2009) considers subjective understandings as well as social and economic factors in the formation of young people's aspirations and attitudes about military service.

32. Available at http://www.paloaltoonline.com/weekly/morgue/2005/2005_06_15.guest15kirst.shtml. Moreover, California has more community colleges than any other state, and 80 percent of the state's Latino students attend community colleges (ibid.).

33. The program coordinator for the Santa Clara Biotech Education Partnership, an organization funded by the Johnson & Johnson Foundation and Genentech Foundation, concurred that this was the case at Morton.

34. Teachers cited students' feelings of alienation toward Silicon Valley's information economy and techno-entrepreneurship. Memorably one teacher commented that Academy students were not as "selfish" as Valley tech professionals (see chapter 4 for a discussion of the attitudes of teachers and other public-service sector professionals toward Silicon Valley's tech sector).

35. In 1999 HP splintered, and Agilent Technologies was founded. Many employees moved from HP to Agilent at this time. Both companies were experiencing lean times during my fieldwork.

36. According to a representative of the Bay Area School-to-Career Action Network (BAYSCAN), a foundation-funded nonprofit organization that provides marketing and communications services for the School-to-Career program supporting the Biotech Academy, the School-to-Career concept encompasses all youth and all aspects of industry, from entry-level positions to the graduate level.

37. After the curtailment of federal School-to-Career funds in 2000, California's then governor Gray Davis set up a system wherein state funding for School-to-Career academies assumed the responsibility of raising private-sector contributions to supplement program budgets. As my contact at BAYSCAN pointed out, this effectively pitted school districts against one another in a competition for private resources.

38. According to a safety officer at the school district office, the ID badge policy was inspired by "the corporate world," while also ensuring that non-students had no access to high school campuses.

39. In 1991 San Jose initiated what came to be a nationally recognized Gang Prevention Task Force, under the administration of former mayor Susan Hammer. A longtime and current administrator at Morton in charge of prevention and suppression programs for youth at risk for gang activity is a former member of the Task Force.

40. This policy was adopted during the 1990s in response to gang problems in the neighborhood where the school was located.

41. A thirty-year veteran of the most widely known and active church-affiliated community group in San Jose, People Acting in the Community Together (PACT), chronicled for me the rise of a concern with the right to safety among Latino residents in the Morton High School attendance area. Interviews I conducted with Morton parents demonstrated the pervasiveness of these feelings as did a 1999 survey conducted by the County of Santa Clara, which revealed that gangs and personal safety were top concerns for local parents of all ethnicities (*Santa Clara County Children's Report* 2002). Similarly, in a 2000 *San Jose Mercury* survey, Bay Area Vietnamese parents listed gang eradication in their communities as a number one priority. However, as the region descended into the recent recession, leaving the County of Santa Clara with a 160 million dollar deficit, transience and basic needs like hunger and multiple families in one home replaced gangs and crime as the chief concern (cited in ibid.).

42. This initiative was well known, invoked by many community activists and a few city officials with whom I spoke

43. This point was made by community activists in San Jose that I interviewed independently.

44. This is one of the talking points that markets San Jose on the city's website, http://www.sanjoseca.gov.

45. Nonetheless, a report by the United Way of Silicon Valley cited Santa Clara County Probation Department statistics that indicate there was an increase in the number of serious offences committed by youth in Juvenile Hall (http://uwsv.org/service2c.htm).

46. The report citing these trends includes graphs produced by the California Department of Justice, Criminal Justice Statistics Center.

47. http://www.aclunc.org/news/print_newsletters/asset_upload_file367_4410.pdf.

48. For example, Pauline Lipman (2003) discusses these policies in Chicago, and their relation to school environments for low-income African Americana and Latino students.

49. San Jose's city attorney countered that the suspected gang members were infringing on the rights of people to live in peace. The State Supreme Court upheld the injunction in 1997 (*ACLU News* 1997; http://www.metroactive.com/papers/metro/02.13.97/tattto02-9707.html).

50. The County of Santa Clara budget increased by seven million between 1994 and 2000 (County of Santa Clara).

51. Whereas real per capita income increased 32 percent in Santa Clara County during the 1990s (compared to 13% for the nation), the household income of the county's bottom 20 percent remained below 1992 earnings at the millennium.

52. http://www.wpusa.org/Focus-Areas/eco_cardea.pdf. See Gilmore 2007 for a discussion of the politics and economics of incarceration in California.

53. For example, in her 2003 State of the County address, the chairperson of the County Board of Supervisors at the time, Blanca Alvarado, stated that because of reform efforts, there was a 28 percent decrease in the average daily number of youth in Juvenile Hall between 2002 and 2003.

54. This statistic was quoted in Blanca Alvarado's 2003 "State of the County Address."

55. This figure is cited in the Santa Clara Juvenile Justice Commission Report for January 17, 2006 (http://www.sccsuperiorcourt.org/juvenile/JJCReports/2006/JuvHallIn-spRpt.1.06.pdf).

56. See Best 2006 for a discussion of the policing and profiling of Latino youth in the public space of San Jose. Her discussion focuses on the policing of the popular and meaningful pastime of cruising, a tradition with deep roots in the Mexican American community and one that symbolizes the collective identity and struggle of the community. She recounts many cases of young people being stopped for "DWB", "Driving while Brown," a shorthand for racial profiling. Narratives about DWB represent, "a repository for the collective consciousness of racial injustice for Latino (and black) youth" (ibid.: 40).

57. For an excellent discussion of the effect of informal mentors and role models on the lives and aspirations of Mexican American youth, see Spina, Stanton-Salazar, and Urso 2003.

58. The somewhat privileged status of Biotechnology Academy participants vis-à-vis other students at Morton recalls Rouse's (1995) notion of a split within the working class in the contemporary United States, in which two groups of workers are hierarchically positioned and represented as more and less deserving in comparison with one another. Programs focusing on bridging the digital divide, which offer enrichment and skill building for some but not all low-income youth, might serve as an example of this process.

59. Since the advent of the Reagan era, one finds in American political discourse an increasing number of references to the evils of "big government" and "tax and spend."

CHAPTER 3. MARKETING THE SELF

1. I attended this ceremony but also transcribed a videotape of the proceedings.

2. In 2000 the median value for a single family home in Palo Alto was $811,800 (U.S. Census 2000). Given Palo Alto's status as an affluent and desirable town with well-regarded public schools, the tech boom rendered the city a seller's market; multiple bids on a given property usually drove the price higher than the asking price.

3. The school's API score is 10 out of 10.

4. At the time of my research, the district had a .3 percent drop-out rate compared to California's rate of 11.7 percent (District Fact Sheet; U.S. Census Bureau 2000).

5. When I conducted this research, the school was 75 percent Caucasian, 13 percent Asian, 5 percent African American, 4 percent Hispanic, and 3 percent other.

6. According to California state law, Basic Aid Districts receive only $120 per year per student, an allotment that the then governor Gray Davis was trying to reallocate to the state's coffers to ameliorate California's budget crisis in 2003.

7. Census information for Palo Alto reveals that 16.8 percent of its households had an income of $200,000 or above in 2000 (U.S. Census Bureau 2000). The 1990 U.S. Census did not delineate the $200,000 and above income bracket, although it did specify that

20.5 percent of households in Palo Alto reported an income of $100,000 or more (U.S. Census Bureau 1990). Moreover, within the North Santa Clara County consortium of cities of which Palo Alto is a member, there was a 457 percent increase in the number of households earning $150,000 or more in annual income between 1989 and 1999, a rate of increase that exceeded that of the county, the Bay Area, and California ("Making Sense of the Census," NOVA 2002).

8. In fact, just before my fieldwork on campus, the school newspaper published an editorial demanding an AP option for state-required courses such as economics.

9. In particular, teachers and administrators at the school seemed to focus relatively little on student drug use. I recall speaking with a teacher about a tall blond male student, a swimmer who had been in trouble for drugs in the past and cut class rampantly. Given the tendency of many adults in Silicon Valley and some teachers at Morton to assume a proclivity for at-risk behavior when discussing Latino youth, it was striking when, in the course of our conversation, the Sanders teacher stated that if this student just attended a college-preparatory program for a year—he was bright as well as athletically talented, she said—and changed his attitude, he might be an appropriate candidate for Stanford.

10. The current School Accountability Report Card for Sanders describes a "zero-tolerance" policy for violent or threatening behavior.

11. This fad had begun a few years earlier among a select group of students.

12. So-called deviant behavior such as illegal drug use also apparently served the function of highlighting an individual's distinctive characteristics. Among its other meanings, illicit behavior served as an opportunity to express an authentic and original self. Motivations for abuse of illicit and prescription drugs were explored in the school literary magazine while I was conducting fieldwork at Sanders, and drug use was, in the above article, construed as evidence of a sophisticated boredom.

13. The precise date of the letter is lost, and an archival check is unavailable.

14. Abercrombie and Fitch was an extremely popular brand at Sanders. The company, which markets apparel to teens, has been the subject of boycotts based upon its sexually explicit advertising.

15. Unfortunately I have no interviews with Chinese parents from Sanders. The Chinese American students I interviewed at Sanders were first-generation. All their parents had come to Silicon Valley after completing graduate degrees in China. A few reported having grandparents who had suffered repression during China's "Cultural Revolution" under Mao.

16. During the time I was observing at Sanders, the school literary magazine ran an exposé of the illicit student-run market at Sanders and other local schools for prescription drugs such as Ritalin, the drug for Attention Deficit Disorder (ADD).

17. Between 1989 and 1999 median household incomes in the seven cities (including Palo Alto) that make up Santa Clara County's northern half exceeded inflation rates by 34 percent ("Making Sense of the Census," NOVA 2002). In 1998 Santa Clara County as a whole ranked third in median household income in the country (cited in Benner 2002:215).

18. The market began its initial slide in April 2000.

19. A few high-tech professionals I spoke with commented that this rate was artificially low, as many professionals did not apply for unemployment benefits and so their joblessness was not documented.

20. Between 2001 and 2002 there was an 18 percent decline in jobs within Silicon Valley's "driving industry" clusters (including semiconductor, semiconductor equipment, electronic component, and computer and communications hardware manufacturing, software, innovation services, biomedical, creative services, and corporate offices). The rate of decline slowed to 9 percent during 2003 (*Joint Venture Index* 2004).

21. The principal and other administrators at Sanders noted that the school's average daily attendance (ADA) rate had risen lightly during the 2001–2002 school year, a fact they attributed to formerly more affluent families who had been affected by the recession having to move children out of private schools and into the public system.

22. As Paul Krugman has pointed out, although state spending in California increased during the 1990s boom, these increases were, in fact, recompense for drastic cuts made during the state's fiscal crisis of the early 1990s (Krugman 2003:A21).

23. Forte also notes that, according to the National Science Foundation, China and India graduated 26 percent of the world's new engineers in 1999.

24. In 2000, 63 percent of Asian high school students had completed college preparatory classes for admittance into the CSU/UC system compared to 46 percent of white students (JVSV Network 2000).

25. The academic year of 1998–99 was the first year that the University of California regents' 1996 decision to end consideration of race and sex in admissions decisions and the state's Proposition 209 ending affirmative action were implemented by the University of California. Ironically these policy shifts, meant to end so-called discrimination against white applicants, elevated the acceptance numbers of Asian Americans.

26. Proposition 187 banned undocumented immigrants from receiving public educational and medical services, and required teachers, doctors, and state workers to report undocumented immigrants to the Immigration and Naturalization Service (INS). Proposition 209 banned consideration of race and sex in college admissions as well as in hiring and contracting.

CHAPTER 4. "EVERY YOUTH A START-UP"

1. A common location of such initiatives has been East Palo Alto, California, a historically African American community that is now approximately 59 percent Latino (American Community Survey Demographic and Housing Estimates 2006–2008, U.S. Census).

2. In the 1980s a national movement to create CTCs to address gaps in technological access due to poverty had gained considerable momentum. The implementation of "CTC-net," funded by the National Science Foundation, created a national network of CTCs and thereby increased awareness of the issue of the digital divide and helped make the term a common one. See Sargent 2002.

3. Fifty percent of SV-CAN's Board of Directors hailed from the business community, 25 percent from the education field and 25 percent from local government.

4. I heard this on separate occasions from a number of nonprofit professionals, a consultant on community technology centers at SRI International, and a former Joint Venture employee.

5. These data are taken from the California Employment Development Department, Labor Market Information Division 2001.

6. Benner cites the California Employment Development Department, Labor Market Information Division 2001.

7. I did not attend this event but obtained a video recording of it.

8. SVMG was founded in 1977 by David Packard.

9. Like public schools that may receive private-sector funding for particular programs, nonprofit youth service organizations often receive both private support as well as state grants and other forms of support. This means that youth service nonprofits may have somewhat similar dynamics vis-à-vis private industry.

10. This budget figure was quoted to me by someone who was closely involved with the Initiative.

11. I thank many interviewees who helped me gain a sense of Joint Venture's projects during the 1990s, including one current and three former Joint Venture employees, as well as educators whose schools participated in Challenge 2000.

12. IISME employees, some of whom had the task of securing financial and mentorship support for teacher interns, had a running joke during the 2002–2003 academic year: "Did Larry call yet?" This was a direct reference to Oracle tycoon Larry Ellison, not known for philanthropic largesse, and an indirect reference to the dwindling of the program.

13. Workforce Silicon Valley received federal funding in 1996 under the 1992 School-to-Work Opportunities Act (which resulted in the creation of School-to-Career programs around the country) and private funding from locally based high-tech organizations such as NASDAQ.

14. According to a program director at a nonprofit organization focused on supporting Bay Area School-to-Career programs, the Bay Area School-to-Career Action Network (BAYSCAN), Workforce Silicon Valley, supported from the beginning by industry, is atypical of School-to-Career programs in the country in terms of its math, science, and technology-focused program content and local private funding.

15. The provisions of the E-rate law are available at http://www.fcc.gov/learnnet/254.html.

16. This event was cosponsored by Workforce Silicon Valley, the local chapter of the national entrepreneurial education nonprofit, Junior Achievement, and 3-Com.

17. Available at http://www.fcc.gov/learnnet/254.html.

18. Such subsidization is part of a pattern that began during World War II, when economic expansion became dependent upon the production of a class of scientists, as well as research laboratories, lab assistants, and other supporting technologies and supplies (Lewontin 1997:8).

19. For example, I interviewed the director of an organization called Cultural Initiatives Silicon Valley who spoke excitedly about harnessing the innovative and collaborative spirit of the Valley to foster a greater emphasis on arts and culture.

20. The WSV Annual Conference was first initiated in 1998.

21. For a detailed discussion of how the notion of "schools as scapegoats" became hegemonic during the 1980s, see Bartlett et al. 2002.

22. Benner (2002) defines work as "the actual activities workers perform, the skills, information, and knowledge required to perform those activities, and the social interaction involved in the process of performing that work." In contrast, he defines employment as "the contractual relationship between employer and employee, including compensation systems and employment practices" (ibid.:4).

23. Katz (2002) reads the subsequent and widespread backlash against the assumption of this tax burden in the U.S and other countries as evidence of compounded resentment on the part of workers in the United States and other locales who have not only lost economic ground (through the reduction of benefits and the decrease in real wage rates since 1973 (Harvey 2005:25) but now have been forced to assume responsibility for social reproduction (ibid.).

24. Agilent split off from HP to become a separate company in 1999, and Linda worked for many years for HP before moving to Agilent.

25. See, for example, Joe Rodriguez's column in the *San Jose Mercury News*, where he refers to the "buffoonery and incompetence" of the Alum Rock Union Elementary School District (Rodriguez 2002:B1).

26. For a critical discussion of such combined social services in public schools, see Cousins 2009.

27. See, for example, http://www.forbes.com/2001/05/07/0507facescan.html.

CHAPTER 5. A FEAR OF SLIPPING

1. Pop-cultural examples abound. Martin Scorsese's recent bio-pic, *The Aviator* (2004), a hagiographic chronicle of the oddities and pursuits of billionaire Howard Hughes, and *A Beautiful Mind* (2002), a depiction of the Nobel prize-winning, schizophrenic mathematician, John Forbes Nash, are recent Hollywood celebrations of "peculiar genius."

2. I draw here on Charles Taylor's definition of the "social imaginary" as a shared reality diffused through stories, legends, and popular images (Crapanzano 2004:7).

3. One HP employee informed me that the old decentralized structure of HP, characterized by separate companies under the rubric of HP with independent functions like personnel or IT departments, was slowly dismantled beginning in 1990. HP was subsequently restructured, outsourcing many aspects of its business (Pollack 1990).

4. For example, HP was the source of the concept of the tech collaborative called the "Digital Village," begun in 1999 in East Palo Alto. The Digital Village involved progressive youth development organizations in East Palo Alto, and was designed to address issues regarding the economic and educational digital divide in the East Palo Alto community.

5. The Equal Employment Opportunity Commission Report of 2002 was cited in Steen 2002. A more recent national figure is available at http://www.newsweek.com/2010/03/16/keep-young-and-beautiful-especially-at-work.html.

6. See, for example, a *Democracy Now* investigative report on the fall 2009 U.C. Regents Tuition Hike, in response to California's budget crisis, at http://www.democracynow.org/2009/11/20/students. This story addresses the corporatization of the UC system and the abandonment of its original mission.

7. For a similar argument about middle-class subjecthood and the potential of cross-class alliances, see Heiman 2009.

CHAPTER 6. A FLEXIBLE POLITICS OF CITIZENSHIP

1. The construction of gender and sexuality at Sanders expressed racial and class privilege because, at Sanders, daring sexuality could be read as a willingness to risk expressing oneself freely, as heroic individualism, and as a sign of potential leadership

qualities rather than as a sign of aggression and at-risk pathology, as would likely be the case for Latinas at Morton.

2. Although Willis's theory of cultural reproduction holds that the production of cultural forms in a capitalist system entails the possibility of the creative production of "alternative outcomes," he ultimately suggests that the "penetrations" of the system that the "lads" make do not disrupt the social relations and hierarchies of capitalism. Instead, cultural "meaning systems" (of race and gender) ultimately serve as "limitations" to these young men that result in their reinsertion into "the system" as manual workers (1977:174–175). In contrast, I am uncertain about the ultimate effects of the pattern of aspiration I have identified. This is partially because of the insecure and knowledge-based nature of the postindustrial economy. In this context, college is the next preferred step, and the volatility of structural conditions make the realization of particular aspirations a long and uncertain process. I have also suggested the possibility that "giving back" represents an emergent critique of privatization as well as an orientation that promotes the reproduction of regional class and racial hierarchies.

3. Sullivan carefully explores the differential effects of structural conditions such as schooling and economic access and marginality on white, Latino, and African American young men's economic stability, employment, and crime, showing that the extent and duration of young people's involvement with crime and the function of crime as an informal economic activity have much to do with structural economic conditions that differ along racial lines.

4. This emphasis on personal responsibility recalls Margaret Thatcher's often invoked neoliberal claim during the 1980s that "there is no such thing as 'society,' there are only individuals" (quoted in Kelly 2001:106).

5. Mitchell suggests that, during the Fordist era, multiculturalism encouraged citizens to work "*through* difference *for* the nation [emphasis in original]," an ethos that promoted the growth and expansion of a Fordist regime of accumulation throughout the world" (2003:392).

6. The work of many of the scholars (e.g., Goldstein 2001) represented in the volume *The New Poverty Studies* (Maskovsky and Goode 2001) exemplifies this emphasis.

7. In keeping with Mitchell's historicization of the new school patriotism, the Pledge of Allegiance was reintroduced at Morton only a few years ago.

8. As Amy Best notes, legislative and policy acts meant to promote public safety through curtailing the freedoms of youth "express how we have come to associate youth with risk and danger, often blaming them wholesale for a set of social circumstances that they had little role in creating" (Best 2006:9).

9. This exploration into the ways in which people draw selectively on their own experience and on dominant narratives and generate new meanings and conditions through performance draws on Cindi Katz's (2004) recent exploration of Walter Benjamin's notion of the mimetic faculty. In her analysis of Sudanese children's play, Katz observes that imitation can spark invention; in other words, new realities are synthesized through performance (ibid.:96).

10. I am reminded of Paul Willis's point that, in thinking through processes of class identification, "we must accept a certain autonomy of processes at this [cultural] level which both defeats any simple notion of mechanistic causation and gives the social agents involved some meaningful scope for viewing, inhabiting, and constructing their own world in a way which is recognizably human and not theoretically reductive" (1977:172).

11. In the conclusion to *Fast Cars, Cool Rides*, Amy Best (2006:154–156) somewhat similarly sums up the political-economic context of San Jose youth.

12. It is interesting to note, as George Packer (2010) does, that Barack Obama celebrates personal responsibility, as did George W. Bush and Bill Clinton.

13. Disinvestments in social reproduction may be, among other things, disinvestments in the public school system, parks and public space for children, community programs, and health benefits, all once guaranteed by the public and private sectors (Katz 2002).

14. I thank Vincent Crapanzano for suggesting this term to me, which he uses in the introduction to *Waiting: The Whites of South Africa* (1986).

15. As Roger Rouse has pointed out, "People have been encouraged to think of . . . class positions solely in terms of the phenomenal forms through which class is commonly expressed: occupation, income, patterns of expenditure, and, more broadly, 'lifestyle' . . . the class structure has been both marked and made explicable by reference to cultural factors—to people's character, their attitudes and values, and more generally their way of life" (Rouse 1995: 386, 388).

16. For an example of such a disruption, see Cahill 2006:334–353.

References

Agilent Technologies. 2001. *Annual Report: Agilent in Citizenship.*

Angwin, Julia, and Laura Castaneda. 1998. "The Digital Divide: High-Tech Boom a Bust for Blacks and Latinos." *The San Francisco Chronicle*, A1.

Aronowitz, Stanley. 1973. *False Promises: The Shaping of American Working Class Consciousness.* New York: McGraw-Hill.

———. 2003. *How Class Works: Power and Social Movement.* New Haven, Conn.: Yale University Press.

Aronowitz, Stanley, and Henry Giroux. 1993. *Education Still under Siege.* 2nd ed. Westport, Conn.: Bergin and Garvey.

Bartlett, Lesley, et al. 2002. "The Marketization of Education: Public Schools for Private Ends." *Anthropology and Education Quarterly* 33 (1): 5–29.

Bellantoni, Christina. 2001. "Program Sets At-Risk Youth on New Path." *Silicon Valley Business Ink.* 2001. November 2.

Benner, Chris. 2002. *Work in the New Economy: Flexible Labor Markets in Silicon Valley.* Oxford: Blackwell.

Bergstein, Brian. 2002. "HP Deal Too Close to Call." *Palo Alto Daily News*, March 18, 10.

Berry, Jennifer Deitz. 2002. "Board Looks to Curb 'Insatiable Appetite.'" *Palo Alto Weekly*, April 12, 3.

Best, Amy. 2006. *Fast Cars, Cool Rides: The Accelerating World of Youth and Their Cars.* New York: New York University Press.

Bjorhus, Jennifer. 2002. "Slow-Down Sending Tech Jobs Overseas." *San Jose Mercury News*, October 21, 1A

Bourdieu, Pierre. 1977. *Outline of a Theory of Practice.* New York: Cambridge University Press.

———. 1987. *Distinction: A Social Critique of the Judgment of Taste.* Cambridge, Mass.: Harvard University Press.

Bourdieu, Pierre, and Jean-Claude Passeron. 1990. *Reproduction in Education, Society, and Culture.* New York: Sage.

Bowles, S., and H. Gintis. 1976. *Schooling in Capitalist America: Educational Reform and the Contradictions of Economic Life.* New York: Basic Books.

Bronson, Po. 1999. "Newcomers." In Bronson, *The Nudist on the Lateshift and Other True Tales of Silicon Valley.* New York: Broadway Books.

Brown, Enora. 2003. "Freedom for Some, Discipline for 'Others.'" In *Education as Enforcement: The Militarization and Corporatization of Schools*, ed. Kenneth J. Saltman and David A. Gabbard, eds., 127–153. New York: Routledge.

Burchell, Graham. 1996. "Liberal Government and the Techniques of the Self." In *Foucault and Political Reason: Liberalism, Neoliberalism, and Rationalities of Government*, ed.

Andrew Barry, Thomas Osborne, and Nikolas Rose, eds., 19–37. Chicago: University of Chicago Press.

Cahill, Caitlin. 2006. "'At Risk'? The Fed-Up Honeys Re-Present the Gentrification of the Lower East Side." *Women Studies Quarterly* 34, nos. 1–2: 334–363.

California Employment Development Department. 2001. Labor Market Information Division.

Castells 1996. "The Net and the Self: Working Notes for a Critical Theory of the Information Society." *Critique of Anthropology,* March, Vol. 16. No. 1. pp. 9–38.

Castells, Manuel, and Peter Hall. 1994. *Technopoles of the World: The Making of 21st Century Industrial Complexes.* New York: Routledge.

Centrie, Craig. 2004. *Identity Formation of Vietnamese Youth in an American High School.* El Paso, Texas.: LFB Scholarly Publishing.

Century Foundation. 2004. "Life and Debt: Why Middle-Class Families Are Stretched to the Hilt." Reality Check series. http://www.tcf.org/publications/pdfs/pb481/baker_debt.pdf.

Chavez, Leo. 2008. *The Latino Threat: Constructing Immigrants, Citizens, and the Nation.* Stanford: Stanford University Press.

City of San Jose, Office of the Mayor. 2002. Press release. December 11.

Clarke, John. 2003. "Turning Inside Out? Globalization, Neoliberalism, and Welfare States." *Anthropologica* 45:201–214.

Cousins, Linwood. 2009. "It Ain't as Simple as It Seems: Risky Youth, Morality, and Service Markets in Schools." In *Childhood, Youth, and Social World in Transformation,* ed. Lynn Nybell, Jeffrey Shook, and Janet L. Finn. New York: Columbia University Press, pp. 92–113.

Crapanzano, Vincent. 1986. *Waiting: The Whites of South Africa.* New York: Vintage.

———. 2004. *Imaginative Horizons: An Essay in Literary-Philosophical Anthropology.* Chicago: University of Chicago Press.

Cruikshank, Barbara. 1999. *The Will to Empower: Democratic Citizens and Other Subjects.* Ithaca, N.Y.: Cornell University Press.

Davis, Deborah. 2007. "Yo Soy El Army." Available at http://www.metroactive.com/metro/09.19.07/news-0738.html.

Davis, Mike. 1990. *City of Quartz.* London: Verso.

Donzelot, Jacques. 1991. "Pleasure in Work." In *The Foucault Effect: Studies in Governmentality,* ed. Graham Burchell et al., eds., 251–281. Chicago: University of Chicago Press.

Ehrenreich, Barbara. 1989. *Fear of Falling: The Inner Life of the Middle Class.* New York: HarperCollins.

Elias, Norbert. 1978 [1939]. *The Civilizing Process: The History of Manners.* New York: Urizen Books.

Emerson, Ralph Waldo. 1883 [1844]. "Self-Reliance." In Emerson, *Essays,* 45–89. Boston: Houghton-Mifflin.

English-Lueck, J. A. 2002. *Cultures @ Silicon Valley.* Palo Alto, Calif.: Stanford University Press.

Federal Register. 2002. Vol. 67, no. 39 (February 27): 8934.

Ferguson, James. 1994. *The Anti-Politics Machine: "Development," Depoliticization, and Bureaucratic Power in Lesotho.* Minneapolis: University of Minnesota Press.

Findlay, John. 1993. *Magic Lands: Western Cityscapes and American Culture after 1940.* Berkeley: University of California Press.

Fisher, Melissa S., and Greg Downey, eds. 2006. *Frontiers of Capital: Ethnographic Reflections on the New Economy*. Durham, N.C.: Duke University Press.

Foley, Douglas E. 1990. *Learning Capitalist Culture Deep in the Heart of Tejas*. Philadelphia: University of Pennsylvania Press.

Foner, Eric. 1999. *The Story of American Freedom*. New York: Norton.

Fordahl, Matthew. 2002a. "Hewlett Booted from HP Board." *Palo Alto Daily News*, April 2, 8.

———. 2002b. "HP to Cut 1,800 More Jobs." *Palo Alto Daily News*, September 26, 10.

Forte, Sanford. 2003. "Foreign Engineers Will Change Our Economic World: Prepare Yourself." *San Jose Mercury News*, May 22.

Foucault, Michel. 1979. *Discipline and Punish: The Birth of the Prison*. New York: Vintage.

Freeman, James. 1989. *Hearts of Sorrow: Vietnamese American Lives*. Palo Alto: Stanford University Press.

Gilmore, Ruth Wilson. 2007. *Golden Gulag: Prisons, Surplus, Crisis, and Opposition in Globalizing California*. Berkeley: University of California Press.

Gillmor, Dan. 2002a. "Hewlett Wins Moral Victory." *San Jose Mercury News*, May 1, 11A.

Gillmor, Dan. 2002b. "HP Has Lost Its Way, but That's Just the Tip of the Iceberg." *San Jose Mercury News*, March 3, 1F.

Goldstein, Donna. 2001. Microenterprise Training Programs and the Discourses of Self-Esteem. In *The New Poverty Studies: The Ethnography of Power, Politics, and Impoverished People in the United States*, ed. Judith Goode and Jeff Maskovsky, 236–273. New York: New York University Press.

Goode, Judith, and Jeff Maskovsky, eds. 2001. *The New Poverty Studies: The Ethnography of Power, Politics, and Impoverished People in the United States*. New York: New York University Press.

Gordon, Colin. 1991. "Governmental Rationality: An Introduction." In *The Foucault Effect: Studies in Governmentality*, ed. Graham Burchell, Colin Gordon, and Peter Miller. Chicago: University of Chicago Press.

Graeber, David. 2007. "Army of Altruists: On the Alienated Right to Do Good." *Harper's Magazine*, January, 31–38.

Harvey, David. 1996. *Justice, Nature, and Geography of Difference*. Oxford: Blackwell.

———. 2005. *A Brief History of Neoliberalism*. New York: Oxford University Press.

Hayes, Dennis. 1989. *Beyond the Silicon Curtain: The Seductions of Work in a Lonely Era*. Boston: South End.

Heiman, Rachel. 2009. "'At Risk' for Becoming Neoliberal Subjects: Rethinking the 'Normal' Middle-Class Family." In *Childhood, Youth, and Social World in Transformation*, ed. Lynn Nybell, Jeffrey Shook, and Janet L. Finn. New York: Columbia University Press.

Herbert, Bob. 2004. "Admit We Have a Problem." *New York Times*, August 9, A15.

Herhold, Scott. 2002. "HP's Way? We Learned 3 Lessons in Tough Love." *San Jose Mercury News*, March 20, 1C, 6C.

Hewlett, Bill, and David Packard. 1995. *The HP Way: How Bill Hewlett and I Built Our Company*. New York: HarperCollins.

Hossfeld, Karen. 1988. Divisions of Labor, Divisions of Lives: Immigrant Women Workers in Silicon Valley. Unpublished dissertation. University of California, Santa Cruz.

"'HP Way' Changed the Valley." 2002. Editorial. *Palo Alto Daily News*, March 18, 11.

Huang. 2005. "White Flight in Silicon Valley as Asian Students Move In." *Wall Street Journal* online. http://www.realestatejournal.com/buysell/markettrends/20051123-hwang.html.

Hyatt, Susan Brin. 2001. "From Citizen to Volunteer: Neoliberal Governance and the Erasure of Poverty." In *The New Poverty Studies: The Ethnography of Power, Politics, and Impoverished People in the United States,* ed. Judith Goode and Jeff Maskovsky, 201–236. New York: New York University Press.

Joint Venture Silicon Valley (JVSV) Network. 1998. *Silicon Valley 2010: A Regional Framework for Growing Together.* San Jose, Calif.: Joint Venture.

———. 1999. *Internet Cluster Analysis.*

———. 2000. *Joint Venture Silicon Valley Index 2000.*

———. 2002. *Silicon Valley Workforce Report.*

———. 2003. *Joint Venture Silicon Valley Index 2003.*

———. 2004. *Joint Venture Silicon Valley Index 2004.*

Jung, Carolyn. 1997. "In These Parts: For Many Recent Arrivals, the Bay Area Is a Promised Land." *San Jose Mercury News,* January 19.

Kaplan, David. 1999. *The Silicon Boys and Their Valley of Dreams.* New York: William Morrow.

Katz, Cindi. 2001. "The State Goes Home: Local Hyper-Vigilance of Children and the Global Retreat from Social Reproduction." *Social Justice* 28 (3): 47–55.

———. 2002. "Stuck in Place: Children and the Globalization of Social Reproduction." In *Geographies of Global Change: Remapping the World,* 2nd ed., ed. R. J. Johnston, P. J. Taylor, and M. J. Watts, , 248–260. Oxford: Blackwell.

———. 2004. *Growing Up Global: Economic Restructuring and Children's Everyday Lives.* Minneapolis: University of Minnesota Press.

———. 2008. "Me and My Monkey: What's Hiding in the Security State." In *Indefensive Space: The Architecture of the National Insecurity State,* ed. M. Sarkin, 305–323. New York: Routledge.

Kelly, Peter. 2001. "The Post-Welfare State and the Government of Youth at Risk." *Social Justice* 28, no. 4: 96–113.

Krugman, Paul. 2002. "For Richer." *New York Times,* October 20.

———. 2003. Op-Ed. *New York Times,* August 8, A21.

———. 2004. "The Death of Horatio Alger," *The Nation,* January 5.

Kwan, Joshua L. 2001. "How the Valley Found Its Future in Chips." *San Jose Mercury News,* June 13. Available at http://wwwo.mercurycenter.com/local/center/150essence.htm.

Lardner, James. 1998. "Too Old to Write Code?" *U.S. News & World Report,* March 16, 39, 45.

Lefebvre, Henri. 1991. *The Production of Space.* Oxford: Blackwell.

Lareau, Annette. 2003. *Unequal Childhoods: Race, Class, and Family Life.* Berkeley: University of California Press.

Leibovich, Mark, and Paul Saffo. 2002. *The New Imperialists: How Five Restless Kids Grew Up to Virtually Rule Your World.* New York: Prentice Hall.

Levinson, Bradley, Douglas E, Foley, and Dorothy Holland, eds. 1996. *The Cultural Production of the Educated Person.* Albany: State University of New York Press.

Lewis, Michael. 2000. "The Artist in the Grey Flannel Pajamas." *New York Times Magazine,* March 5.

Lewontin, Richard. C. 1997. "The Cold War and the Transformation of the Academy." In *The Cold War University,* ed. Noam Chomsky, 171–195. New York: New Press.

"Letter to the Editor." 2002. *Palo Alto Daily News*, August 27.

Lipman, Pauline. 2003. "Cracking Down: Chicago School Policy and the Regulation of Black and Latino Youth." In *Education as Enforcement: The Militarization and Corporatization of Schools*, ed. Kenneth J. Saltman and David A. Gabbard, 81–103. New York: Routledge.

Lovato, Roberto. 2007 "Bad Schools, Good Soldiers, and the 'All Volunteer' Military." *Hispanic Outlook in Higher Education* 7, no. 11: (March 12).

Lutz, Catherine. 2002. "Making War at Home in the United States: Militarization and the Current Crisis." *American Anthropologist*, n.s., col. 104, no. 3 (September): 723–735.

Lyon-Callo, Vincent. 2000. "Medicalizing Homelessness: The Production of Self-Blame and Self-Governing within Homeless Shelters." *Medical Anthropological Quarterly* 14, no. 3: 328–345.

MacLeod, Jay. 2009 [1987]. *Ain't No Makin' It: Aspirations and Attainment in a Low-Income Neighborhood*. 3rd ed. Boulder, Colo.: Westview.

"Making Sense of the Census: A Look at the Demographic, Social, and Economic Characteristics of Northern Silicon Valley." 2002. North Santa Clara County Workforce Board (NOVA) report.

Mariscal, George. 2004. "Nowhere to Go: Latino Youth and the Poverty Draft. Public Affairs. Available as of January 2011 at http://www.politicalaffairs.net/articile/articleview/295/1/36.

Martin, Emily. 1994. *Flexible Bodies: The Role of Immunity in American Culture from the Days of Polio to the Age of AIDS*. Boston: Beacon.

———. 1996. "The Society of Flows and the Flows of Culture." *Critique of Anthropology* 16 (1): 49–56.

———. 2000. "Flexible Survivors." *Cultural Values* 4 (4): 512–517.

———. 2009. *Bipolar Expeditions: Mania and Depression in American Culture*. Princeton, N.J.: Princeton University Press.

Maskovsky, Jeff, and Ida Susser, eds. 2009. *Rethinking America: The Imperial Homeland in the 21st Century*. Boulder, Colo.: Paradigm.

Maurer, Bill, and Richard Warren Perry. 2003. "Introduction." In *Globalization under Construction: Governmentality, Law, and Identity*, ed. Bill Maurer and Richard Warren Perry. Minneapolis: University of Minnesota Press.

McHugh, Josh. 1999. "Burning Passion." *Forbes Magazine*, October 4, 99–101.

Mitchell, Katharyne. 2003. "Educating the National Citizen in Neoliberal Times: From the Multicultural Self to the Strategic Cosmopolitan." *Transactions of the Institute of British Geographers* 28:387–403.

Mullings, Leith. 2005. "Interrogating Racism: Toward an Antiracist Anthropology." *Annual Review of Anthropology* 34:667–693.

Murr, Andrew, and Jennifer Ordonez. 2003. "Tarnished Gold." *Newsweek*, July 28, 33.

Nolan, Chris. 2002. "HP Heritage." *Palo Alto Daily News*, March 19, 14.

Nolan, Kathleen, and Jean Anyon. 2004. "Learning to Do Time: Willis's Model of Cultural Reproduction in an Era of Postindustrialism, Globalization, and Mass Incarceration." In *Learning to Labor in New Times*, ed. Nadine Dolby and Greg Dimitriadis, 133–151. New York: Taylor and Francis.

Nybell, Lynn, Jeffrey Shook, and Janet L. Finn, eds. 2009. *Childhood, Youth, and Social Work in Transformation*. New York: Columbia University Press.

Oanh, Ha K. 2002. "Immigrants Tap into Ready-Made Support Network." *San Jose Mercury News*, November 11, 1A.

O'Malley, Pat. 1996. "Risk and Responsibility." In *Foucault and Political Reason: Liberalism, Neoliberalism, and Rationalities of Government*, ed. Andrew Barry, Thomas Osborne, and Nikolas Rose, 189–209. Chicago: University of Chicago Press.

Ong, Aihwa. 1999. *Flexible Citizenship: The Cultural Logics of Transnationality*. Durham, N.C.: Duke University Press.

———. 2003. "Zones of New Sovereignty in Southeast Asia." In *Globalization under Construction: Governmentality, Law, and Identity*, ed. Bill Maurer and Richard Warren Perry. Minneapolis: University of Minnesota Press.

O'Riain, Sean. 2000. "Networking for a Living: Irish Software Developers in the Global Workplace." *Global Ethnography: Forces, Connections, and Imaginations in a Postmodern World*. Berkeley: University of California Press.

Packer, George. 2010. "Obama's Lost Year." *New Yorker*, March 15.

Palo Alto Daily News. 2002. "Letter to the Editor." August 27.

Palo Alto Daily News. 2003. January 13, 50.

Pastor, Manuel, Jr., P. Dreier, and M. Lopez-Garza. 2000. *Regions That Work: How Cities and Suburbs Can Grow Together*. Minneapolis: University of Minnesota Press.

Pellow, David N., and Lisa Sun-Hee Park. 2002. *The Silicon Valley of Dreams: Environmental Injustice, Immigrant Workers, and the High Tech Global Economy*. New York: New York University Press.

Perez, Gina. 2006. "How a Scholarship Girl Becomes a Soldier: The Militarization of Latino Youth in Chicago Public Schools." *Identities: Global Studies in Culture and Power* 13:53–72.

———. 2008. "Discipline and Citizenship: Latino/a Youth in Chicago JROTC Programs." In *New Landscapes of Inequality: Neoliberalism and the Erosion of Democracy in America*, ed. Jane L. Collins, Micaela di Leonardo, and Brett Williams, 113–131. Santa Fe, N.M.: School for Advanced Research Press.

———. 2009. "JROTC and Latino/a Youth in Neoliberal Cities." In *Rethinking America: The Imperial Homeland in the 21st Century*, ed. Jeff Maskovsky and Ida Susser, 31–49. Boulder, Colo.: Paradigm.

Pitti, Stephen J. 2003. *The Devil in Silicon Valley: Northern California, Race, and Mexican Americans*. Princeton, N.J.: Princeton University Press.

Poletti, Therese. 2002a. "Carly Fiorina's Journey to CEO." *San Jose Mercury News*, March 10, 1A, 17A.

Poletti, Therese. 2002b. "Weak Economy Standing in HP's Way; Sales Outlook Slow; 15,000 Jobs to be Cut." San Jose Mercury News, June 5, 1A.

Poletti, Therese, and Elise Ackerman. 2001. "HP to Purchase Compaq in $25 Billion Stock Deal." *San Jose Mercury News*, September 4, 1A, 12A.

Pollack, Andrew. 1990. "Hewlett Packard in a Realignment." *New York Times*, October 6, sec. 1, 33.

Pred, Allan, and Michael Watts. 1992. *Reworking Modernity: Capitalisms and Symbolic Discontent*. New Brunswick, N.J.: Rutgers University Press.

Pritchett, Price. 1999. *New Work Habits for the Next Millennium*. Dallas, Tex.: Pritchett and Associates.

Quinn, Michelle. 2002a. HP: How Did it Come to This? San Jose Mercury News, March 17, 1A

——. 2002b. "Hewlett Emerges as Hero to Dissenters." *San Jose Mercury News*, March 20, 1A.

——. 2002c. "Home Prices Soar in Bay Area." *San Jose Mercury News*, June 25, 1C.

——. 2002d. "HP's Road Ahead." 2002. *San Jose Mercury News*, May 5, 1A, 18A.

Rivlin, Gary. 2004. "The Tech Lobby, Calling Again." *New York Times*, July 25, sec. 3, 1.

Roberts, Susan M. 2003. "Global Strategic Vision: Managing the World." In *Globalization under Construction: Governmentality, Law, and Identity.* ed. R.W. Perry and B. Maurer. Minneapolis: University of Minnesota Press.

Robins, Kevin, and Frank Webster. 1999. *Times of the Technoculture: From the Information Society to the Virtual Life.* New York: Routledge.

Rodriguez, Joe. 2002. "Parents Push Reform Idea in San Jose District." *San Jose Mercury News,* June 6, B1.

Rose, Nikolas. 1996. "Governing 'Advanced' Liberal Democracies." In *Foucault and Political Reason: Liberalism, Neoliberalism, and Rationalities of Government*, ed. Andrew Barry, Thomas Osborne, and Nikolas Rose, 37–65. Chicago: University of Chicago Press.

——. 1999. *The Powers of Freedom: Reframing Political Thought.* Cambridge: Cambridge University Press.

Rouse, Roger. 1992. "Making Sense of Settlement: Class Transformation, Cultural Struggle, and Transnationalism among Mexican Migrants in the United States." *Annals of the New York Academy of Sciences* 645:25–52.

——. 1995. "Thinking through Transnationalism: Notes on the Cultural Politics of Class Relations in the Contemporary United States." *Public Culture* 7:353–402.

Sachs, Aaron. 1999. "Virtual Ecology: A Brief Environmental History of Silicon Valley." *WorldWatch*, January/February.

Saltman, Kenneth J., and David A. Gabbard, eds. 2003. *Education as Enforcement: The Militarization and Corporatization of Schools.* New York: Routledge.

Santa Clara County Association of Realtors. 2003. Housing Statistics Year End. http://www.sccaor.com/fileadmin/stats/yearend/2003.htm.*Santa Clara County Children's Report.* 2002.

Santa Clara Housing Task Force. 2002. "Supplemental Materials: Housing Need."

Sargent, Mark. 2002. "Community Technology Centers: A National Movement to Close the Digital Divide." Available at http://www.glef.php/article.php?id=Art_992&key+188.

Saxenian, Anna Lee. 1996. *Regional Advantage: Culture and Competition in Silicon Valley and Route 128.* Cambridge, Mass.: Harvard University Press.

Schneider, Jane, and Peter Schneider. 2004. "Power Projects: Comparing Corporate Scandal and Organized Crime." In *Corporate Scandal; Global Corporatism against Society,* ed. John Gledhill, 11–20. New York: Berghahn Books.

Scott, Allen J. 1998. *Regions and the World Economy: The Coming Shape of Global Production, Competition, and Political Order.* New York: Oxford University Press.

Shankar, Shalini. 2008. *Desi Land: Teen Culture, Class, and Success in Silicon Valley.* Durham, N.C.: Duke University Press.

Sieber, Robert Timothy. 1976. "Schooling in the Bureaucratic Classroom: Socialization and Social Reproduction in Chestnut Heights." Ph.D. dissertation, New York University.

Siegel, Lenny. 1985. *The High Cost of High Tech*. New York: Harper and Row.

Silicon Valley Citizens for Affordable Housing. 2003. "Full Circle: The Economic and Fiscal Impacts of Affordable Housing: A Silicon Valley Perspective." Report by Silicon Valley Citizens for Affordable Housing.

Smart Valley. 1998. *A History of Smart Valley*. Palo Alto, Calif.

Smith, Gavin. 1999. *Confronting the Present: Towards a Politically Engaged Anthropology*. Oxford: Berg.

Smith, Neil. 1996. *The New Urban Frontier: Gentrification and the Revanchist City*. New York: Routledge.

Sonnenfeld, David A. 1993. "The Politics of Production and Production of Nature in Silicon Valley's Electronics Industry." Paper presented at the Annual Meeting of the American Sociological Association, Miami, Florida, August 13–17.

Spina, Ricardo D., D. Stanton-Salazar, and Stephanie Urso. 2003. "Informal Mentors and Role Models in the Lives of Urban Mexican-Origin Adolescents." *Anthropology and Education Quarterly* 34, no. 3: 231.

Spring, Joel. 1986. *American Education: An Introduction to Social and Political Aspects*. 4th ed. New York: McGraw-Hill.

Stacey, Judith. 1990. *Brave New Families: Stories of a Domestic Upheaval in Late Twentieth Century America*. New York: Basic Books.

Stack, Carol B. 1975. *All Our Kin: Strategies for Survival in a Black Community*. New York: Harper and Row.

Steen, Margaret. 2002. "Older Job Seekers Facing Tough Market." *San Jose Mercury News*, August 18, 1A, 14A.

Steinberg, Jacques. 2003. "The New Calculus of Diversity on Campus." *New York Times*, February 2.

Steinmetz, George. 2003. "The State of Emergency and the Revival of American Imperialism: Toward an Authoritarian Post-Fordism." *Public Culture* 15 (2): 323–345.

Stephens, Sharon, ed. 1992. *Children and the Politics of Culture*. Princeton, N.J.: Princeton University Press.

Sullivan, Mercer. 1989. *"Getting Paid": Youth Crime and Work in the Inner City*. Ithaca, N.Y.: Cornell University Press.

Suryaraman, Maya. 2002. "Private Funding Divides Schools, Raises Equity Issues." *San Jose Mercury News*, March 31, 1B, 4B.

Susser, Ida. 1982. *Norman Street: Poverty and Politics in an Urban Neighborhood*. New York, NY and Oxford: Oxford University Press.

———. 1996. "The Shaping of Conflict in the Space of Flows." *Critique of Anthropology*, March, Vol. 16, no. 1, pp. 39–47.

Sylvester, David A. 2002. "Silicon Valley: An Economic Snapshot," *San Jose Mercury News*, January 14, 4E.

Taqi-Eddin, Khaled, and Dan Macallair. 1999. "Shattering Broken Windows: An Analysis of San Francisco's Alternative Crime Policies" for the Center on Juvenile and Criminal Justice. San Francisco, Calif. Available at http://www.cjcj.org.

Task Force on Education for Economic Growth. 1983. *Action for Excellence*.

U.S. Census. 2000. American Community Survey. Available at http://www.census.gov.

Wadhwa, Vivek, Annalee Saxenian, Ben Rissing, and Gary Gereffi. 2007. "Americans New Immigrant Entrepreneurs." Duke University Master of Engineering Management Program Report. Available at http://ssrn.com/abstract=990152.

Williams, Alex. 2005. "Wheels and Deals in Silicon Valley." *New York Times*, December 4, sec. 9, 1, 6.

Williams, Raymond. 1994. "Selections." In *Culture/Power/History*, ed. Nicholas Dirks, Geoff Eley, and Sherry B. Ortner. Princeton, N.J.: Princeton University Press.

Willis, Paul. E. 1977. *Learning to Labour*. New York: Columbia University Press.

Wong, Nicole. 2002. "Anatomy of the Palo Alto Process: Model Democracy or Death by Indecision?" *San Jose Mercury News*, September 22, 1.

Workman, Bill. 2000. "Philanthropist Encourages Wealthy to Help United Way: Organization Works to Recover after Scandal." *San Francisco Chronicle*, December 8.

Zavella, Patricia. 1987. *Women's Work and Chicano Families: Cannery Workers of the Santa Clara Valley*. Ithaca, N.Y.: Cornell University Press.

———. 2001. "The Tables Are Turned: Immigration, Poverty, and Social Conflict in California Communities." In *The New Poverty Studies: The Ethnography of Power, Politics, and Impoverished People in the United States*, ed. Judith Goode and Jeff Maskovsky. New York: New York University Press.

Zhou, Min, and Carl Bankston. 1999. *Growing Up American: How Vietnamese Children Adapt to Life in the United States*. New York: Russell Sage.

Zlolniski, Christian. 1994. "The Informal Economy in an Advanced Industrialized Society: Mexican Immigrant Labor in Silicon Valley" *Yale Law Journal* 103, no.8.

———. 2006. *Janitors, Street Vendors, and Activists: The Lives of Mexican Immigrants in Silicon Valley*. Berkeley: University of California Press.

Index

achievement gap, 118; corporate discourse about, 122, 123

ageism, 175–176

anti-immigrant sentiment, 64, 148

aspiration formation: career aspirations (*see under* middle-class youth; working-class Latino youth); and class status and hierarchy, 80; and diminishing opportunities for poor youth, 64; framing discussion of, 5–6; and gender, 21, 72; and idealized techno-entrepreneurial model of citizenship, 6, 130; paradoxical nature of, 29; and regional educational priorities and perceptions of youth skills, 119; and social debt (*see under* working-class Latino youth); social reproduction and citizenship formation, 23–25. *See also* "giving back"

"aspiration management," 13, 22, 23, 24, 25, 41, 62, 69, 87, 96, 187; defined, 41; and middle-class youth, 67–117; and working-class youth, 29–66

"at risk" youth: middle-class, 113; national and global discourses about, 187; pervasive school discourse about, 54, 64; proliferation of discourse about in San Jose, 60; state disinvestment and privatization of responsibility for, 15, 64, 146; working-class of color, in Silicon Valley, 15; working-class Latino, 29–66

Attention Deficit Disorder (ADD), 102, 108, 208, 223n16

Attention Hyperactivity Disorder (ADHD), 102, 108, 208

authenticity. *See under* middle-class (established professional) adults; middle-class youth

Benjamin, Walter, 227n9

Benner, Chris, 216n6, 218n5

Best, Amy, 215n7, 220n26, 227n8

"big government," 147

Biotechnology Academy, 18, 20, 29–66, 118, 188–189; admission to four-year colleges, 62; and contradictory forms of regulation, 190; and corporate internships, 33–35; and corporate mentorship, 49, 50, 53, 140; and corporate partnerships, 47, 48; and critical thinking skills, 138; curriculum of, 46, 47, 49–53, 62, 128–129, 139–140; mission of, 46; and national skill imperatives, 141; and private sector influence, 130; and private sector influence on teacher practice, 127, 151–152

bodily discipline, 51, 54, 198

Bourdieu, Pierre, 216n11

Bronson, Po, 4, 157, 158, 159, 160, 173

career aspirations. *See under* middle-class youth; working-class Latino youth

Castells, Manuel, 113, 141, 215n4

Chavez, Cesar 53, 198

Chinese-Americans, white middle class discourse about, 89, 109–110

citizenship: exclusionary politics of 64; status, 44; techno-entrepreneurial ideal of, 6; young people's engagement with ideals of, 22, 23, 44, 185, 196–202; jokes about, 44. *See also* anti-immigrant sentiment; citizenship, responsible

citizenship formation, 6, 22, 25; and differential framing of personal responsibility, 16, 23, 187; flexible process of, 16,
21, 23, 185; and reconfiguration of state's
relationship to citizenry, 187; schooling
and "strategic cosmopolitan" subjects,
195–202; and social reproduction, 21;
success of project of, 188

citizenship, responsible, 21, 53, 64, 146, 202

civilizing process, 10, 11, 24; defined, 10–11; and
negative representations of youth "at-risk,"
144; neoliberal ideas and subjecthood, 144;
and stylistic meanings of class, 11; techno-
entrepreneurial variant of, 11, 144

class: American commonsensical understanding of, 11; barriers and language,
219n13; conflict and generational difference, 78; entitlement, 78–80, 112, 190;
entitlement and use of space, 78–79;
identification, 6, 14, 17, 192; identification and elite style, 75, 91; identification and process of class formation, 11;
identification and racism, 86; identification and Willis's critique of reductive
causation, 227n10; and parent-school
relations, 78; polarization, 9; and racialized discourse about public goods and
services, 110

Clarke, John, 202

Clinton, Bill, 126, 137

college, 82, 90, 91, 92, 105, 191

community college, 44, 86, 91, 220n32

concerted cultivation, 111–112

corporate citizenship, 10, 14, 48, 118,
219n15; and e-rate legislation, 131–134;
and HP as model, 133; and Applied
Materials, 133; and creation of education
manager positions, 134

"cultural politics of class," 25

De-Bug: Voice of the Young and Temporary
(Web magazine), 212

"digital divide," 11, 24, 48, 119–120; and
access to technology, 11; and "at risk"
youth, 12; corporate ambivalence to
term, 121; corporate framing of, 130; and

corporate motivations for engaging, 134;
and generation of public sector critique,
148; historicization of local use of term,
216n18; HP definition of as "e-inclusion,"
133; and interregional competition, 135;
and youth skills and values, 11

diversity, 71, 80

"dot-commers," 105, 161

drug use, 79, 86, 95, 223n9, 223n12; prescription drugs, recreational use of, 88

East Palo Alto, 1–25, 119, 147, 148, 164,
224n1, 226n4

East San Jose, 164

economic insecurity. *See under* middle-
class (established professional) adults;
working-class Latino youth

education, public: disinvestment in, 143;
and federal representations of system
as "failed," 142; and high-speed Internet
access, 126; institutions as "subjects,"
24; and local business leaders' role in
promoting neoliberal model, 143; and
manufactured crisis of, 143; and national
neoliberal politics of reform, 29; and
neoliberal accountability discourse of
"excellence," 195, 198; and "new white
flight," 110; private-sector appropriation
of right to manage public education, 131;
private-sector critique (*see also* privatization, 124, 147; private-sector critique
about workforce preparation, 123–131,
136; and private-sector emphasis on
"accountability," 130; and private-sector
focus on youth skills (*see also* youth
skills), 129–131, 134, 136; and private-
sector influence on teacher practice,
126–128; and private-sector practice
of "documentable results," 125; and
private-sector school partnerships, 126;
representations of teachers as lazy, 152;
and school accountability, 15, 130; as site
of social reproduction and citizenship
formation, 15; and "teaching to the test,"
16, 189; teachers as critics of tech private
sector, 155

education and training of youth: and fostering desire over content learning, 139–140;
increasing local private sector dominance
over, 144; private-sector influence on and
"revitalization" of, 124–131; regional civic
agenda regarding: 12, 48, 118; and regional
"culture," 144; shifting ideas about skills,
138–141; in Silicon Valley, 117–156. *See also*
"soft skills"; youth skills)
education market, 131–134, 143; and digital
divide, 131, 135, 143, 144
educational inequalities, public, 16, 18–20,
70, 123; and Basic Aid, 20, 70, 217n35,
222n5; and differential tracking of working and middle-class children, 208; and
fundraising, 106–107; and Proposition
13, 143; and private sector appropriation of, 131; racial and ethnic hierarchy
within local system, 9, 122
Ehrenreich, Barbara, 110–111, 209
Elias, Norbert, 10
Ellison, Larry, 159, 225n12
Emerson, Ralph Waldo, 11
entrepreneurial ethics, critique of: local,
170–172; national middle-class populist,
172
entrepreneurial ideal citizen, 160. *See
also* techno-entrepreneur as model of
conduct
entrepreneurialization of self/self-enter-
prise, 14, 194, 200
E-rate Telecommunication Act of 1996, 131,
225n15
exceptionalism of new entrepreneurial
elite: of Palo Alto, 77; of region's highly
educated professionals, 76; of students,
68, 76, 77, 78
extreme sports, 3, 4, 111

fear of slipping, 103–111; and social and
moral entrapment, 103
Ferguson, James, 62
Fiorina, Carly, 165–168; and break with HP
Way, 166; and lay-offs, 166–167, 170; and
symbol of new, heartless and ethically
questionable HP, 170–172; of risk-taking

culture, 166; as symbol of youthful tech
elite, 176. *See also* entrepreneurial ethics
flexible employment, 218n5
flexible work, 12
Foucault, Michel, 14, 62, 153, 216n21
freedom of expression, 69, 71–75, 78,
81–84, 112; as pragmatic self-cultivation,
87. *See also under* middle-class youth
frontiers of knowledge, 50, 139, 140–141

gangs, 18, 18, 31, 54, 55, 58, 61; jokes about, 45;
Norteno and Sureno, 55, 56
gender: and patterns of aspiration), 21, 42,
72; and status symbols, 82. *See also under*
aspiration formation
Gillmor, Dan, 168, 173, 175
"giving back," 21, 24, 40–42, 57, 62, 63, 65,
144, 190, 204, 219n23; "hidden injuries
of class," 22
globalization, processes of, 4, 5, 25, 107, 111,
134–135, 143, 187, 200, 215n4
Gore, Al, 131
governmentality, 14. *See also* neoliberal,
governmentality
graduation, high school), 67–69
Graeber, David, 219n22

Hammer, Susan, 59
Hewlett, Walter, 166–168, 171, 172, 173;
as symbol of established professional
middle-class decline, 176
Hewlett-Packard (HP), 47, 48, 132, 133;
garage as symbol of Silicon Valley "culture," 163; as good corporate citizen, 164;
and organizational effectiveness, 149
HP-Compaq merger, 163, 165–167; critique
of e-commerce as inauthentic innovation, 168, 181; and discourse about
corporate greed and corruption, 172–173;
and nostalgia for an idealized Silicon
Valley Past, 167–170, 175, 180–181
HP Way, 163–165, 164; as counter-narrative
to boom-time, "free agent" environment, 165; and cultural critique of "new
entrepreneurial" present, 165, 172–173;
employees' testimonies about, 168–16

incarceration rates, 60; of youth in California, 60; of youth in Santa Clara County, 54, 60

individual responsibility. *See* personal responsibility

Industy Initiatives in Science and Math (IISME), 127, 133, 142, 153, 225n12

interregional competition, and global capitalism, 135

Joint Venture: and 21st Century Education Initiative, 126–127, 150; and Challenge 2000, 125, 150; and emphasis on measurable results in digital divide campaign, 150; and focus on regional digital divide, 121, 123; and regional goals, 120–121; Silicon Valley Network, 8, 13, 120–122

Katz, Cindi, 143, 209, 216n10, 229n9

Kaplan, David, 160

knowledge economy, 141, 142

Latinos: and agricultural history of Silicon Valley, working-class adults, 30; first generation immigrant experiences, 32, 38, 39, 45

layoffs, 13, 86, 104–105, 108, 220n30; and HIB-visa debate, 108

Learning to Labour (Willis), 22

Lefebvre, Henri, 4; and representations of space, 4

Lewis, Michael, 158, 158

liberalism, 14, 216n21

low-wage service work, 6, 7, 19, 30

MacLeod, Jay, 22

Marine Corps, 34, 35, 36, 37, 39, 40

market, downward slide of, 12, 223n18; discussion of, among middle class youth, 77; and relationship to "manic style" of selfhood, 160

Martin, Emily, 113, 194; and "manic style" of selfhood, 160; optimized mania and productivity, 179

middle class, 5, 11, 215n6; increasing disappearance of, 8

middle-class (established professional) adults, 17, 160; anxiety of, 6, 13, 25, 105, 109, 175, 176–179, 180–181; attitudes towards "new entrepreneurial" middle class, 162, 173–176; awareness of shifting social and economic conditions, 180; and children's acts of self-definition and self-cultivation, 163; and children's futures as markers of class status and privilege, 111; and cultural critique of "new entrepreneurial" present, 165, 172–17; and cultural politics of class and age, 175–176, 180; defined, 8, 9; disappearance of, 8; entrapment of, 25, 181–182; erosion of status and security, 9, 16, 24, 103–111; and experience of tech boom, 161, 174, 176–179; identification with techno-entrepreneurial values and success, 13, 105–106, 161, 179–181; intensifying social and economic insecurity and pressures on, 17, 24, 69, 103–111, 162, 163, 179; nostalgia for a pre-"New Economy" past, 25, 168, 175, 181 (*see also* HP-Compaq merger; HP Way); nostalgia for era of relative economic security, 111, 175–176; nostalgia as politics of distraction, 180–181; and responses to idealized "New Economy" free agent, 160, 161 182; self-comparison with "new entrepreneurial middle class and elites, 106, 162; and stigma of being risk-averse, 176–179;. *See also* white middle-class racial anxieties. *See also* techno-entrepreneurial ideal subject

middle-class youth, 5, 16, 67–114; and anxiety about grades, 81, 85, 105; aspirations as self-fulfillment, 112–113; attitudes toward materialism, 83, 89, 91, 93, 110, 113, 181; authenticity, phoniness, or shallowness, 82, 86, 90, 92, 93–95, 110, 113, 181–182, 223n12; career aspirations, 72–73; and comparing wealth, 88, 93–94, 105; competitive performance, 81–87; creativity and creative exploration, 69, 73, 75, 81–83, 94–95, 112; definitions of success, 80, 81, 91; and discourse of brilliance, 76–77, 112; dispositions towards authority, 55; entrapment of, 180, 181; ideas about failure, 84–88; instrumentalization of interests, authenticity, 85, 87, 95–96, 189, 190; intensification of social and economic insecurity and pressures on, 17, 24, 69, 189; freedom of expression, 69, 71–75, 78, 81–84, 112, 189; and parental pressure, 85, 99–103; perceptions of marginality, 88, 90, 93–95; passions, creative and intellectual, 69, 71, 78, 82, 84; and performance of sophistication, 95; racism of (*see also* Sanders High School, racism on campus), 83, 86, 89–90; and self-marketing, 96–99, 113; sexual identity, expressions of, 74, 75, 112; social and academic markers of success, 68, 69, 82, 83; stress and anxiety, 83–88, 191

militarization, 22, 37; and diminishing opportunities for poor youth, 42; ritualization of, 68

military recruitment, 35; of Latinos, 37

Mitchell, Katharyne, 195, 227n7

Morton High School, 29–66; classroom dynamics at, 55–56; dress code, 55, 57, 75; families' economic status and insecurity, 30; gang reputation of, 18, 19, 31, 45, 54; multiculturalism at, 53; neighborhood demographics, 18, 19; on-campus definitions of "at-risk," 54; ordering of social space and bodies on campus, 54, 58; parents, 18, 30, 32, 38, 45; parents' occupations, 30; parents' unemployment, 30; school demographics, 30; and surveillance, 130; teachers, 32, 55, 56; transience, 18, 31, 221n41

multiculturalism, 53, 195; and accumulation, Fordist regime of, 195, 227n5; articulating with nationalism, 198

municipal government: critique of mismanagement, 148

Nation at Risk, A (federal report), 127, 142

neoliberal: framing of multiculturalism as failure, 195; governance, historicization of emergence of, 216n21; governance of poor people in the United States, 204; governmentality, 14, 62, 64, 188, 194; ideology (*see also* personal responsibility), 14, 15, 16, 24, 64, 65; subject formation and the cultural politics of class, 213

neoliberal subject formation, 16, 25, 65, 188; ambivalence toward, among established professional middle class adults and youth, 182; and workplace, 160

neoliberalism, 11, 14, 111, 124, 146; and critique of the public sector, 124, 143, 147; discourses of entitlement in California (*see also* white middle class racial anxieties), 64, 110; and education as augmentation of human capital, 14; and local discourse about techno-entrepreneurship and personal success, 65; and private sector solutions to social problems, 124; and public educational priorities 16, 142, 143; and students as consumers, 15

"New Economy," 5, 25, 69, 70, 175, 191, 215n5

"New Economy" free agent (ideal self): defined, 158, 160, 161; and leisure activities, 159

"new entrepreneurial" practices and values, 5, 23, 25. See also techno-entrepreneurial success/practices/values

"new entrepreneurial" upper-middle class, 8; definition and provenance, 162

No Child Left Behind Act of 2001, 20, 37, 197

non-profit social service institutions, 24, 146; critique of local institutions, 146–148; and focus on "results," 150; and local private sector emphasis on pace of transformation, 150

nostalgia: for era of relative economic security, 111, 175–176; for idealized, Silicon Valley past, 165, 167–170, 180–181; as politics of distraction, 180–181; for a pre-"New Economy" past, 25, 168, 175, 181

Obama, Barack, 228n12

Ong, Aihwa, 5, 194

organizational effectiveness/efficiency, 125, 148–153; and emphasis on "results," 150, 151; HP's commitment to, 164; and "one-stoppism," 150; public and non-profit sector agencies' endorsement of, 149

outsourcing, 107

"over-programmed generation," 99, 100

Palo Alto, 19; and class privileges, 112; and crime, 19; education levels in, 70; housing values, 71, 222n2; and median home price, 19; and median household income, 19, 108, 222–223n7; social and economic transformation of, 70, 71; and tech and service managerial and professionals' employment, 71

parental pressure, 85, 99–103; and racialization of Chinese parents, 101–102, 109–110

parents' entrapment, 103–111. See also fear of slipping

partying, 83, 84, 88; as task to remain competitive, 84. See also middle-class youth

passion(s), creative and intellectual, 69, 71, 78, 81; edification of and career aspirations, 72; instrumentalization of, 85, 98; and myth of meritocratic Silicon Valley, 158

patriotism, 197, 227n7

peer pressure, 81, 82, 87, 94

People Acting in the Community Together (PACT), 59

Perez, Gina, 206, 220n31

personal freedom, 69

personal reliability, 50, 51, 55, 57, 63

personal responsibility, 21, 24, 46, 63, 64, 65, 75, 146, 187, 198–199, 202, 203, 227n4

personal success, middle-class youth and, 6; academic markers for, 68, 69; ambivalence about, 92; social markers of, 68, 69; contradictory definitions of, 69, 81, 96; corporate mentors as embodiments of, 53, 140; equated with personal responsibility or an "at-risk" status, 198; as evidence of entrepreneurial character traits, 161, 162; marginality and alternative definitions of, 99. See also techno-entrepreneurial success/skills/values

Pledge of Allegiance, 56, 197, 198

Plugged-In, 119, 147

post-industrial, 22, 192, 227n2

prisons, 123

private tutors, 81, 102

privatization, 15, 64, 111, 144, 187, 212; critique of, 227n2; dynamics of, within public education, 64, 111, 118, 130, 131; regional dynamics of within nonprofit social service organizations, 118, 148–156; of responsibility for "at-risk" status, role of state disinvestment in, 15, 64, 146. See also "at risk" youth

productivity, 160; "new entrepreneurial" emphasis on, 179

Project Crackdown, 58, 59. See also San Jose

Proposition 13, 20, 107, 143

Proposition 98, 20

Proposition 39, 20

Proposition 187, 224n26

public sector, the: and nonprofit institutions as "subjects," 24; as skeptics and moral critics of tech private sector, 153–156; workers represented as inefficient and lazy, 151–152; worries about declines in corporate support with tech bust, 153

public social services: critique of as wasteful, 146–148, and imposition of local private sector temporality, 150; local perception of need for reform, 148; and private-sector expertise, 148–149

quality-of-life, 134–135

racial anxiety, of white established professional middle class, 109–110

racial hierarchy, within regional information economy, 9, 33, 70, 216n16

racial profiling, 61, 222n56

racist discourse: against Latino immigrants, 64; and middle-class youth 83, 89–90. See also under Sanders High School, racism on campus

Reagan, Ronald, 142, 147, 222n59
recession, 218n3, 221n41
regional "culture," 30. *See also* Silicon
  Valley
regulation of bodies: lack of, at Sanders, 73,
  74; at Morton, 54; regulation of space,
  54, 74; in San Jose, 59, 60. *See also* freedom of expression; surveillance
Reich, Robert, 141
reinventing education and workforce
  development, 124–131
Reserve Office Training Corps (ROTC), 32,
  53, 68, 206, 220n29
resistance, 188
risk and risk management: global preoccupation with, 12; individualized,
  15, 57, 63, 65, 146, 188, 190; national
  concern with "at-risk" youth, 12; poor
  youth supplanting state's role, 146;
  and working class Latino youth, 46,
  57, 58, 62
risk-taking, 4, 53, 105, 117, 158, 165, 191;
  Burning Man festival as example of,
  159; Fiorina, Carly, as symbol of, 171;
  and "New Economy" free agent, 159;
  vs. "plugging away," 178–179; and representations of Silicon Valley CEOs,
  159; Venture Trippers as epitome of,
  158. *See also* Silicon Valley, "culture"
  of; techno-entrepreneurial success/
  skills/values
Roberts, Susan, 200, 215n4
role models, 63, 64, 129, 222n57. *See also*
  working-class Latino youth
Rose, Nikolas, 194
Rouse, Roger, 11, 25, 222n58, 228n15

Sanders High School, 19, 67–114, 173, 181,
  189; curriculum, 74; and demographics,
  19, 70; graduation rates, 70; informal
  connections to tech sector and elite,
  71, 77; and joblessness, 104; ordering of
  social space, 83; racism on campus, 83,
  86, 89, 92; and tech industry talk, 71. *See
  also* class, entitlement
Sandhill Challenge, 117, 118, 119

Santa Clara County, 7, 13, 58, 59; budget
  during tech boom, 60; and demographic
  shifts, 109; and housing affordability,
  108; and median household income, 18,
  223n17; overrepresentation of Latino and
  African-American youth in custody, 60,
  61; and real per capital income, 13, 122;
  School-Linked Services, 31, 59, 60; and
  School-to-Career programs, 129
San Jose, 9, 18, 58, 59; Anti-Cruising
  Ordinance, 59; erosion of public space,
  61; Gang Prevention Task Force, 59;
  gang suppression and prevention
  efforts, 18, 58, 59; and median household
  income, 18; population of, 18; Project
  Crackdown, 58, 59; redevelopment of,
  58–59; "revitalization" of, 187; and right
  to safety, 58–62; and Strong Neighborhoods Initiative, 154; social transformation of during boom, 174; surveillance of
  youth of color, 61, 222n56
SCANS skills, 33, 47, 51, 142, 196; defined,
  33, 219n12
School. *See* Biotechnology Academy; Morton High School; Sanders High School
school market. *See* education market
school safety, 3–28, 67–114, 74
School-to-Career, 18, 20, 29, 48, 129, 138,
  142, 225n14
self-enterprise/entrepreurialization of
  self, 14, 194, 200
self-esteem, 49, 63, 145, 204
self-improvement, 12, 15
self-marketing, 53, 96–99, 103, 113–114, 190,
  206; and double consciousness, 207; and
  marginality as selling point, 207
self-presentation, 53. *See also*
  self-marketing
self-transformation, 15; narratives about
  "at-risk" youth of color, 145, 146; and
  role of regional "culture," 145–146;
  sexual identity, 74; as solution to social
  and educational inequality, 144
September 11th, 56, 68; and harassment of
  Latino immigrants, 61
Shankar, Shalini, 215n7

About the Author

ELSA DAVIDSON is Assistant Professor of Anthropology at Montclair State University in Montclair, New Jersey.